Sacred Places asks why certain types of prehistoric places are thought of as sacred, and explores how the physical presence of such sacred sites is less important than what these places signify. So this is not another guide book to sacred places but instead provides a unique and thought-provoking guide to the mental worlds – the mindscapes – in which we have created the idea of prehistoric sacred places.

Recurring throughout this book is the idea that we continually create and re-create our ideas about the past, about landscapes, and the places within those landscapes that we regard as sacred. For example, although such concepts as 'nature', 'landscape', 'countryside', 'rural' and the contrast between profane and sacred are all part of our everyday thinking, in this book Bob Trubshaw shows they are all modern cultural constructions which act as the 'unseen' foundations on which we erect more complex myths about places.

Key chapters look at how earth mysteries, modern paganism and other alternative approaches to sacred places developed in recent decades, and also outline the recent dramatic changes within academic archaeology. Is there now a 'middle way' between academic and alternative approaches which recognises that what we *know* about the past is far less significant than what we *believe* about the past?

Bob Trubshaw has been actively involved with academic and alternative approaches to archaeology for most of the last twenty years. In 1996 he founded *At the Edge* magazine to popularise new interpretations of past and place. He has written over twenty books, booklets and CD-ROMs.

Previous publications by Bob Trubshaw and published by Heart of Albion include:

How to Write and Publish Local and Family History Successfully

Explore Mythology

Explore Folklore

Good Gargoyle Guide: Medieval carvings of Leicestershire and Rutland

Rutland Village by Village

Interactive Little-known Leicestershire and Rutland (CD-ROM)

Little-known Leicestershire and Rutland

Ancient crosses of Leicestershire and Rutland

Holy wells and springs of Leicestershire and Rutland

Standing stones and mark stones of Leicestershire and Rutland

Sacred Places

Prehistory and popular imagination

Bob Trubshaw

Heart of Albion

Sacred Places:
Prehistory and popular imagination
Bob Trubshaw

Cover illustration and design by Bob Trubshaw.

The front cover depicts Wayland's Smithy, Oxfordshire – an example of the Neolithic 'technology of memory', a chamber tomb constructed to intentionally endure, to connect the past with the present, to connect the dead with the landscape, and to cast a shadow into the indefinite future.

ISBN 1 872883 67 2

Published by
Heart of Albion Press
2 Cross Hill Close, Wymeswold
Loughborough, LE12 6UJ

albion@indigogroup.co.uk

Visit our Web site: www.hoap.co.uk

Printed in the UK by Booksprint

Contents

List of illustrations

Acknowledgements

Cornelius Hortolf and Jeremy Harte kindly provided extensive comments on a previous draft of this book. I am greatly indebted for their suggestions which helped to clarify my thinking and writing. However I have retained a number of comments where our opinions differ.

An overview of this nature cannot be accomplished without being influenced by the work of a wide range of authors and a great many conversations, letters and emails with like-minded people. Although I cannot thank everyone individually, a number of other people have helped the preparation of this book in a variety of ways: Richard Alexander, John Billingsley, Philip Burton, Kathryn Denning, Paul Devereux, Bob Dickinson, Chris Fletcher, Ronald Hutton, John Michell, Neil Mortimer, Tony Myers, Nigel Pennick, Richard Pollard, Alby Stone, Adam Stout, Steve Taylor, Steven Waller, Robert Wallis, Helen and Alastair Ward, Anthony Weir, and Andy Worthington. I am most grateful to them all.

My thanks also to John Billingsley, Anthony Weir and Andy Worthington for kindly providing additional photographs, and to Richard Pollard of Leicestershire Museums for helpfully arranging photographs of polished stone axes.

Preface

The title of this book, *Sacred Places*, suggests the subject matter is the physical landscape and specific places which, for whatever reasons, have been deemed distinct from the mundane and secular. However this is misleading because, as the words 'popular imagination' in the subtitle suggest, my interest is less with the places themselves and more with how we think about sacred places. Indeed this book is essentially a history of ideas – an account of how we have constructed meaning and significance about specific types of places, and how that meaning and significance has evolved.

The word 'prehistory' in the subtitle also limits the scope to prehistoric sacred places – which excludes the sacred places of literate cultures such as Classical Greece, the Roman empire, Buddhism, Christianity, Islam and many other faiths. In practice the scope of the book is focussed on British prehistoric sites, with the emphasis on specifically *English* popular imagination. The types of prehistoric places most likely to be regarded as sacred are the more monumental ones constructed from 'megaliths', such as stone circles and chamber tombs, although henges without surviving stones, hill forts, burial mounds, standing stones and holy wells are also included in the broader scope of 'alternative' archaeologies. In contrast academic archaeologists usually restrict their recognition of prehistoric sacred sites to causewayed camps, henges (with or without stones), Neolithic chamber tombs and later burial mounds.

Sacred Places is not a guide book to sacred places themselves but rather a guide to the mental worlds – the 'mindscapes' – in which we have created the idea of prehistoric sacred places. The vast increase in tourism in recent decades has brought about far greater numbers of visitors to well-known prehistoric sites such as Stonehenge, Avebury and Newgrange. The consequence of increasing popular awareness of prehistoric sites has also led to increased visits to less well-known places, often known only to local enthusiasts or non-locals equipped with specialist guide books.

Yet, despite the comparative ease with which prehistoric sacred sites can now be visited, in practice they are places which we mostly think about rather than directly experience. We sit at home reliving our memories of sacred sites we have visited – perhaps augmented with photographs or videos – or read guide books and pore over maps planning future excursions to places which we regard as suitably alluring.

This book is both 'descriptive' and 'prescriptive', in that it both looks back and looks forward. The descriptive, backward look has been written from the perspective of my active interest in both 'alternative' and academic archaeology over the last twenty years. However despite straddling both camps, I am not a neutral bystander (even if such a hypothetical person could exist in reality). 'I was there' between 1990 and 1998 as editor of the quarterly magazine *At the Edge* (which had the subtitle 'Exploring new interpretations of past and place in archaeology, folklore and mythology') and its precursor *Mercian Mysteries*. In this small way I acted as 'gatekeeper' and helped popularise the evolving alternative and academic approaches, although other people had much greater influences.

During the last five or so years the once-active 'alternative archaeology' community has mostly dissipated. A few groups keep alive some of the approaches first developed thirty or more years ago, but mostly the ideas have been absorbed and adapted by modern day pagans, whose interests and ideas overlap but who do not share the same approach as 'old school' alternative archaeologies.

More importantly, during the last ten or so years academic archaeology has changed radically, although few of these ideas find their way into popular publications. So, whereas in the 1970s and 80s there was almost no middle ground between the academics and those they deemed the 'lunatic fringe', now that middle ground is densely populated by the younger generation of academics, whose ideas are based on what might be regarded as post-modernist approaches to the past.

After *At the Edge* merged with *3rd Stone* magazine in 1998 I deepened my own understanding of how archaeology and folklore fit into the 'bigger picture' of the humanities, including the implications of post-modernist thinking. Two very different academic disciplines have been of significance, cultural studies and the cognitive sciences (especially cognitive linguistics). Such influences create a curious hybrid of ideas, some of which have been developed in *Explore Folklore* (Trubshaw 2002) and *Explore Mythology* (Trubshaw 2003). While reading these two books is not essential before reading this book, they do help to 'set the stage' for some of the deeper discussions. Furthermore, I have tried to keep the overlap between this book and these previous ones to a minimum (by providing cross-references where appropriate). As a result *Explore Mythology* deals with a number of aspects of 'landscapes and mindscapes' that are not touched upon in this book, such as sacred centres, boundaries, crossroads, and the way the cardinal directions manifest in cosmologically-significant landscapes.

This book was drafted between October 2002 and June 2003. At the same time as I started on the draft I was also compiling articles for a new web site, Foamy Custard (www.indigogroup.co.uk/foamycustard). The title is an acronym for 'FOlklore, MYthology, CUltural STudies And Related Disciplines and the aim was to explore the overlaps between these disciplines, especially as they related to present day ideas, lore and myths. Foamy Custard developed further some of the ideas I had summarised in *Explore Folklore* and *Explore Mythology*. More recently Simon Danser's book *The Myths of Reality* (Danser 2005) has developed and expanded the fundamental ideas of Foamy Custard.

Copies of the first draft of this book were circulated mid-2003 to a variety of people which resulted in some very helpful comments. I was then diverted by other writing and publishing projects and only resumed writing in December 2004, after preparing *The Myths of Reality* for publication. The eighteen month gap between the first and final drafts enabled me to look anew at some of the ideas, notably from the perspective of Danser's ideas about the processes by which social groups construct meaning and significance. Indeed, this book might be thought of as exploring specific examples of the wider-ranging 'social construction of reality' explored by Danser.

While reading *The Myths of Reality* is not essential to understanding this book, it provides a broad understanding of how we continually recreate the meaning and significance we give to the past according to ever-evolving present day concerns – not least Romantic 'rural idylls' invented in the nineteenth century and widely popularised in the first half of the twentieth century, combined with the overwhelming nostalgia that has fuelled the 'heritage industry' in recent decades.

Recurring throughout this book is the idea that we continually create and re-create our ideas about the past, about landscapes, and the places within those landscapes that we regard as in some way sacred. This was the underlying emphasis of the alternative archaeology community long before it was acceptable in academe, although in all fairness the academics have been far more rigorous and innovative in pursuing this approach. However, the near-total absence of periodicals and books aimed at popularising this approach has led to an ever-widening gap between interested amateurs and the latest thinking of the professionals.

Prehistoric sacred places are deemed sacred in quite a different way to the recognition of the sacredness of churches, synagogues, mosques, Buddhist, Jain or Sikh temples, and the like. Principally this is because visitors to such places, whether they are believers or not, accept the sacredness of the buildings as a 'given'. Undoubtedly there is a wide range of beliefs and attitudes about what constitutes this sense of sacredness, but these debates exist within the long-traditions of each faith, and are often directly or indirectly based on formal beliefs passed down through the hierarchy of theologians and clergy. In contrast the ideas about the sacredness of prehistoric places have largely evolved in the last four decades and with little or no formal hierarchy of opinion leaders.

In addition the nature of churches, mosques and temples is essentially architectural – they are always recognisable as buildings, which have clearly-defined boundaries. With prehistoric sites we are aware that they have been *constructed* but they are architecturally more ambiguous and, typically, only tenuously separated from their surroundings.

The sense of sacredness as a 'given' also tends to persist even when the church is ruinous, as is the case with the numerous picturesque abbeys abandoned at the Reformation. However the dramatic settings, sometimes desolate ruination and the sense of monumentality of ruined abbeys are echoed by the larger prehistoric monuments. To this extent there is a 'spectrum of sacredness', with living churches and temples at one end, through disused and ruined ecclesiastical buildings, to major prehistoric monuments, and fading away into the prehistoric sites that have left less visible evidence.

Despite the domination of Christianity over the British landscape for the last 1,500 years – especially the pre-Reformation landscape where chapels, crosses and holy wells augmented the cathedrals and churches – the Bible gives us little or no sense of sacred places. The British sense of sacred places has arisen from secular and essentially Romantic sources (especially visual art and literature, as will be discussed in the first chapter). We have constructed the meaning and significance of sacred places in recent centuries and envisage the past according to these modern day Romantic ideas.

As already noted, this construction of the past according to present day ideas is the recurrent theme of this book. The main interest is the way we think of certain types of prehistoric places as being in some way sacred. The emphasis is how prehistoric monuments are regarded as sacred *in the present day* rather than, say, speculating about their sacredness to the people who built them, or their descendants who respected this sacredness for many centuries afterwards.

The first two chapters book explore the diversity of the meaning and significance that modern day thinking gives to prehistoric places, and look at how such ideas have developed and evolved. For example, our ideas about such concepts as 'nature', 'landscape', 'countryside' and 'rural' have become entirely normal aspects of modern day thinking and seem quite 'natural' to us. However these, and many other related words, are artificial constructions, the underlying foundations on which we construct more complex myths about places.

The third chapter switches from how we think about places to how we experience places. Or, more specifically, attempts to open up a greater variety of ways of experiencing places than the 'minimalism' of modern day tourism usually encompasses.

The following three chapters look at how both alternative and academic approaches to sacred places have arisen and developed, and especially at how a 'middle way' has evolved in recent years. This middle way recognises that what we *know* about the past is of far less significance than what we *believe* about the past. A mix-and-match attitude to beliefs enables the past to be understood in a variety of different ways. Some of these ways will be more relevant than others, depending on what objectives the person has at the time. At the risk of mixing metaphors to excess, these different beliefs about the past can be regarded as 'conversations' with the past. So, just as we might imagine a number of people with different approaches to the past gathered together and sharing ideas and beliefs in a manner that might be thought to be greater than the 'sum of the parts', so the remainder of this books brings together several different beliefs to create imaginary conversations about aspects of the past.

Some final qualifying statements. At times in this book I refer to prehistoric 'societies' and 'cultures'. These are terms of convenience and do not imply that such entities can be clearly defined, least of all over any significant period of time. Likewise it is sometimes convenient to contrast modern western thinking with non-western cultures and pre-modern societies (western or otherwise). For simplicity I have used such terms as 'traditional societies' and 'traditional people', although these should not be taken as implying that there is any homogeneity across time and/or place between societies and cultures referred to in this generalised manner.

Dates are shown as **CE** (for 'common era', traditionally referred to as anno Domini or 'AD') and **BCE** (for 'before common era', traditionally referred to as 'before Christ' or 'BC').

1: Thinking about places

We are never conscious of things in their true nature, only of the excerpts we make of them.
Jaynes 1976

The landscape is not seen for itself, but as a commentary upon the human condition, as a speculation upon the tension between order and disorder.'
J.M.W. Turner

A richness of meanings

Words such as 'nature', 'landscape', 'country', 'countryside', 'rural', 'urban', 'place', 'space', 'vista', 'route' and 'map' are used in everyday speech without much thought as to their exact meanings, the distinctions between them, and still less to their origins. Yet each of these words relates to complex interwoven ideas rarely recognised in their everyday usage. Academics might be tempted to say that these words are 'problematical', but that has an undesirable negativity. Instead let us put a positive spin on them and think about their 'richness of meanings'.

What is the difference between a 'space' and a 'place', for instance? Whereas space is an abstract analytical concept, place is somewhere specific and tangible. We relate to physical places in a way that we cannot to abstract notions of space. Whereas 'space' is more about what is conceived and thought about, 'place' is what is perceived and lived in. The modern mind might think of space as being a broader concept into which places are situated. However a little thought reveals that humans have had a sense of place long before the more abstract concept of space. An understanding of place must precede the idea of space. Whereas we can conceptualise an empty space, the idea of an empty place suggests only where no people are present, but is otherwise physically present.

Places are not simply physical. They have meaning and significance, which are conveyed in myths and legends, and possibly in ritual activities. Certain places gain importance from promises made during rituals there, so that in future they are increasingly appropriate for ritual activities – whether celebrating New Year at Trafalgar Square, or for 'rites of passage' at a church or prehistoric stone circle.

Places mean different things to different people, and perhaps even different things at different times. Places are the venues where we live out our lives, and as such places range from entirely secular to entirely sacred, with plenty of variation in between. We live out our lives in such places as houses, shops, pubs, parks, fields, woods, prehistoric sites and churches. Specific examples of each of these types of places may have more significance than others, and each type of place – and each specific place – can change in significance over time.

Modern sense of place has been greatly diluted by people spending so much time in dehumanised places – what might be termed 'architectural spaces' – such as supermarkets, shopping malls, office blocks, hotels, railway and tube stations, airports, and motorways. While they are places they do not have the depth of meanings that are typically associated with traditional notions of place and have only rather negatively-valued meanings (Douglas Adams wittily noted 'It is no coincidence that in no known language does the phrase "As pretty as an airport" appear.'). Even our own homes are becoming less like specific places as we spend more time watching TV or in front of a computer – physically 'at home' but mentally elsewhere.

Meaning and memory

Places have significance to us because they have 'meaning'. That meaning needs to be, in some way, retained and remembered. Simon Schama's study of place and memory (Schama 1995) looked in breadth and depth at the complexities of how cultures create and remember meanings for significant places.

However such 'remembering' also takes place at quite mundane and everyday levels too. For example, the 'meaning' of a place is often summarised in the name we give to the place. The study of place names is far more than unravelling the complex changes to spelling and derivation of the original terminology. It is also more than relating places to the topography, even though a great number of British place names incorporate subtle descriptions of the terrain.

No place name is arbitrary. No matter how little of the original meaning has been remembered, all names link into a society's associations, people and stories. Within a few miles of where I sit writing this the place-names encapsulate the otherwise lost ideas of Anglo-Saxon people living about 1,200 years ago. There is Walton (which translates as 'native British settlement'), Dalby ('the settlement in the dale'), Willoughby ('the settlement in the willow trees'), Hoton ('the settlement on the heel-shaped hill'), Wymeswold ('Wygmund's wold' i.e. woodland with fields), Prestwold ('the priest's wold') and Burton ('the fortified garrison' – created later to defend against Viking attacks). Eighteenth century antiquarians identified the site of a Roman town known as Vernemetum, which means 'Especially Sacred Grove' and presumably refers to a late Iron Age ritual site which has left no visible evidence and has never been excavated by archaeologists.

Sometimes places are given additional significance by being linked with legends or myths. In northern Europe stories giving significance to sacred places rarely emphasise a transcendental presence, a 'spirit of place' or *genius loci*, although these are common in Classical Mediterranean cultures. Even if these legends are *post hoc* explanations (as, for example, when prehistoric or Anglo-Saxon ditches become called the 'Devil's Dyke') they add to the associations of a specific place. By adding a vivid narrative, place-related memories materialise as myths.

Our sense of places exists in the interplay between physical topography and 'mind scapes' conveyed in legends and myths. The meaning of a place needs to be passed on in the form of story or narrative, even if this has become 'fossilised' or shrunken to merely the name of the place whose original significance is lost or largely unknown. Places, like all other aspects of culture, only have significance by providing them with 'narratives of meaning'. Much of the rest of this book explores different aspects of such narratives, whether they be traditional folklore, academics' belief systems about the past, or modern pagan beliefs.

The meanings we give to a place may help to create the sense of belonging for a society and, intentionally or otherwise, exclude others from 'belonging' there. The meaning we attribute to places readily becomes political. Conversely, people who do not 'belong' – such as Gypsies and other travellers – have for centuries been despised by people who feel they belong somewhere. In many non-Western societies women leave the place of their birth and upbringing to live with their husbands. As some feminist writers have recognised, such women are far more 'placeless' than men.

In summary then, the significance of a place has less to do with the physical landscape than with the meanings we give to the location. More specifically, these meanings are remembered and sustained in the narratives we create about these places.

Places and routes

If we have 'places', what about all that lies between them? Do the places meet up? Are there intentional 'spaces' in between? Are places linked together, either conceptually or by routes? And if so, are 'routes' just another type of rather long and thin place, or are they something rather different from 'places', or indeed the 'space' they traverse?

And who travels these routes? Are they humdrum routes we use for commuting to work or popping to the shops? Are they deeply rooted in our history, whether made by eighteenth century Enclosure Awards, or by the Romans, or even by prehistoric feet? Were they once – or perhaps still are – traversed by pilgrims? Or have medieval pilgrims given way to modern day tourists? Or are the routes invisible in the material world but known through myths, such as Irish 'fairy paths', Australian 'Dreamtime tracks', or various shamanistic 'spirit lines'?

The answers to such questions about places and routes reveal much more about how we *think* about the landscape than its physical manifestation. Even the word 'landscape' reveals a richness of meanings. As Raymond Williams noted, 'A working country is hardly ever a landscape. The very idea of landscape implies separation and observation' (Williams 1973 (1985: 120)). We separate 'practical' and 'aesthetic' ways of thinking about the land. This is a highly culturally-specific distinction. Immigrants to Britain such as Asians and Afro-Caribbeans, even second and third generation descendants, are rarely interested in visiting the countryside for the pleasures of, say, rambling, picnicing or visiting historic buildings. While there are undoubtedly a number of reasons for this, a key one must be that Asian, African and Caribbean attitudes to the land see it as a practical place where people work in the fields cultivating crops, not as somewhere to be 'enjoyed'. The aesthetic appreciation of landscape is not inherent in non-western mindscapes.

Nature, landscapes and mindscapes

What could be more 'natural' than a 'nature'? Yet 'nature' is a concept of human thought, an idealistic concept – a vague collective of hills, streams, plants and animals but excluding humans. The exclusion of people from the 'natural world' is a profound contradiction, but this is not the only paradox in the way we think about nature. For, on the one hand, nature represents an idealised paradigm of inter-dependence and co-operation while, on the other, nature is regarded as red in tooth and claw.

Likewise landscapes are more mental than physical. Western mentality thinks of landscape primarily in terms of who owns what. As a result boundaries become one of the most significant aspects of landscapes. Not everything in a landscape is necessarily created by people, but the idea – or, rather, ideas – of landscape are most certainly entirely invented by people. Clearly we construct landscapes by planting trees and hedges, clearing and managing woodland, digging ditches, ploughing and planting crops, erecting buildings, and – increasingly with the advent of mechanisation – have transformed landscapes with canals, railways, roads, cities, suburbs, motorways, airports, industrial estates, derelict areas, and all the rest. But the way we *think about* landscapes is more important still. While we may only be constructing ideas and concepts, these are fundamental to our notions of 'reality'. We need not make any physical changes to the land as a result of these transformations in our thinking, although more usually some changes to the 'real world' result from changes to our concepts about reality. Above all, changes are *thought* about before they are put into effect. Once they are put into existence, the changes to the real world affect the way we think and act – so, a boundary fence or a new bridge blocks or enables physical access, while planting or clearing trees creates concealment or enables visual 'access'.

Some of the most artificial ways of thinking about the landscape hide behind the ubiquitous phrase 'countryside'. In Britain, and especially England, over the last hundred-or-so years some deeply-ingrained 'invented traditions' have come to dominate thinking about rural areas. Beyond rural England extends an even more archetypal landscape, the 'wildernesses' of Wales, Scotland and Ireland. So significant are they in defining the character of their country, large areas are deemed 'national' parks. Into this wilderness venture intrepid 'ramblers' who distinguish themselves by an Otherworldly dress code that signifies their separation from urban life.

The sacred places explored in this book might be thought of as existing within both 'real' and 'perceived' landscapes. However, such a distinction is unreal as the term 'landscape' essentially refers to the way we perceive physical reality. The *topography* may be real but the way we think about it as *landscape* results from the ways we consciously and otherwise construct our perceptions of 'reality'. This book seeks to step outside this 'consensus reality', at least temporarily.

As will become clearer as this chapter progresses, words such as 'landscape', 'countryside' and 'nature' are much more to do with 'mindscapes' than physical reality. But this is not a modern phenomenon. People in all times and all places have engaged with the world in ways that depend on their specific social and historical circumstances. Such involvement is never static. Ideas are continually created, contested and adapted. For this reason 'nature', 'landscape', 'countryside' and similar words are less nouns than verbs in that they describe something that is an ongoing process of both physical change and, more especially, changing significance.

Thinking outside the monoculture

Western culture traps us inside a web of implicit assumptions and values. To step outside these implicit ideas is always difficult, increasingly so as Western cultural values relentlessly promote themselves as 'common sense'. Our 'common sense' derives from a secularised Protestant outlook combined with a dumbed-down, 'Disneyfied' attitude that reduces the most subtle or complex of concepts to simplistic dualistic distinctions.

Where the Western cultural system differs from previous ones is the extent to which it presents itself as the 'natural' option. Western culture succeeds not because it is forced on anyone but because subtle interactions between education, media, commerce and government all beguile the people into thinking there is no alternative. The technical term is 'hegemony'.

The main characteristic of Western hegemony is the assumption that there is only one way to see the world. More exactly, it assumes that, even if there are any other approaches to reality then they are 'superstitious' and otherwise inferior. Its trump card is to swiftly absorb subversive attitudes into nostalgia. This could be seen as one aspect of the invented tradition of the British countryside, explored later in this chapter. A more readily recognised example is the way in which the Sex Pistols' anarchical hits of the mid 1970s were rapidly absorbed into the entirely unthreatening and generally nostalgic *Best of the 70s* compilation CDs. (The pop music industry has proven to be expert at emasculating subversive subcultures, for instance by elevating white boy Elvis Presley as the king of the black R'n'B genre; promoting Jamaican reggae in the toned-down versions of UB40 and Eric Clapton's *I Shot the Sheriff*; making rap safe by promptly putting it into the mouths of pretty white boys such as Duran Duran or Vanilla Ice; using drum and bass as the soundtrack of TV adverts for executive cars; and more recently with Ali G's trite and unthreatening parodies of black street culture. The New Age ethos is also a prime example of radical ideas that have been commodified and trivialised.)

Because of the ease of travel and communication, together with the Western-orientated aspirations of many Third World inhabitants, the Western hegemony is causing all 'traditional cultures' to adapt and mutate at a pace never seen before. At the same time Western tastes for 'exoticism' mean that selected aspects of traditional cultures are absorbed into the 'mainstream'. We are fast approaching a worldwide monoculture.

This book is about 'thinking outside the monoculture'. This in no way means a romantically-inspired return to the past, or even turning one's back on modernity and 'heading for the hills'. The aim is to restore some subtleties to our experiences of places, especially those we chose to perceive as in some way sacred.

This Western monoculture makes it difficult to step outside the matrix and conceive of places in other ways. Too often 'other ways' are just deemed 'alternative' ways to the ones we are accustomed to, 'other' to the monoculture's 'normality'. Only people brought up as children in what the mainstream might call 'alternative communities' are spared the inevitable perspective of seeing everything non-mainstream dismissed as 'alternative'. However every 'alternative' comes with its own cultural baggage, its own ideologies and myths, its own fallacies and flaws. No one has any claim on the 'One True Way' of thinking about our surroundings and, as will be explored in much of the rest of this book, no one has the One True Way of understanding past cultures, especially those made more mysterious by the mists that enshroud all prehistoric societies.

Rather than slip and slide on these superficial distinctions, let's delve down to where some of the most pervasive concepts about our surroundings have their origins. Four words act as shorthand for some very complex 'invented traditions' that are pervasive in modern day Britain. They are 'landscape', 'nature', 'countryside' and 'heritage'.

The invention of landscape

'Landscape' derives from an Old German word, *landschaft*, used by the Anglo-Saxons to mean a small piece of cultivated land. The word died out in English during the eleventh century but reappears in Dutch during the late sixteenth century as *landschap*, a technical term used by painters to describe the new fashion for 'landscape' painting. Previously depictions of rural scenes provided only a background to human subjects in the foreground. For reasons unknown, the specialists in such 'background painting' created a fashion for works without any foreground figures.

The interest in 'backgrounds' is probably part-and-parcel of the Renaissance's rediscovery of Ptolemy, a Greek polymath of the second century CE, who invented the concept of 'geography' (as an objective view of the world) and what he termed 'chorography', a more subjective sense of place.

However knowledge of Ptolemy, geography and chorography all died out. Not until 1336 do we have a record of someone climbing a mountain simply to admire the view. This person was the Italian poet Francesco Petrarch (1304–74) who helped to rediscover the Classical tradition. He describes how in 1336 he felt 'intoxicated' by the view from the summit of Mount Ventoux and came down thinking he had transgressed a fundamental law by seeing the land spread out around him, as if he were God, or at the very least Moses when he received the word of the law from Jehovah on Mount Sinai (Lachman 2003: 217–20).

Ptolemy's abstract way of thinking about geography and map-making were rediscovered in the fifteenth century. Two centuries later his sense of chorography manifested in such works as Johannes Vermeer's *View of Delft* (c.1661) and the landscapes of Claude Poussin (1593–1665) and Claude Lorrain (1600–82).

An approximate contemporary of Ptolemy, a doctor called Pausanias, represents a different aspect of chorography. He travelled around Greece in the second century CE describing the sites of Classical antiquity at a time when their remains survived. His aim was to provide a guide to travellers so they might see for themselves the achievements of Classical Greece, at a time when Greece was subject to Roman rule. The sacred sites he describes encompass man-made temples and natural sites such as springs, caves, mountains and groves. Pausanias was especially interested in surviving statues. Indeed his descriptions fail to distinguish between man-made temples and entirely natural sites, although it is probable that in many cases natural sites had been augmented in antiquity with statues and perhaps also temples. (See Alcock and Osborne 1994; Bradley 2000: 20–8)

Pausanias was more than an antiquarian or art historian, as he combined the history of religion with what we would now think of as the attributes of both a field archaeologist and a guide book author. As a 'chorographer' he recovered an all-but-lost sacred landscape to serve nationalistic idealism, thereby anticipating the invention of notions of idealised landscapes that have predominated in Britain during the last hundred-or-so years, to be discussed in the next section.

Art historians conventionally attribute the origins of landscape painting to the Bavarian painter and printmaker Albrecht Altdorfer (c.1480–1538). However these are less studies of nature than settings for human subjects where the background takes greater precedence than in the work of his older contemporaries.

While popular notions of art history attribute the depiction of more realistic landscapes to Leonardo da Vinci (1452–1519) (indeed his earliest surviving work is a sketch of the Tuscan countryside). However his lesser-known contemporaries Giovanni Bellini (c.1430–1516) and Piero di Cosimo (1462–c.1521) seem to have been the true pioneers.

In contrast to these 'background' painters, the aesthetic appreciation of landscape from a vantage point arises from novel Renaissance theories of visual representation, especially those put forward by Leon Battista Alberti (1404–72) in his *Ten Books on Architecture* (published posthumously about 1498). Key to this was the use of linear perspective, almost certainly augmented by tracing from images created using a *camera obscura*. Claude Poussin (1593–1665) became the most famous exponent of such landscape art, although Vermeer's *View of Delft* (c.1661) and a large number of topographical prints also fit into this new mode of seeing. Gone was the 'collage of close-ups' that characterised the landscapes of, say, Hieronymus Bosch (1460–1516) or Peter Breughel the Elder (c.1525/30–1569). Perspective is an essentially humanistic development – it aims to represent how the human eye (or, rather, how the human 'I') – views the world. It is not, for example, the omnipresent 'God's eye view' as used in some previous representational schemas. The illusion of perspective is also an ideological illusion.

'Capability' Brown's 1760s landscaping at Chatsworth House, Derbyshire.

Not everybody approved of 'Capability' Brown's transformations. One critic is supposed to have said to him: "Mr Brown, I very sincerely desire that I may die before you." "Why so?" enquired Brown. "Because I should like to see Heaven before you had improved it." (MacDermott 2003: 42)

Landscape as a way of viewing

There is more to landscape painting than the adoption of perspective and a more fully-formed notion of landscape emerged in the seventeenth and eighteenth centuries as a way of viewing. The first recorded use of the word 'landscape' in English is in 1632 and the term came to denote a broad view of a natural or imaginary scene. By the nineteenth century the term 'landscape' shifted from denoting a genre of painting and became adopted as a way of referring to those parts of the real world considered equivalent to the subject matter of such paintings.

The conflation of subject and object continued. Just as landscape paintings depicted their subject from a specific viewpoint, so nature and the estates of the nobility began to be seen from specific 'vantage points', perhaps even imposed by creating prospect mounds or gazebos for the purpose. Estates were 'landscaped' by the likes of William Kent (1685–1748), 'Capability' Brown (1715–83) or Humphrey Repton (1752–1818) to comply with such idealised ways of seeing. The world was seen as a sequence of *vistas*, whether in the original sense of 'a long narrow view' (as between rows of trees) or in the more panoramic sense that the word is now often used.

With the advent of photography in the second half of the nineteenth century 'nature' was further promoted from the fixed 'ideal viewpoint' of the camera and became the dominant western way of seeing.

Prospect mound at Kirby Bellars near Melton Mowbray, Leicestershire.

The word 'landscape' owes much more to art history than to geography. Above all it is a way of looking at the world that is specific to Renaissance and modern Western thinking. It is not an *a priori* way of apprehending the world. Writers who refer to 'prehistoric landscapes' or the ways in which non-Western societies see 'their landscape' are either using the word 'landscape' as a convenient shorthand for the different ways people of other times or places conceptualised their surroundings, or have failed to recognise that 'landscape' is a concept specific to our own culture.

There are two deeply-rooted aspects which make the modern Western concept of landscape distinct from non-Western ones. The first is that it is entirely visual, whereas non-Western cultures often give equal or greater prominence to auditory interaction with the surroundings. Secondly, the deeply-embedded notion of seeing landscapes from specific viewpoints removes our sense of travelling through space. Indeed when the scene is frozen in a painting or photograph the image becomes literally timeless. Because this static notion of landscape is so ingrained in western thinking, we see tend to see rural topography as implicitly timeless. Yet almost all our interaction with our surroundings is as much about time as space. In the next chapter we will explore further these two specific problems with our concept of landscape.

The invention of nature

If our ideas about landscape are derived from Renaissance paintings, 'nature' comes from a more literary vein, albeit deeply rooted in a sequence of social and political strata.

There have been broadly four ways of thinking about nature in Europe during the last few hundred years:

1. In medieval times 'nature' equated to the whole of God's creation, with the human world being rather fluidly differentiated from the rest of the natural world. People were not usually conscious of the distinction between the concepts of the 'human world' and the 'natural world'.

2. By the end of the Renaissance a more secular and rational abstraction had been conceived – the idea of 'humanity', which was defined by distinction from 'nature'. The adoption of perspective by Renaissance artists undoubtedly helped foster this 'alienation' from nature, in that a landscape painting is viewed as an object, by a viewer who is entirely 'outside' the topography depicted.

3. During the eighteenth and nineteenth centuries humans increasingly intervened in 'nature', whether by agricultural improvement, science, and the various technical and social changes of the industrial revolution, so that all aspects of nature became regarded as something akin to objects. This was the Age of the Enlightenment, where 'Reason' was diametrically opposed to 'Nature'.

4. Within the last three decades this way of thinking about nature as quite distinct from humanity has been moderated in various ways by the concerns of ecologists, James Lovelock's 'Gaia hypothesis', and pagans who regard the Earth as a goddess.

These changes underlie more specific shifts in perceptions of nature. Most people are aware that such 'beauty spots' as the Lake District were regarded as threatening wildernesses until the nineteenth century, notably until the poet William Wordsworth (1770–1850) turned to the natural world of his native Cumbria for inspiration. As late as 1874 Gustave Flaubert wrote that 'The Alps are out of all proportion to human existence. They are too big to be useful. This is the third time that they have provoked a disagreeable reaction in me and I hope it is the last.' (Cited in Beaumont 1985: 87)

In the eighteenth century landscape painting developed as part of the activities on the 'Grand Tour'. The pioneer English watercolour painter Paul Sandby (1731–1809) came back from Italy and, for the first time, depicted the landscapes of Scotland and Wales in a similar manner. The Wye Valley, South Wales, the Scottish Highlands, North Wales, and the New Forest followed in the 1780s under the direct influence of William Gilpin (1724–1804). The influence of other watercolourists in the 1760s made the Lake District fashionable.

About a hundred years later a further change in the visual awareness of nature arose in the 1880s when a group of artists, among them Guy Dawber (1861–1938), began to spend their summers at Broadway. This visual awareness was paralleled in literature with the creation of 'Wessex' by Thomas Hardy (1840–1928). Together a fashionable cult of the Cotswolds (hitherto a little-regarded area) was triggered in 1895 with the arrival of a famous actress and various members of the nobility, who were visited by a great many guests, included the leading writers and artists of the day. The publication of four guide books in 1904 completed 'the transformation of Broadway from a sleepy straggling village into one of the showpieces of rural England'. (Marsh 1982: 30)

The founding of the National Trust in 1895 quickly led to the preservation of both historic buildings and 'picturesque' open spaces (see Marsh 1982: 55–9). The priorities of the National Trust fitted in closely with the widespread influence of John Ruskin (1819–1900) and William Morris (1834–96). Starting in 1901 the National Trust became responsible for the preservation of large parts of Ruskin's beloved Lake District.

Long before Wordsworth painters and writers in the sixteenth century had played a major part in creating the modern concepts of nature. In 1546 Pietro Arentino (1492–1556) writes of 'discovering' the beauty of Venetian sunsets after seeing them depicted in Titian's vibrant paintings. Similarly, the 'discovery' of Alpine scenery *follows* the spread of prints and paintings with mountain panoramas in the sixteenth century. One of the first literary appreciations of an Alpine region bears a striking resemblance to Peter Breughel the Elder's *Landscape with St Mary Magdalene* (c.1555). The similarity can hardly be accidental.

As Flaubert's instincts still confirm, 'nature' was once to be feared. Until we felt securely in control we could not begin to look positively at mountains, wild animals, and other previously unsubdued aspects of nature. Only with the Romantic movement's response to urbanisation does nature become regarded as beautiful. The mystical love of nature is a by-product of the change from a largely rural Britain to a largely urban one during the nineteenth century. The active protection of animals, birds and plants in the wild is an even more recent change in attitudes.

Modern western benign attitudes to nature should not be projected onto earlier times and other societies. Indeed, one of the fundamental concepts of many different cultures is the contrast between 'ordered' society and 'chaotic' nature. As we will explore in Chapter 7, creating such distinctions may be one of the defining features of Neolithic peoples in Europe.

The English rural landscape is far from natural. Since at least the ninth century landowners have invested heavily in farming and estate management to maximise both profit and opportunities for recreations such as hunting. Enclosure Acts in the mid-eighteenth to early nineteenth century not only created the pattern of small fields regarded as typical of lowland Britain but also to all intents and purposes eliminated 'subsistence farming' in their quest for maximising profits. The wealthiest aristocrats created landscaped parks around their houses at vast expense as extravagant examples of conspicuous consumption. The English landscape is not merely a product of human enterprise, it is a profoundly political statement of ownership and hegemonic domination. The main players are the tenant farmers who made the aristocracy wealthy, and yeoman farmers who transformed the landscape during the seventeenth and eighteenth centuries to fulfil their own economic motives. Upon this political stage our notions of nature evolved (see Thomas 1983).

11

The invention of the rural idyll

A widespread human myth is of the 'good old days', a never-quite-specified time approximately contemporary with one's grandparents when everything was better than it is today. Rural England has long been the venue for such myths.

William Keith, in a pioneering study of the rural idyll in English literature, put this sharply in focus when he noted 'Rural values, like all others, are continually in a state of flux; every generation encounters new changes and challenges.' (Keith 1975: 14)

Keith places Isaak Walton's *The Compleat Angler*, written in 1653, at the root of the English rural idyll:

> *The Compleat Angler* begins – and therefore, to all intents and purposes, the English rural tradition begins – with three men, Piscator, Venator and Auceps, meeting on a road leading out of London this 'fine, fresh May morning'. The setting is at one and the same time familiar and original. Inevitably we recall the congregation of pilgrims at the Tabard Inn at the opening of *The Canterbury Tales*, but, whereas Chaucer presents us with a journey from the secular city to the sacred cathedral of God, Walton shows us three men leaving London for the enjoyment of the countryside. True, the river Lea may at first sight appear a trivial goal compared with the shrine at Canterbury, yet the overall tone of Walton's book is more sober and, despite the Parson's concluding and comprehensive sermon (interestingly paralleled by Piscator's speech in the final chapter), more pious than that of Chaucer's poem. While at Canterbury pilgrims turn a holy duty into a diverting recreation, Piscator converts a secular hobby into a contemplation and celebration of God's gifts to man on earth. Implicit here, I suggest, is the idea later to be expressed with memorable conciseness by William Cowper that "God made the country, and man made the town".
> (Keith 1975: 26, quoting from Isaak Walton's *Compleat Angler* p19 and William Cowper's *The Task* 1, p749)

Man not only made the town but it was these townspeople who predominately made the myth of the rural idyll. As Keith states, 'It is worth noting that Piscator, Walton's mouthpiece, is also a townsman.' (Keith 1975: 27).

Walton was followed by Gilbert White and numerous other literary rural idealisers. Alongside these the work of the political Radical William Cobbett (1763–1835) also created a widespread belief that rural life had been ideal when each man had a cottage, a pig and use of the common – a scenario that was largely being superseded by the effects of Enclosure. Cobbett's idealism was disseminated in popular broadsheet ballads, which gave the underlying ideals such widespread currency that by the 1830s they have become truisms. This rural idyll was prevalent in nineteenth century literature and not directly opposed at the time. (Hutton 1999: 433 fn19, contra Mandler 1997b).

Rural writers such as Isaak Walton and Gilbert White only became popular in the Victorian era with the advent of an urban readership. Reading about the countryside was, and still is, not merely a substitute for visiting the countryside but often preferable to the reality. The rural idyll may be a widespread and deeply-rooted myth, but there is a complex conflict between the myth and both the reality of rural life and the practicalities of travel, weather, refreshments, accommodation and such like.

As already noted, the transformation of nature into something desirable takes place at the same time as Victorian England was becoming increasingly urban. Early urban development soon developed into squalid living conditions where basic sanitation was lacking and epidemics of diseases such as cholera could not be controlled. One of the Victorian obsessions was attributing illnesses to 'bad air'. Quaint as these notions are now that we understand bacteria and viruses, they are fundamental to the positive perceptions of the rural environment, where the air was considered to be generally 'good'. Indeed modern tourism, with its fetish for the seaside, has its origins in Georgian England and the supposed ozone of the coast air (although we now know that 'stimulating sea breezes' smell not of ozone but of rotting seaweed).

The notion of 'bad air' is now regarded as totally fallacious. Nevertheless, it was a primary cause in the creation of an imagined tradition that has become increasingly important in Britain – what we think of as 'the countryside'.

The invention of the countryside

Before we explore the invention of 'the countryside' we need to understand another quirk of nineteenth century values. At a time when Britain dominated the world and was setting the pace for industrialised nations, the preferred architectural style for public buildings was an accurate recreation of the 'Gothic' of about 1300. Why, while every other aspect of British life reflected the overwhelming forces of modernism, were churches and town halls, indeed even the rebuilding of the Houses of Parliament, done in a manner that suggested a loss of confidence in modernity?

This apparent chink in the self-confidence of the dominant nation can be traced to changes in ecclesiastical fashions in the 1830s. These turned against the eighteenth century Church of England liturgy that was dominated by sermons. Instead the reformers substituted the celebration of 'communion' (the Protestant successor to the Catholic Mass) along with hymn singing – more-or-less what was a typical CofE service for much of the twentieth century. This new ecclesiastical fashion required changes to the interiors of the churches. As many of the rural churches were dilapidated and long overdue restoration this led to a major programme of church renewals during the middle decades of the nineteenth century. The leading architects, such as Charles Barry, A.W.N. Pugin and Gilbert Scott all favoured the 'Gothic' style with its emphasis on 'heavenward-pointing' columns and arches as, by the early part of the nineteenth century, the Gothic had become associated with profound religious thinking.

If the Gothic was good enough for the country's cathedrals and churches then, by gosh, it was good enough for town halls and railway terminals too. The fashion for Neo-Gothic brought with it respect and admiration for original medieval architecture. Alarmed at the destructive 'restorations' of medieval buildings typical of Victorian architects, William Morris founded The Society for the Protection of

Ancient Buildings (SPAB) in 1877. Morris achieved some of his objectives with the passing of the Ancient Monuments Protection Act 1882.

Morris's SPAB emulated the first of the 'heritage pressure groups', the Commons Preservation Society which had been born in 1865. The same spirit of concern for what we now think of as 'heritage' widened from the preservation of Gothic architecture to the 'countryside' with the creation of the National Trust in 1895. The formation of the National Trust was part of a wider group of radical and Liberal protests which sought to provide land access benefits for the working classes but, by the 1920s, these organisations had moved to the political right and were more concerned with protecting property than enabling access.

For example, a leading figure in the Commons Preservation Society at the time, Sir Lawrence Chubb, thought the Kinder Scout mass trespass on 24 April 1932 was funded by 'Russian money'. In the 1930s the National Trust turned its attention away from preserving and providing access to places of natural beauty and instead became preoccupied with country houses, hitherto an incidental aspect of their interests. At this time the Conservative party under Stanley Baldwin began to associate itself explicitly with an idealized myth of the countryside.

> Baldwin assiduously cultivated an image of himself as a kind of rural
> Everyman (despite the fact that his money came from the iron industry) and
> the illusion he created was so successful that it not only remains more or
> less intact to this day (think John Major and his evocation of 'village cricket
> and warm beer' as what was best about Britain) but it also began to
> undermine the efficacy of the claims on the countryside that were made by
> the radicals and the Romantics.
> (Worthington 2004: 101–2)

The National Trust is a quintessentially British compromise which holds land and properties in private ownership for the benefit of the nation and the public. The radicalism that led to its founding has long been replaced by a populist rhetoric which thinly disguises deeply unequal class interests and the need to be a major player in the 'big business' of the country's tourism and heritage industry.

Little could the founders of the National Trust realise how profound the changes to rural Britain would be in the next fifty years, and to what extent the Trust would both serve to create and maintain an illusion of a 'lost' (but ultimately illusory) countryside. In all fairness the National Trust did not create this illusion, although it has most effectively nurtured it.

So where does the invented tradition of the British countryside arise, and how does it shift so quickly along the political spectrum? Intriguingly, these ideas and changes are largely attributable to the success and longevity of what might be thought of as one of the 'institutions' of British publishing – *Country Life*.

Country Life was founded in 1897, the year of Queen Victoria's Diamond Jubilee, and two years after the creation of the National Trust. Unlike almost all other periodicals of its time the emphasis was visual rather than literary. It was well-designed and used newly invented high-quality photographic printing technology.

These images presented a romantic vision of 'unspoilt' villages, rolling landscapes, country houses, and the nation's heritage of cathedrals, castles and historic cities.

By this time most of the population lived in suburban surroundings. These were the people who predominately bought this romantic rural idyll. The influential thinker John Ruskin (1819–1900) had added his weight to the belief that the countryside provided an antidote of order and tranquillity that was lacking in industrial society (although there is no record of him enquiring whether the rural population thought they were living in 'order and tranquillity').

By the Edwardian era the readership of *Country Life* was predominantly female. For many decades the cover featured a débutante from the minor aristocracy, photographed in a conventional flattering style. Every issue featured a country house, photographed with all evidence of its inhabitants eradicated. Not even a copy of *The Times* on a study desk or a handy pair of bedroom slippers cluttered the images, in contrast to far-from-minimalist furnishings typical of late Victorian interiors.

The emphasis was on rural leisure rather than toil. *Country Life* promoted sports suitable for gentlemen, such as the then new fashion for golf (indeed the idea for the magazine was first discussed on a golf course). Hunting and shooting were also promoted as part of this romanticised tradition, an early emphasis that, controversially, remains a mainstay of current editorial attitudes.

Above all *Country Life* made the countryside glamorous, and nurtured the aspirations of successful businessmen to sell up their urban houses and acquire the appearances of a gentleman by taking up rural residence.

> More than any other magazine, *Country Life* was to become the manual of gentrification for the late Victorian and Edwardian middle classes. It was created at a crucial period in the formation of the attitudes and ideas which were to dominate British society well into the twentieth century.
> (Strong 1996: 30)

The reality of rural Britain was totally at odds with *Country Life*'s romantic image. Changes in the rural economy during the eighteenth and nineteenth had been every bit as dramatic as the industrialisation and massive growth of urban areas. Georgian England had been marked by the social consequences of enclosure and the loss of common lands. While improving the efficiency of farming by concentrating land and power into the hands of the gentry, the result was the creation of a large number of landless poor. When these were not required for military service the problems of vagrants and beggars became difficult for the authorities to contain. In parts of England many families eked out their survival in such poverty-stricken trades as framework knitting. Only as the nineteenth century unfolded, and industrialised urban areas grew, did this poverty steadily migrate from rural settlements to the slums of the new cities.

But all was not well at the top end of the social scale either. The power of the landed classes was steadily undermined by politicians. In 1883–4 the Third Reform Act finally separated voting rights from property. More damaging to the financial basis of the gentry were the imports which depressed agricultural prices from the 1880s until

1945 (for instance, in 1930 land was worth what it had been in 1850). The assets of the land-owning dynasties were further diminished by death duties. These were first introduced in 1894 and increased from 8 percent to 15 percent in 1909. Income tax also rose in 1909 and those with an income over £3,000 per year were subject to a 'super tax'. The Parliament Act of 1910 rendered the House of Lords virtually impotent. The landed classes had all-but lost out to socialism and the First World War completed what the politicians had started. The new county and district councils (with all the associated legislation) took over the power vacuum.

One of the consequences was that the country houses, fetishised in picturesque photography in the editorial pages of *Country Life* and sold or let in its advertisement pages, were increasingly sold off, the contents and fittings auctioned, and – in many cases – allowed to go to ruin. Remarkably, this large-scale 'dissolution' of the country houses during the middle decades of the twentieth century did not render *Country Life* defunct. The reasons provide a remarkable insight into the invention of 'the countryside' in Britain during the last hundred years, as Roy Strong has analysed in his history of the first hundred years of *Country Life* (Strong 1996).

There was a long tradition, going back to Tudor times, of fortunes made in trade and commerce being invested in a country estate. But by the Edwardian era it did not make sense to own a substantial estate. Nevertheless, the new ideal of rural life was modelled on the economically and politically redundant aristocracy.

> At the time when the landowning classes lost their political and social power, they were to retain their cultural hegemony over society through the projection of their culture as the model way of living for the middle classes. By the 1880s, over eighty percent of the population was urban-based, and one might have thought that towns and cities were where future aspirations should logically have been focussed.... Instead, they centred around a totally new vision of rural life, part of a phenomenon which we now recognise as an invented tradition.
> (Strong 1996: 29)

> Conservatism and a suspicion of change began to pervade society, which found a creative expression for these values in a largely fictional view of the countryside, where ancient stoic virtues were seen to flourish... After decades of massive economic and social change, these alternative attributes quickly assumed an aura of spiritual authority and consequently underpinned a new sense of collective identity from which the attributes of industrialised society were excluded.
> (Strong 1996: 33)

The aspirations of the professional and urban-based readers of *Country Life* saw the life of a country gentleman as particularly desirable. Each week's issue provided a 'pantheon of images that gradually formed a powerfully enticing illustration of national identity.... The overwhelming impression ... was (and still is) of continuity and tradition.' (Strong 1996: 36)

The illusion crossed ideological boundaries. To the socialist the 'lost idyll' was one where an honest craftsman could practice his skills within the security of an unchanging village community. Simultaneously '... Tories could envisage an age when the social hierarchy lay undisturbed, guided by the landed classes who dominated local affairs as their natural right.' (Strong 1996: 36–7)

Country Life came to embody the quintessence of English ideals. These ideals continue to perpetrate the cultural influence of the aristocracy who, in almost all other respects, had no significant influence after the 1920s. The major social changes of the 1920s included the advent of the five-day working week and thus the 'invention' of the weekend. Developments in private motoring increased the interest in the countryside that had already been aroused by the railways and bicycles, leading to vastly more 'day trips' at weekends. Country houses, ruined castles, parish churches and picturesque villages were the prime destinations, although prehistoric sites were of interest too.

Country Life was written for the upper classes, even though the majority readership was middle class. Towards the opposite end of the social scale *The Clarion* was aimed at the upper working classes, especially those with middle class aspirations. It had started off with a socialist agenda but by the 1920s was promoting cycling, walking and the enjoyment of rural pleasures. The editor of *The Clarion* was Robert Blatchford who wrote a book called *Merrie England*. As the title suggests, it promotes a romanticised rural idyll. The popularity of this idyll is indicated by the sales of *Merrie England* exceeding a million copies.

Even greater commercial success was attained in the 1930s by the King's England series of guidebooks written by Arthur Mee and the Shell guides. These too promoted the romance of the rural idyll and, to a large extent, shaped the concepts of 'countryside' which we still hold today.

Country Life had an effective monopoly on the advertising of 'superior' country properties and this income kept the magazine alive during the middle decades of the twentieth century, even though the conservatism of the editorial content became increasingly anachronistic. During the 1970s this conservatism led to *Country Life* being the focus for the new 'heritage lobby'. Awareness of 'heritage', and the threats to it, have subsequently gone from strength to strength but, as will be discussed in the next section, exactly what is meant by the term usually remains slippery.

In the mid-1980s rivals to *Country Life* such as *Countryman*, *The Field*, *The Lady* and *This England* began to promote this fantasy traditional lifestyle. And the emerging concept of poorly-defined 'heritage' combined with increased interest in rural living prompted the launch of other periodicals, notably *Country Living*, which appealed to the new middle class interest in the countryside. Indeed, so pervasive was the notion of rural 'escapism' that it could be gently satirised by the television sit-com *The Good Life*.

Although England is essentially urban, for the majority of people their ideals are rural, even though these ideals are based almost entirely on illusions rather than reality.

The invention of heritage

During the last twenty-five years the word 'heritage' has become increasingly used, initially by pressure groups but now as part of 'bureaucrat-speak' where familiar words are linked together by national and local government officials in sentences that defy all attempts to unravel their meaning.

The *Concise Oxford Dictionary* provides four meanings for 'heritage', of which 'a nation's historic buildings, monuments, countryside, etc. especially when regarded as worthy of preservation' is the only relevant one. But, as we have just explored, this begs the question as to how we think of 'countryside'. Because of the imperceptible changes to the editorial approach between the 1930s and the 1970s, the invention of 'the countryside' by *Country Life* in the early decades of the twentieth century merges seamlessly with the magazine's central role in the invention of 'heritage' in the 1970s. Justifiable concerns for ecology and the depredations of motorway building were put into the same pot as support for hunting and attacks on EEC/EU 'interventionist' farming policies and broader political issues, creating what I think of as 'heritage soup'.

Numerous pressure groups seek to preserve the 'traditional countryside' invented in the twentieth century. Indeed, one of the most active takes its role in the conservation of this myth further and styles itself the Society for the *Protection* of Rural England. Partly in response to these new pressure groups the British government passed the National Heritage Act in 1983. One of the actions was to create a body known as English Heritage to care for and promote the nation's heritage. English Heritage has responded to this difficult challenge in ways that have rather too often generated controversy and created the impression that it is inward-looking, authoritarian and inflexible (one of the most public of these contretemps arose over 'Sea Henge'; see Chapter 5). Suffice to say that the cynicism with which English Heritage is too often regarded has tainted the word 'heritage' further.

The *Concise Oxford Dictionary* fails to take account of how the word 'heritage' is now used for much wider cultural legacies, so that phrases such as 'musical heritage', 'literary heritage' and the like are not regarded as spurious. The word 'heritage' is now used so abundantly that it is possible to think in terms of the early twenty-first century being enacted within a 'heritage cult'. The heritage industry too readily reduces the complexities of changes over many centuries to a poorly-differentiated sense of 'oldness'. What they offer is the preservation and promotion of a consoling but largely spurious past, epitomised by neatly mown areas of grass and a nice tea shop. How the past is 'consumed' is far more important to the heritage industry than how ideas about the past are 'produced' (a distinction explored further in Chapter 6; see also Shanks 1992: 71–3; 106–8). This mish-mash approach to the past further blurs the ingredients of 'heritage soup'.

Since the start of the heritage industry in the 1980s, its capitalist and materialistic ideologies have been critiqued by a number of writers (notably Samuel 1984; Wright 1985; Lowenthal 1985; 1996; and Hewison 1987; Brewer 1995; Hunter 1996; Mandler 1997a; Arnold, Davies and Ditchfield 1998). The promotion of heritage has become a ubiquitous aspect of modern culture. Like much else it is neither all bad nor all good and continually evolves.

Heritage can be thought as a way of reconstructing the past as artefacts and commodities which appeal to present-day fads and fancies. Heritage has little (and often nothing) to do with promoting the sort of ideas and meanings about the past that are developed by specialists or academics. 'Heritage centres' too frequently offer a dumbed-down rendition of the past, with specific myths and ideologies being promoted at the expense of the greater diversity (and complexity) of interpretations which informed research offers.

For most people the past is consumed through different aspects of the heritage industry. Inevitably this consumption of the past is how the meaning of the past is produced, as consumption and production of meanings are two sides of the same process. The ever-evolving mythic past promoted by the heritage industry are reconstructions of the past according to present day considerations.

The romance of ruins

However we should not entirely blame the modern heritage industry for creating romantic myths about the past. There is something inherent in the English personality which has been seduced by the romance of ruined buildings and old documents. This goes all the way back to the author of the first history of England, the *Historia Ecclesiastica Gentis Anglorum*, written by Bede (c.673–735) – who seems to have a fondness for earthworks and ruins. Two centuries later King Alfred (c.848–c.900) was also an enthusiastic historian. Indeed, what we might now think of as antiquarianism was crucial to both religious and social status for the Anglo-Saxons.

In later centuries John Milton (1608–74), William Blake (1757–1827) and William Wordsworth (1770–1850) helped to create and sustain a romantic vision of Britain's past. Even William Shakespeare (1564–1616) puts the following words into the mouth a soldier:

> … from our troops I strayed
> To gaze upon a ruinous monastery,
> And as I earnestly did fix mine eye,
> Upon the wasted building…
>
> (*Titus Andronicus* Act 5)

And Shakespeare's younger contemporary, John Webster (c.1580–1634), betrays similar concerns in his dark tragedy *The Duchess of Malfi*, which is obsessed with death and decay:

> I do love these ancient ruins;
> We do never tread upon them, but we set
> Our foot upon some reverend history

Webster would have read William Camden's *Britannia* (first published in 1586) which has been described as 'an earnest attempt to convey the political wisdom of the recent past.' (Richardson 2004: 113). Camden, who lived from 1551 to 1623, is the *de facto* father of English antiquarianism as, although John Leland was an generation earlier (1506–62), his *Itinerary* was only published posthumously in 1710 (see Chapter 5 for a further discussion of Leland). However Camden makes few observations about prehistoric sites and is predominately interested in the Roman period; even the much-expanded posthumous editions of *Britannia* did little to redress the balance.

*The yawning arch betokening slow decay at Newstead, Nottinghamshire.
Modern day visitors need to provide their own wine and monk's skull to
have the complete Bryon experience.*

By the time of Lord Byron (1788–1824) the love affair with ruins went so far as to live in a house adjoining the ruins of Newstead Abbey, whose 'yawning arch betokens slow decay', and drink wine there out of a monk's skull. Even such disparate characters as Percy Shelley (1792–1822) and Edward Gibbon (1737–1794) were inspired to write by visits to ruins – *The History of the Decline and Fall of the Roman Empire* was conceived during a visit to the remains of the Capitol in Rome.

By the late eighteenth century no garden makeover was complete without the creation of a picturesque ruin. So well-known was the English predilection for ruins that J.W. von Goethe (1749–1882) was able to include the following mocking remark:

> Are Britons here? They go abroad, feel calls
> To trace old battle-fields and crumbling walls…
> (Mephistopheles in *Faust*)

Old John, the well-known folly in Bradgate Park, Leicestershire, built in 1784. Old John was probably designed by John Hope, who had designed a similar folly for Mow Cop (on the Cheshire/Staffordshire border) in 1754.

Old John provides shelter to view the surrounding landscape in comfort, especially the hunting and horse trials which took place in close proximity to the tower. The archway was originally part of a longer wall which, although constructed as a mock ruin, was originally part of now-demolished stables.

Local folklore tells that this monument was erected in its present tankard shape to commemorate either a faithful retainer or a miller killed on the hill top. However the putative 'Old John' commemorated in this way seems to be a post hoc invention, as the hill was known as 'John Hill' at least forty years earlier than these supposed deaths (Ramsey 2002).

Napoleon may have famously accused Britain of being a nation of shopkeepers but a more accurate observation would have been to regard us as a nation of nostalgics, sustaining myths of romantic rural idylls.

Nothing but nostalgia

Such tendencies to nostalgia have multiplied many-fold in recent decades. The pace of technological and social change means that artefacts and attitudes of our grandparents' era rarely have any utilitarian value today. We can only value them nostalgically, as part of our 'heritage' and such like.

Laurie Lee's evocative although somewhat imaginative biography *Cider with Rosie*, published in 1959, became widely known (not least because for many years it was a set text for some GCE and GCSE English examinations). He describes life in a poor but self-sufficient Cotswold village in the 1920s and records the tough conditions of this now-vanished rural way of life, although the overall tone is very much one of nostalgia. The same is true of Flora Thompson's study of life in late nineteenth century Oxfordshire, *Lark Rise to Candleford*, published in 1945. Lee and Thompson write in a manner which is easy to read and both delight in recounting the traditional practices of their villages. This generates a sense of 'lost idyll' which more than counterbalances the poverty, hard work, disease and sheer stoicism which these writers also recount.

When Edith Holden's natural history diary for 1906 was rediscovered after 70 years and published in 1977 as *The Country Diary of an Edwardian Lady* this fuelled a huge wave of nostalgia and led to numerous me-too books and a whole industry of kitsch artefacts decorated with motifs from the book. Sixty to thirty years on from their publication, these three books remain as the key inspirations for the currently pervasive English nostalgia.

In Britain anyone under the age of about 40 has been brought up within a culture largely fabricated from notions of nostalgia, mostly woven by commercial concerns and the whims of mass media, into which tourism and heritage are thoroughly intertwined. Such nostalgia is pervasive but far from homogenous. Indeed, the same place or object can evoke a wide variety of reconstructions of the past, mostly dependent on prior knowledge and belief systems.

Complex constructions of nostalgia are deeply embedded into present day culture. Places and artefacts of historic interest which no longer have any practical importance are utilised to create mythic references to aspects of the past – usually carefully selected aspects that sanitise away the poverty, social inequality and poor health of the people who sustained stately homes and generated the wealth which enabled such conspicuous consumption.

A place or object – restored or conserved to its present day existence – is used to signify specific cultural reconstructions of the past (perhaps better thought of as 'simulations'). The heritage industry has long been creating such nostalgic simulations of the past. This is as true of prehistoric sites as it is for stately homes or decommissioned Cold War nuclear bunkers. The urge to simulate the past takes many forms, from military re-enactment groups at medieval castles to Druids at Stonehenge on midsummer morning.

In recent years the 'visitor centre' syndrome has increasingly infected prehistoric sites too, with Newgrange in Ireland and Carnac in Brittany providing some of the more dramatic examples, while quite subtly-nuanced presentations (such as the Keiller Museum at Avebury in Wiltshire) make their own statements about how the past can be reconstructed, or 'simulated', including in these 'statements' the possibility of multiple interpretations.

Summary

While only some of these elaborate notions of the past are closely related to how we think about landscape or the countryside, how we think about sacred places is derived from four interwoven strands. Starting with the most recent, these are:

- pervasive and complex nostalgia;

- muddled ideas of heritage;

- the invented tradition of the countryside;

- the earlier invention of nature and landscape.

Needless to say this interweaving readily results in some rather complex (and at times rather confused) thinking about sacred places. This complexity is explored in the rest of this book.

Sources

Adams 1979; Baker 1992; Baudrillard 1983; 1990; Bender 1993b; Bennett1993; Bradley 2000: 20–1, 33–4; Burchardt 2002: 103–6; Cavallaro 2001: 42–3; Collingwood 1960; Cosgrove 1984, 1993; Danser 2005; de Cunzo 2003; Fowler 1995; Gombrich 1966; Hill 1980: 77; Hirsch 1995; Hoskins 1955; Howkins 1986; Howkins and Dyck 1987; Hutton 1998; Keith 1975; Lachman 2003: 217–20; Knapp and Ashmore 1999; Lefebvre 1991; Letcher 2001; Mandler 1997; Marsh 1982; Meinig 1979; Olwig 1984; Schama 1995; Sheldrake 2001; J. Thomas 1993: 21–2; K. Thomas 1983; Tuan 1974, 1977, 1986; Williams 1972, 1973, 1980; Wilton and Lyles 1993: 83, 321, Wood 1993; Woolley 1999: 3.1–3.6 and 5.1–5.4; Worthington 2004: ch.5.

2: The mythology of places

> A visitor to the Flinders Ranges [Australia] may see a hill, a rock, a waterhole or copper where traditionally an Adnyamathanha person would have seen that and more: the huge serpent Akurra, a Dreamtime Spirit's head, a Dreamtime Spirit's urine, and emu meat thrown by two Dreamtime Spirits passing by... it is quite common for Dreamtime Spirits to leave behind them their faeces and urine, the former generally in the form of rock, the latter in the form of waterholes. Blood is left behind in the form of red ground. When both the birds Marnbi and Yuduyudulya leaves their feathers behind, it is in the form of white quartz, and when the eagle leaves his feathers behind, it is in the form of flintstone.
> (Tunbridge 1988: xxxiv)

The invention of such concepts as 'landscape', 'nature', 'the countryside' and 'national heritage' can be placed under a broader umbrella of mythologising our surroundings. As such these concepts, which are pervasive in the way we in Britain think, are placed on exactly the same basis as 'traditional' and historical cultures.

Perhaps one reason why we tend not to think of our own approaches to our surroundings as myths is because 'traditional' myths appear to have greater complexity. Some of this apparent complexity is merely the consequence of their unfamiliarity. But some of the complexity is 'real'. For example, modern myths are essentially about the 'horizontal plane' of the Earth's surface, whereas traditional myths are more 'three-dimensional' in that they often incorporate vertical space, inextricably linking both heaven and the underworld with the 'manifest' mundane world.

The cosmic axis

Many traditional cultures have the idea of a 'cosmic axis' (or *axis mundi*) linking the three zones. This cosmic axis is often symbolised by a 'world mountain' or 'world tree' and, indeed, in some regions specific mountains or trees may be regarded as symbols or manifestations of this world tree. Standing stones, columns and architectural pillar-like structures (such as stupas, pagodas and the spires of Gothic churches) may also represent this cosmological axis. In some traditional societies the structure of the house is seen as depicting the cosmological order, with the smoke rising from the heath to a central smoke hole in the roof being a domestic manifestation of the cosmic axis.

From north American totem poles to Hindu lingam stones the image of the cosmic axis is all-but omnipresent, although the interpretations vary greatly in different cultures. The idea of the cosmic axis was first developed by Mircia Eliade in his 1964

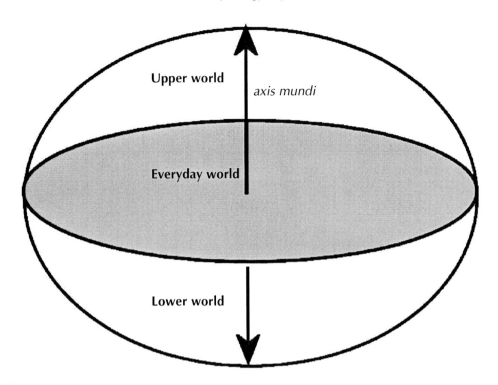

Three-level cosmological model proposed by Mircea Eliade.
(See also the Scandinavian world tree, Yggdrasil, on page 112.)

book *Shamanism* in a chapter called 'Celestial ascents: Descents to the underworld'. Although very influential, Eliade's views have been extensively critiqued by various researchers in the last ten or so years. In the context of this discussion of the cosmic axis it is sufficient to note that Eliade tried to create a universal 'one size fits all' theory whereas later researchers recognise a far more complex and varied range of beliefs. (See Trubshaw 1997a; 2003a: Ch.10 for a more extensive discussion of the cosmic axis.)

The concept of the cosmic axis brings with it the idea of a 'central place', a focus for either the house (and the word *focus* is the Latin word for 'hearth'), a settlement, a region or a nation. In its turn the sense of 'centre' creates a distinction with places that are more peripheral. Indeed, traditional myths often have more about 'boundaries' than about 'central places', especially boundaries that are in some way 'fluid', 'mutable' or 'liminal'. Both central places and boundaries will recur later in this book (for a more extended discussion see Trubshaw 1995; 2003a: Ch.2).

However traditional concepts of landscape extend further than a cosmic axis linking the visible surroundings with the heavens and the underworlds. Indeed the multifarious geographies of the 'otherworld' quickly become bewildering. We risk getting lost in the haunted wildwood of medieval Europe, or encountering ghosts of the dead travelling along invisible 'spirit paths' – perhaps on their way to being assisted across a river dividing the world of the living from that of the dead. Caves, springs and other subterranean entrances are, predictably enough, where the

A Buddhist stupa.

underworld is most easily accessible. Mountains are both colossal and inhospitable. Their summits are unsuited for human habitation; it is only natural that they are the abode of the gods.

The Otherworlds

Despite our modern mentality reasoning that Otherworlds have a clear distinction from the 'real' world, the reality of much traditional thinking is less about *the* Otherworld than *an* Otherworld. Or, more commonly, Otherworld*s*. Furthermore, these Otherworlds are not essentially 'elsewhere' but rather regions of this world that, for the traditional society concerned, are difficult to access (commonly to the west, the land of the setting sun and, by implication, the land of the dead).

Otherworlds are as unmappable as mist. Otherworlds change with each telling of the story. A *Rough Guide to Hades* would be out of date long before it could be published. Instead, we should follow John Carey's directions, where the Otherworld is 'any place inhabited by supernatural beings and itself exhibiting supernatural characteristics' (Carey 1987: 1). Rather than a destination, the Otherworld is a potential 'intrusion' into the mundane world. In ways that will be explored throughout much of this book, 'sacred places' might be regarded as places where the potential for Otherworldly 'intrusions' are greatest. This approach fits comfortably with Pausanias's 'chorography' of Classical Greece (which features springs, caves and groves) and, among many others, with medieval Irish and Welsh accounts of *Tír na nÓg* and *Annwn* (see Chadbourne 1998).

Quite commonly, Otherworlds can be accessed through lakes and springs. Or they are situated on the other side of a river; or – most commonly of all – on islands in the sea. Mythical sea journeys, such as the *Odyssey*, link together various Otherworlds and Otherworldly creatures.

When we start to think of the 'votive deposits' made by Iron Age people in watery places such as bogs and the increasing archaeological evidence that the main way of disposing of human corpses at this time was to commit the loved one's remains to fast-flowing water (as it still is in India and elsewhere), then we begin to see the extent to which earlier people regarded water as a boundary between the mundane world and the Otherworlds.

Sources of drinkable water are essential to life. The era of piped water has existed for less than 80 years in most parts of rural Britain (although longer in the cities) yet we have quickly forgotten the importance of reliable wells. Water is integral to initiation rites the world over, including Christianity. The Well of Zamzam is one of the places venerated at Mecca and perhaps the reason the most important shrine in the Muslim world is situated where it is. Ritual bathing unites modern day Muslims with Hindus, and both with Classical Greeks, among many others. Sacred springs are associated with healing, divination, inspiration and – as with the Roman lead tablets found at Bath – with asking the gods to curse suspected wrongdoers.

The lore of places

For all that this discussion has so far generalised about concepts of 'places' and 'landscapes', such generalisation is alien to traditional thinking. In complete contrast to attempts by academics to generalise about 'landscapes', traditional people think in terms of *specific places*. Klara Kelley and Harris Francis set out to study Navajo sacred places.

> When we started our work... we expected people to answer questions
> about what local places were important to them by providing lists of
> places. Instead, people told stories, or at last alluded to them, about Navajo
> origins, about Navajo encounters with colonialism, and about their own
> personal encounters with immortal beings. The names of places are
> embedded in these stories, which explicitly tie many places together into
> landscapes...
> (Kelley and Francis 1994: 41)

If the deserts of Arizona and New Mexico seem somewhat exotic, then consider medieval Ireland. During the tenth to twelfth centuries a substantial number of tales, the *Dindshenchas*, were recorded, although most of these substantially predate their first written record. *Dindshenchas* translates as 'lore of place' and the tales create a 'primordial past' where mythological kings, queens, heroes and quasi-divine beings forge the natural and cultural landscape. They do not represent a history of Ireland but rather a 'mythic memory' that stood outside of historic time.

> ... the literal representation or the country was less important than its
> poetic dimension.... The terrain was studied, discussed and referenced.
> Every place had its own identity and legend. *Dindshenchas,* the celebration
> of place-names, was a feature of this poetic topography, what endured was
> the mythic landscape.
> (Foster 1988)

Several of these tales recount how rather Otherworldly women are buried on hills, and annual fairs were established on the hills in their honour. These include Ard

Macha (Armagh) and the nearby Emain Macha (Navan Fort), Tailtiu (Teltown on the confluence of the Boyne and Blackwater rivers) and Tara. These women are ambiguous in status and character, but are never referred to as goddesses (although other Otherworldy women in Irish myths may be aspects of 'land goddesses' or the 'sovereignty goddess'; see Low 1996: 32–4). These 'women of the land' fit comfortably with the interest that the Irish poets who composed the *dindshenchas* had in observing and celebrating all aspects of nature, and for praising heroes and saints using metaphors that draw on the excellence of the natural world.

N.B. Aitcheson's exemplary study of Armagh (see Trubshaw 1996b for a summary) includes this overview:

> The landscape is ordered by dominant socio-political groups. Its structuring is as much a cognitive process as a physical one, and is achieved principally through the dissemination of information. This is exemplified by the *dindschenchas* ('lore of places') and by the prominence which the landscape in general, and monuments – such as Navan Fort – in particular are accorded in the epic literature.
> (Aitcheson 1994: 290)

Michael Dames' book *Mythic Ireland* (1992) takes up ideas from the *dindshenchas* and combines these with modern scholarship and archaeology to 'remythologise' the landscape of Ireland in a manner more accessible to modern minds. (See also Chapters 5 and 8 for discussions of Dames' 'remythologising' of the Avebury landscape.)

Non-western concepts of 'landscape'

The eighth to eleventh century *dindshenchas* reveal a way of thinking about the land that is very different from modern ideas, even modern ideas about 'sacred landscapes'. Nevertheless Irish ideas about landscape do evolve into mediaeval ideas, which in turn evolve into our more recent ideas. With 'traditional' ways of thinking in non-Western countries the differences in approaches to 'landscape' can be exceptionally varied and difficult to fully appreciate.

However differently traditional societies think of their surroundings compared to modern concepts of landscapes, these traditional 'landscapes' all share the concept of being in the 'background' of social life. With care we can use modern ideas of 'landscape' to explore more traditional approaches. In turn our understanding of traditional approaches can be reflected back to provide ways of reassessing Western preconceptions.

Sadly, much of the interest in traditional approaches to landscape is a direct consequence of the rapid encroachment by modern cultural values and Western 'development'. Even more so than with Western notions of landscape, in non-western countries there is often even more emphasis on establishing cultural identity from the surroundings, both specific places and broader regions. Frequently the traditional concepts of landscape differ greatly from colonial concepts. Not only cultural identity but social order (indeed even 'supernatural order') can be deeply rooted in the surroundings. There should be no expectation that such ways of regarding the landscape are simple or easily summarised – rather, different approaches can be 'nested' and each can be every bit as quixotic as other aspects of traditional cultures often appear to Western minds. (See Carmichael *et al* 1994 and Knapp and Ashmore 1999: 14–18 for a more detailed discussion of approaching non-western landscapes).

Western minds expect to see our surroundings as vistas receding to a more-or-less distant horizon. Even when we are the middle of a vast conurbation, we still get our bearings from the streetscapes and associated landmarks. Such visual cues are lacking in tropical jungles where sight is blocked in all directions and 'space' is an alien abstraction. Indeed, jungle dwelling people relate to their surroundings through sound rather than vision, as we will explore in the next chapter.

Roger Keesing describes how the Kwaio of the Solomon Islands deal with this problem:

> The landscape of the Kwaio interior appears, to the alien eye, as a sea of green, a dense forest broken periodically by gardens and recent secondary growth, and an occasional tiny settlement... To the Kwaio eye, this landscape is not only divided by invisible lines into named land tracts and settlement sites, it is seen as structured by history.
> (Keesing 1982: 76)

The Kwaio, typically for jungle dwelling people, 'see' their surroundings as an ever-evolving process of kinship. The poor soils mean that cultivation plots are soon depleted and allowed to return to jungle vegetation, meaning that different kin groups have a deeply 'historical' relationship to the surroundings. Settlement sites are also linked by kinship as adult sons leave their father's settlements to establish their own settlements. Peter Gow has explored these relationships in western Amazonia (Gow 1995) and reveals how kinship and the land are mutually implicated. Western notions of 'property ownership' lack the overlapping interactions of kinship and, generally, lack the 'historic depth' that kinship relationships invoke.

'Historic depth' can, and frequently does, extend back into mythic times. Famously the indigenous peoples of Australia believe that their country was created during the Dreamtime by ancestral beings who journeyed through the hitherto-featureless land. They created the features of the landscape, and they left behind songs, sacred objects and rituals that commemorate their creative activities (Morphy 1993: 232). (See also the quotation at the head of this chapter.)

One aspect of these Dreamtime legends has been widely popularised thorough Bruce Chatwin's somewhat garbled accounts of what he calls the 'song lines' (Chatwin 1987), more properly *'tjuringa* lines' or 'dreaming tracks'. Chatwin's travel writing reflected his life which transcends notions of 'reality' and 'fiction'; he referred to *The Songlines* as a novel and not a travelogue when he was interviewed for *Granta* magazine in 1987.

Chatwin is broadly correct when he describes Aboriginal ideas of landscape as not being blocks of land defined by frontiers but as a network of tracks. Perhaps we can believe Chatwin when he reports that one his informants stated that 'All our words for 'country' are the same as the words for 'line'.' Thankfully a better-informed approach to the Dreamtime soon appeared in the works of James Cowan (1989;

1992; 1994) and Howard Morphy (1991; 1993; 1994) but Chatwin's superficial and overly-inventive approach still pervades popular (mis)understanding.

Christopher Tilley provides a useful overview of Aboriginal approaches to landscape (Tilley 1994: 37–57). He summarises the complexities:

> The Aboriginal landscape is one replete with a highly elaborate totemic geography linking together place and people. Formed in the Dreamtime, the landscape provides an ancestral map for human activity. It is sedimented in history and sentiment. The landscape is not something 'natural' and opposed to people, but totally socialized.
> (Tilley 1994: 38)

We need not venture anywhere as exotic as the Australian outback to find our own 'dream time'. Western culture traces itself back to Classical Greece. The Greeks themselves traced themselves back to the origin of time with a series of myths that were recorded by Hesiod about 700 BCE in his *Theogony* (which translates as 'the origins of the gods').

> Chaos was born first and after her came Gaia the broad-breasted, the firm seat of all the immortals who hold the peaks of snowy Olympos, and the misty Tartaros in the depths of the broad-pathed earth…
>
> … and Eros, the fairest of the deathless gods; he unstrings the limbs and subdues both mind and sensible thought in the breasts of all the gods and all men.
>
> Gaia now first gave birth to starry Ouranos, her match in size, to encompass all of her and be the firm seat of all the blessed gods.
> (*Theogony* 116–22; 126–29; translated by A.A. Athanassakis 1983)

Other accounts of the Greek creation myth elaborate how Gaia is the consequence of union between Ouranos, the sky, and Chthon, the deep and unseen 'Otherworld'. Such sexual cosmogony implicit in landscape has been discussed in detail by Kenneth Olwig (1993); for an assessment of the analogous 'engendering' of the landscape in India see Elinor Gadon (1991).

Gender and space

Julian Thomas made the curious comparison that 'Like landscape, women are painted by men to become visual commodities, consumed by other men.' He summarises the work of Susan Ford, who notes that the way we typically look at landscape is decidedly masculine and 'distanced', and archaeologists have adopted some of the most 'distanced' presentations of landscape, such as aerial photographs, distribution maps, site plans, and the like (J. Thomas 1993: 23–5; Ford 1991).

This leads Thomas to observe:

> They all imply a considerable distance between subject and object, and they all present a picture of past landscapes which the inhabitant would hardly recognise. All attempt to lay the world bare, like Eliot's 'patient etherised upon a table', or like the corpse under the pathologist's knife. In

the same way, we seek to dissect landscape, to probe into everything and to make it all visible. ...Knowledge and power are here closely connected. Given that these methodologies have much in common with modern technologies of surveillance and control, we seem to be seeking to monitor and discipline the past.
(J. Thomas 1993: 25)

In contrast to these modern masculine myths of power and control, traditional peoples have entirely different ways of thinking about and engendering the landscape. Cultural uses of space, even if not explicitly engendered, are linked to gendered activities such as hunting, sewing, butchering, cooking, dancing, discussions between 'elders' and the like. Activities we think of as asexual, such as ploughing, are regarded by some traditional cultures as masculine penetration of the female Earth. Or the making of ceramic vessels may be thought of as akin to the pots being born from the soil.

Experiencing places in time

Just as our ways of perceiving the landscape are culturally constructed, so too is the way we regard time. The relevance of time to sacred places is a fairly specific one, in that almost by definition they are places that have sustained their significance over extended periods of time, often much longer than a few human lifetimes. They in some way embody ideas about the past.

By their very nature, monuments are intended to survive over long periods of time. Some prehistoric sites were in active use for hundreds and, occasionally, thousands of years. Other monuments, ranging in date from Neolithic to Roman times, are known to have been brought back into use in the medieval period as high-status sites. To what extent this helped legitimise new élites and involved the invention of 'traditions' can be demonstrated for places such as Yeavering and the Boyne Valley, although the majority of sites inevitably remain silent (Bradley 1993: 116–19; Holtorf 2002).

Above all, monuments 'function' not by their physical presence alone but by the ideas they embody. However such ideas are not fixed – they may adapt and change during the active life of a specific monument, or may be different for superficially-similar monuments built in different regions. As or when the original concepts are lost then new 'traditions' can be readily imposed on the visible remains. This means the meaning of landscapes can be transformed without any changes in the topography (Bradley 1993; Knapp and Ashmore 1999: 10).

Clearly such transformations are easier to follow when there are historical records than when interpreting the silent evidence of prehistory. Simon Schama's famous book and TV series *Landscape and Memory* in 1995 provides plenty of evidence for the complexities of places, memories and deeply-held cultural beliefs. For example, capitalisation can be seen as the annexation of space by time, epitomised by British concerns with land which (at least until recent decades) have been dominated by possession and the authority of the landed classes. So, until the 1970s, archaeologists too regarded the spaces between 'sites' as 'territory', 'resources' and discussed issues of land use, reflecting these long-held concerns of capitalism.

Ethnology provides examples of quite other approaches to places and time. The Australian 'Dreamtime' alone has provided a vast literature (for relevant summaries see Hirsch 1995:19 and Ch.9; Tilley 1994: 37–54; Molyneaux and Vitebsky 2001: 31; 80–1). Caroline Humphrey draws attention to the way Mongolian concepts of space are inextricably linked to time (Humphrey 1995). Not surprisingly the Irish Otherworld also reveals both the 'otherness' of Otherworldly time, but – more surprisingly perhaps – also reveals the 'otherness' of 'everyday' medieval Irish views of time, compared to modern day ones (Chadbourne 1998: 170–1). I have also discussed the way societies create their concepts of time (Trubshaw 1997c; 2003a: Ch.3).

Sacred and profane places

The remarks so far in this book have been intended to outline the richness of ideas that are implicit in the way we think about our surroundings. However it is now appropriate to focus on the specific topic of this book, sacred places. However, identifying somewhere as 'sacred' implicitly identifies other places as in some way more 'profane'. Natural as this simple dualism might be to modern Western minds, it is distracting rather than helpful.

The sacred:profane dualism can be detected in Biblical practices (at sacred places such as mountain tops), Classical religion (where special rules of behaviour were enforced for temples) and the groves of north European heathenism. The concept of sacred was very much of appropriate ritualised behaviour at specific places. However we should be careful about assuming that these are the *only* sacred places. Considerable ritualised behaviour also took place in domestic contexts during Biblical, Classical and heathen eras, yet we do not think of homes as 'sacred places'.

We have to keep pinching ourselves to make sure we are awake and not simply assuming that traditional cultures share modern day distinctions between sacred and profane places (see Bradley 2003). Rather they may have thought in terms of the ritual appropriate in different places, with no underlying (or, at least, consciously recognised) differentiation between 'sacred places' and 'profane places'.

The modern day dualism results in a minority of places being regarded as in some way 'sacred', in contrast to a largely-undifferentiated mass of 'profane' places. A simple inversion, akin to the pantheism ('God is part of Nature') and panentheism ('God is in everything') more typical of pre-modern thinking, would require specific places to be designated as profane in contrast to the ubiquitous sanctity of the Earth. In practice both approaches are too blunt to be serviceable. That there is a 'spectrum' of sacred and profane places in our surroundings is incontestable, but the two notions are part of a continuum rather than exclusive. Traditional and non-western cultures typically recognise 'sacred' places, but not in distinction to 'profane'. Rather than the western 'piecemeal' approach to sacred landscapes, theirs is more 'holistic', where specific places all combine together to create the sacred.

The sacred is often regarded as 'unknowable', perhaps epitomised by a god who is 'invisible', regarded as 'he who is not', who hides himself; is ineffable; is named as the vortex, abyss, desert, solitude, silence, absence; is the sum of what cannot be said of him; so that in speaking of him we celebrate our ignorance. The sacred then appears to us as *numen*, something not understood by man, and which 'produces a sense of terror, an irresistible fascination, a feeling of inferiority and a desire for expiation and suffering.' (Eco 1987: 93) In historical religions this has been personified as more-or-less terrifying deities, associated with sacred places that may also be 'terrifying', such as dramatic mountain top and cliff top temples.

Traditional sacred places

Even if all the world is seen as sacred, certain places may offer easier access to the deities or the Otherworld. This seems to be the nature of early Greek temples – as previously mentioned, Pausanias's descriptions reveal that temples were intimately linked with springs, caves, groves and mountains. In many societies mountains are seen not only as the cosmic axis, but also the places where Earth comes closest to the deities. Moses went to the summit of Mount Sinai to speak to Yahweh and received the Ten Commandments. The Japanese national icon is the snow-capped peak of Mount Fuji (although many other mountains in Japan are also sacred). The Maoris regard the volcanoes at the heart of the Tongariro National Park as so sacred that no humans can venture there (a belief supported by UNESCO when, in 1993, Tongariro became the first property to be inscribed on the World Heritage List under the revised criteria describing cultural landscapes). A volcanic peak in Wyoming venerated by various Great Plains peoples was also the site selected by Steven Spielberg for the arrival of the aliens in the *Close Encounter of the Third Kind.* (A useful overview of sacred mountains in different cultures can be obtained by following the index entries in Holm and Bowker 1994.)

If mountains have been secularised by ski resorts, cable cars and the seemingly continual accompaniment of mountaineers, then caves usually retain a greater sense of otherworldliness. Even the most touristy 'show cave' of stalagmites and stalactites requires entering a world where, part from electric lights, the modern world seems excluded and the chthonic powers seem closer. If the ability to spontaneously transform modern minds still remains, then for traditional peoples caves offered opportunities for transformation that we might now term 'altered states of consciousness'. The constant temperature, deep darkness lit only locally by flickering light, strange acoustics (an aspect to be explored further in the next chapter), often dramatic natural features, and the ever-present belief that somewhere further on the underworld began all contribute to an environment that is entirely Otherworldly.

Modern people usually have little experience of the total darkness commonplace until electric lights became pervasive. This makes the total darkness of caves a panicky experience. However, non-western people do not necessarily share this fear and may instead regarded caves as womb-like shelters, or places which induce contrasting emotional reactions.

Caves can be regarded as 'immersive' experiences, in the same way that within the last hundred years first cinema, then television, and more recently computer games (and their close-cousins, aviation and military simulators) can also be distinguished from other experiences by 'immersing' all the senses. Films seen in a cinema are much more immersive than watching the video or DVD at home because of the

The torii *at Itsukushima Jinja (*jinja *means 'shrine'), on the holy island of Miyajima (*miya *means 'grand shrine'), Hiroshima Prefecture, Japan. At high tide, the sea laps just under the wooden boards of the shrine buildings, and the* torii *stands surrounded by the water. Photograph by John Billingsley*

darkness, bigger screen, louder sound and fewer opportunities for disturbance. Perhaps the same can be said for doing a ritual in a cave rather than a stone circle. Such immersive environments can readily induce trances.

Some aspects of the 'immersiveness' of caves are also experienced in untamed forests, as can be found in the menacing 'otherness' of forests in medieval romances (and this sense of menace has been greatly intensified in Arthurian fantasies and other neo-medieval literature; see Pluskowski 2002). Sacred groves approached via paths through the surrounding forest would have shared some of the experiential aspects of caves. A recent study by the Forestry Commission revealed that a minority of walkers thought walking among trees to be disturbing. In these politically-correct times the Commission promised to respond by cutting down trees to widen tracks. That many people have ambivalent feelings about forests is undeniable and presumably contributed to the unlikely success of *The Blair Witch Project* in 1999.

Natural sacred places 'evolve' into temples and tombs, and thence to churches and mosques. The columns of early temples mimic the trees of sacred groves and, many centuries later, are still a dominant architectural feature of the interiors of medieval cathedrals and mosques. The earliest Neolithic long barrows have cave-like chambers. The grandeur of large caves is matched only by the interiors of major churches. All churches are cave-like constructions (more so before Gothic architecture enabled large windows) and their spires point to God in a manner shared by sacred mountains the world over.

Just as churches enclosed within a well-defined churchyard, so pre-Christian sacred sites in Europe seem to have been defined areas, usually referred to in Latin as *tenemos*. The Old English word seems to have been *frithgaerd,* literally, 'peace enclosure' but with the sense of 'sanctuary'. Various types of *frithgeard* '... about a stone, or a tree, or a well... ' were prohibited in England under the tenth century laws of Edgar and the eleventh century laws for Northumbrian priests.

Similar concerns about enclosing sacred places can be seen to this day in Japan, where local shrines are defined by boundaries of straw ropes. The entrances are marked by a formal gateway known as a *torii,* now of timber with a double crosspiece although this design imitates earlier forms which were much simpler structures comprising two upright posts with a straw rope stretched across.

Present day notions of 'sacred sites'

Modern mentality can usually recognise that springs, ancient temples, certain caves, stone circles and the like may once have been regarded in a similar way to the way we now 'respect' churches, cemeteries, mosques and the like. But there is a considerable difference between putting up an interpretation board which includes the words 'ancient sacred site' and actually believing in and experiencing the sense of sacredness of such places. Most professional archaeologists and 'heritage managers' are quite happy to bandy about the term 'sacred site'. However, their notions of 'sacred sites' often have little in common with what the phrase denotes for, say, modern day pagans. This is not to say that such pagans necessarily have a well-developed understanding of sacred sites or even always behave in ways that other pagans consider appropriate (see Chapter 5) but suffice to say that for pagansthe words 'sacred site' have a richness of meaning and experience that are difficult for others to grasp.

In essence, sacred places are significant less for their practical significance than for what they signify. Sacred places originally signified where deities and the Otherworld could be accessed. Now the term signifies locations where people in a nostalgically-viewed and poorly understood past are believed to have accessed the deities and/or the Otherworld. Some pagans seek to link their modern day beliefs with these beliefs about the past, 'reclaiming' (or, perhaps more accurately, 'recycling') the past into the present.

Often modern mentality reduces sacredness to 'monumentality'. An ancient monument such as Stonehenge or the smaller Neolithic henges can be readily regarded as a 'sacred site' because there is a perceived continuity with how we regard, say, cathedrals. In the same way a Neolithic chamber tomb (even though excavated and all human remains removed) is perceived with the sanctity we might approach cemeteries or war memorials. Indeed, in 1920 exactly such an empty 'chamber tomb' was created in Britain when Edwin Landseer Lutyens designed the Cenotaph in Whitehall to commemorate the hundreds of thousands of servicemen who had died in the First World War but whose bodies were never recovered:

> Thus was created perhaps the first national holy site... neither Lloyd
> George [the Prime Minister] nor Lutyens... anticipated the spontaneous
> response of the people to the infinite meanings of emptiness... Thousands

of the bereaved left wreaths at the makeshift altar, projecting their grief
onto the void within…
(Laqueur 1994: 156–7)

Similar spontaneous expressions of grief following the death of the Princess of Wales
in 1997 resulted in vast numbers of flowers being left on the steps of major churches
or at other places people 'intuitively' felt were the focal point of their locality. Sadly
no one seems to have 'catalogued' these places perceived as the appropriate
'spiritual centres' of late twentieth century British towns and cities. This spontaneous
recognition of sanctity within even the most urban landscapes is a further clue to the
complexities of sacred places in present day thinking.

Sources

Aitcheson 1994; Bradley 1993; 2003; Carey 1987: 1; Carmichael *et al* 1994;
Chadbourne 1998; Chatwin 1987; Cooney 2000; Cowan 1989; 1992; 1994; Dames
1992; Danser 2005; Eco 1987: 93; Eliade 1964; Ford 1991; Foster 1988; Gadon
1991; Gow 1995; Hirsch 1995:19 and Ch.9; Holm and Bowker 1994; Humphrey
1995; Keesing 1982: 76; Kelley and Francis 1994: 41; Knapp and Ashmore 1999:
10; 14–18 ; Laqueur 1994: 156–7; Low 1996: 32–4; Molyneaux and Vitebsky 2001:
31; 80–1; Morphy 1991; 1993; 1994; Olwig 1993; Pluskowski 2002; Schama 1995;
Thomas 1993: 23–5; Tilley 1994: 37–57; Trubshaw 1995; 1996b; 1997a; 1997c;
2003a Ch.2 & Ch.10; Tunbridge 1988: xxxiv.

3: Experiencing places

The previous chapter explored how places are perceived and structured through ideas created by our innate myth-making processes. However places and landscapes are not simply something we think about. They are something we *experience*. Some people might be happier sitting in a comfortable chair and reading about other people's experiences, or merely looking at photographs, but most realise something is lacking (and not just feeling footsore, tired, too wet and cold or too hot, and wondering how far it is back to the car).

If we have been brought up in the modern world then the world-views of traditional peoples can never be our 'natural' way of thinking. Even if we become experienced anthropologists and spend years living in such societies, we will gain only a 'contrasting' experience of a small sample of non-western cultures. We could read shelves full of reports and analyses of anthropological fieldwork which encompass all such cultures, but we will be still looking at them from the 'outside', as something 'other' to our upbringing. The 'experience' of living inside the culture is lacking.

The problems of understanding ways of thinking which are now lost in the past are clearly even greater as the evidence is less and the experience irretrievably lost. Archaeologists are beginning to speculate on the ideas which led our ancestors to, say, first erect megalithic monuments in the Neolithic (see Chapter 7), but the nature of these speculations reflect in modern day ideas, however much those ideas may be 'deconstructed'.

In the absence of written records all the finer aspects of the ways of thinking of the people who erected prehistoric monuments have been lost forever, although we can make some guesses about the broader issues (and some indication of the complexities of thought several millennia ago is indicated by the hieroglyphic texts that describe in detail the purpose of Egyptian pyramids). Above all we struggle to see the variety of ideas that might have been current in a society at any one time, and how those ideas changed. In the absence of evidence to the contrary it is all too easy to impose a homogenous and enduring 'ancient wisdom' and 'lost knowledge' on to the past.

What we can do is 'compare and contrast' the clues that have come down to us from the past with modern approaches. We might do well to think of this as an iterative 'interrogation' of modern values. In other words, we use clues from the past to change our 'starting point', then look again at the past from this new perspective, trying to find further clues, then use these clues to again critique our approach.

Sacred places as processes

Such 'interrogation' offers a number of opportunities, not least the ability to think outside the monoculture. The first step towards breaking down our presuppositions and beginning to think outside the monoculture is to interrogate how we experience sacred places.

In western languages 'sacred place' is a noun-like phrase. Linguistically, such places are just an example of what we lump together as 'objects'. Yet in Chinese and related languages such as Tibetan there is less distinction between nouns and verbs. So the sense of the word 'cup' is more akin to 'cupping'. In such languages the phrase 'sacred place' is also verb-like. The places are a focus for the rituals that take place there, and together there is a *process* of 'sacred placeness'. More specifically, they can only be experienced as part of movement through the landscape. In this sense, sacred places are part of a 'moving experience'.

The next step towards breaking down our preconceptions is to think outside the pages of books, and to step beyond the idea that sacred places are something to be discussed, written about and photographed. Books are best for discussing 'objects' but far from ideal when the emphasis is on 'processes' and subtle relationships to the surroundings. If we want to more fully appreciate sacred places they need to be experienced *directly*.

We always experience places in the present

Sacred places – indeed all places – are always experienced in the present, no matter how much we may value a prehistoric monument or a cathedral for its impressive sense of 'ancientness'. The history of a place is experienced in vastly compressed time depth. Major prehistoric monuments such as Avebury and Stonehenge were built up over hundreds, even thousands, of years. The same remark could be made of the older cathedrals of Europe. What we encounter today is devoid of any obvious time depth but has merely a 'simultaneous oldness', presented through the conventions of tourism and heritage marketing. Photographs, interpretation boards and guide books are seemingly more 'real' (if only because they can be readily assimilated) than the often complex reality of physical monuments.

The second step towards fully experiencing places is to attempt to think beyond this simplistic 'gee it's old' mentality and use whatever sources of information are available to see how the monument evolved over time – from its earliest inceptions, through to one or more heydays, and then how it has survived later destruction or modification, through to conservation (which may include extensive reconstruction) and whatever form it is in today. (See Chapters 8 and 9 for examples.)

We are always here

The third step towards breaking down our seemingly hard wired assumptions about places is to explore how we relate to where we are. Human nature naturally thinks in terms of a 'home', a place from which we travel to other places. Even if we emigrate and live in another place for many years (and, indeed may even be second- or third-generation offspring of such émigrés) a dialectical relationship exists with the place of origin. When we go on holiday, when we set off visiting 'sacred places', we go 'away'. And yet, incontrovertibly, we are always 'here'. We never get 'there' because when we do it has become 'here'. There is a wonderful Zen exercise that requires the students to imagine while walking that they are remaining stationary while the Earth moves around them. That we find this idea strange is even stranger. After all, our perceptions are *always* here and it is always our surroundings that move around us, whether at the pace of our own walking or a result of motorised transport.

We are omnipresent

This suggests a further step towards cracking open 'consensus reality', which is to challenge the apparently clear and immutable distinction between self and not-self which modern mentality imposes. Challenges to these distinctions are often regarded as pathological, as with schizophrenia – although 'hearing voices' seems to have been a favourite occupation of Old Testament prophets and no doubt a great number of other spiritual leaders and 'wise elders' the world over. A great number of apparently ordinary and almost certainly quite sane people are happy to 'channel' from the Otherworld, or simply make the most of 'inner conversations' experienced during 'guided visualisations', lucid dreaming, and so-called 'altered states of consciousness' (Klimo 1987). Such activities clearly are not pathological, although perhaps at one end of a spectrum that leads to the involuntary auditory hallucinations of schizophrenia.

Modern rationalism may have explained many natural phenomena but, so far, it has not been able to explain how or why humans are 'conscious' or even to come up with an understanding of consciousness that is agreed by relevant scientists. I have been lurking on the email discussion group for the *Journal of Consciousness Studies* for about eight years. Here all relevant issues have been comprehensively debated, but the best these multi-disciplinary academics can do is recognise the so-called 'hard problem' at the core of consciousness. Until these experts have at least a workable hypothesis about what it means to be conscious, we should not to assume our 'common sense' has anything better to offer.

By and large enhancing our appreciation of sacred places does not require entering the problematical territory of self:not-self distinctions, although there will be sections in this book where such boundaries will be regarded as permeable or being entirely different for traditional cultures.

The world was once alive for us all

Most modern minds are the product of materialistic cultures so believing the sun, wind, flowing water, animals, plants and maybe even rocks are spiritual entities is often regarded as mere superstition. But, even though the modern monoculture is the most materialistic culture the world has ever known, we readily recognise this more animistic way of looking at the world. Why do we recognise it so readily? Because such animism is a more 'obvious' interpretative schema than the reductionist materialism of post-Enlightenment western culture. Even in western cultures children adopt somewhat animistic worldviews before education instils alternative schemas.

Further recollection about our own childhood beliefs will reveal that animism does not bring forth a world full of happiness. Rather there also come innumerable bogey men of the shadows and the projections resulting from fear of the unknown. Childhood animism may be a *natural* response to the world but it is also one populated with frightening demons. By postulating their non-existence, scientific rationalism has become the ultimate slayer of demonic powers.

Rupert Sheldrake has also drawn attention to the ambivalent way modern minds approach animism:

> Oddly enough, I think most people in our society take it for granted that the universe is alive, but only in their 'off-duty' moments, at weekends or while they are on holiday. The extreme dissociation from natural processes which is engendered by the technological nature of our modern life has created, it seems, an imbalance in our attitudes towards nature, and many people live a kind of double-life. During working hours they accept a mechanistic world view, or at least go along with it, and in their free time they revert to a kind of Wordsworthian romanticism about natural beauty and unspoilt nature. But if we really begin to take the idea that nature is alive seriously, then we must adopt it not just at weekends when we are gardening or when we are with our pets and children, but in our official life, during working hours.
> (Sheldrake 1989)

Tourism is not pilgrimage

Experiencing places, especially new places and sacred places, is often something we do on our holidays or at weekends – the time when Sheldrake suggests our innate animism is allowed to come out and play. Ah, so tourism is the modern day counterpart to traditional pilgrimage? Far from it. Not only has Protestant Christianity desecrated (literally) the tradition of sacredness of place, creating the anomaly of mankind's first secular landscapes, but the concept of 'tourism' is inextricably rooted in nineteenth century imperialism and colonialism. With the advent of mechanised transport tourism became one of the longest-surviving and pervasive manifestations of imperialism.

> Even though tourists appear to be physically present in Nature or Culture, in effect one might call them ghosts haunting ruins, lacking all bodily presence. They're not really *there*, but rather move through a mind-scape, an abstraction ('Nature', 'Culture'), collecting images rather than experience. All too frequently their vacations are taken in the midst of other peoples' misery and even add to that misery.
> (Bey no date; mid-1990s)

Tourists leave 'home' to admire 'the scenery' and make tentative explorations of the cultural differences, the 'otherness', of their destinations. Whereas increasing tourism erodes the cultural differences, increasing pilgrimage enhances the sense of the numinous. In contrast to the tourist, a pilgrim is seeking a change in awareness, a shift in consciousness. Pilgrimage is *experiential* and immersive in a way that tourism is not. Hakim Bey goes so far as to state that 'Pilgrimage is a form of initiation, and initiation is an opening to other forms of cognition.'

> The wandering dervish who sleeps at a shrine in order to dream of a dead saint (one of the 'People of the Tombs') seeks initiation or advancement on the spiritual path. A mother who brings a sick child to Lourdes seeks

healing. A childless woman in Morocco hopes the *Marabout* will make her fertile if she ties a rag to the old tree growing out of the grave. The traveller to Mecca yearns for the very centre of the Faith, and as the caravans come within sight of the Holy City the *hajji* calls out 'Labbaïka Allabumma!' – 'I am *here,* O Lord!'
(Bey no date)

Bey's colourful style of writing provides a contrasting depiction of tourists:

Nothing ever really touches the life of the tourist. Every act of the tourist is mediated. Anyone who's ever witnessed a phalanx of Americans or a bus load of Japanese advancing on some ruin or ritual must have noticed that even their collective gaze is mediated by the medium of the camera's multi-faceted eye, and that the multiplicity of cameras and videocameras forms a complex of shiny clicking scales in an armour of pure mediation. Nothing organic penetrates this insectoid carapace which serves as both protective critic and predatory mandible, snapping up images, images, images. At its most extreme this mediation takes the form of the 'guided tour', in which every image is interpreted by a licensed expert, a 'psychopomp' or guide of the Dead, a virtual Virgil in the Inferno of meaninglessness – a minor functionary of the Central Discourse and its metaphysics of appropriation – a pimp of fleshless ecstasies.
(Bey no date)

Bey's essay, called 'Overcoming tourism' and available on a number of Web sites, provides numerous ideas relating to exploring sacred places. The major part concerns what 'western' minds can learn from the wandering Dervishes, the Sufi mystics for whom the act of travel transcends the mundane world as becomes an expansion of spiritual joy. His writing is tendentious and intentionally challenging, setting up a dialectical process between his over-stated rhetoric and 'consensus' cultural values.

A brief history of pilgrimage

The wanderings of the Australian Dreamtime Spirits, the Israelites being led by Moses through the desert to their promised land, the Classical legends of Odysseus or Jason, the peregrinatory life of Jesus Christ, the quest for the Holy Grail by the Arthurian knights, Dante's trip to Purgatory, John Bunyan's *Pilgrim's Progress* are all among the great diversity of heroic journeys that are the stalwarts of mythic literature. In contrast, the most mere mortals can aspire to is pilgrimage.

The earliest records we have of large-scale pilgrimage relate to the Classical Greeks. For most of the first millennium BCE Greeks toured well-known shrines and temples. In many cases they were seeking guidance about a specific problem. They visited oracles to gain the god's approval for a course of action. They were initiated into various mystery cults, mostly in the hope of obtaining better rewards in the afterlife. Above all, they visited healing sanctuaries. Divine guidance and intervention were the key objectives of these pilgrims (Dillon 1997).

The Romans maintained the Greek tradition of travelling around the Mediterranean to a variety of sacred sites. This tradition merged seamlessly into early Christian practices. Jerusalem became the paramount destination and, when it was taken by the Moslems in 637–8 CE, led to a generally rather disastrous series of Crusades that blurred the boundaries between pilgrimage and warfare.

Rome and Santiago de Compostella were the other major destinations for medieval pilgrims, although a multitude of more local sites – such as Walsingham and Canterbury – also formed part of this immense and lucrative 'industry'. The social and economic implications of medieval pilgrimage are vast and difficult to put into context. We know that up to 40,000 pilgrims arrived in Rome *every day* during 1450, perhaps because the Holy See had promoted this as a Jubilee Year to attract more pilgrims than usual. On one day in 1496 there were said to be 142,000 pilgrims in Aachen, although we have no way of knowing if this was exceptional or even exaggerated. Throughout the thirteenth and fourteenth centuries there is abundant evidence of churches being rebuilt to accommodate vast numbers of visitors, and of brisk trade in religious relics to entice pilgrims to these places. The trade in souvenirs sold to pilgrims is also mind-boggling – 130,000 badges were sold in a fortnight at Einseideln in Switzerland (Stopford 1994).

The literature on Christian pilgrimage is also vast. Victor Turner (Turner 1974; Turner and Turner 1978; Turner 1979) sees pilgrimage as a 'social process' with its own metaphorical or symbolic relationships to other aspects of the society. Compared to liturgical practices, which follow established customs, pilgrimage activities are more responsive to social change and popular moods, thereby offering greater insight into the beliefs of the pilgrims (see, for example, Eade and Sallnow 1991).

Despite the emphasis of academics on Christian pilgrimage, whether medieval or modern, pilgrimage is not a predominantly Christian practice. The heterogeneous nature of Hinduism ensures that pilgrimage plays a part in its religious practices. The aim of Hindu pilgrims is usually 'to cleanse away one's past sins and to acquire spiritual merit for one's future life after death. The more austere the journey, the more spiritual merit one gains.' The pilgrimage destinations are typically on the banks of rivers and lakes, although the 'liminal' nature of places is also significant as these destinations symbolise the intersection of the spiritual realms with the physical world. Indeed the Sanskrit word for a place of pilgrimage, *tirtha*, is derived from the root word meaning 'to cross over'. (Choudhury 1994: 67–8)

Pilgrimage is also a feature of pre-conquest South American cultures, perhaps intensified during the conquest era when the indigenous people felt most in need of supernatural assistance, then merged into the syncretistic practices of Catholicism in this continent. Evidence has been revealed in Peru (Silvermann 1994) and at Mayan ceremonial centres in Belize (Hammond and Bobo 1994) for such continuity from pre-conquest to modern times.

Archaeologists have similarly begun to look for evidence of pre-Christian pilgrimage in the British Isles. Croagh Patrick is the pre-eminent sacred mountain of Ireland and the focus of annual Catholic pilgrimages in early August, the time of the pagan festivals of Lughnasa. Legend holds that St Patrick spent the forty days of Lent there in 441, spending his time fasting, praying and banishing both pagan spirits and serpents. The earliest recorded pilgrimage was in 1113 CE, at a time when local pilgrimages were beginning to be 'fashionable'. Nevertheless there is abundant evidence for prehistoric ritual in the vicinity of this mountain. While only two prehistoric sites have been identified with any certainty on Croagh Patrick itself, the surrounding area contains the remains of many Bronze Age ritual monuments, with the cone-shape of Croagh Patrick and its quartz summit acting as the focus. The mountain may have been significant in the Neolithic too, but not until the Bronze Age was enough of the natural forest cleared away to provide distant views (Corlett 1997).

By the Iron Age pilgrimage to sacred sites in Ireland seems to have become well organised. In the vicinity of Uisneach, County Westmeath – long held to be the sacred centre of the country – an Iron Age roadway was built over about five miles of bog near Corlea. This was wide enough to take wheeled vehicles and must have required considerable effort to construct. It is in a direct line between Uisneach and a probable Iron Age ceremonial centre at Cruachain, with a long-established crossing over the River Shannon also in line. Was this road merely of practical benefit for local inhabitants, or was it constructed also to enhance the status of the local rulers? Was it even in the nature of a 'toll road', constructed with the intention of generating revenue from those who benefited from using it? Were there sufficient pilgrims plying between these two ritual sites to justify such enormous effort to aid their passage? (Raftery 1994: 104) As ever, the archaeological evidence teases us and leaves such questions unanswered.

In England Roman roads pass close to Iron Age shrines, redeveloped in the Roman era as temples. Which came first – the shrine or the road? Whatever the answer in the Iron Age, clearly the Romans were adopting existing religious sites and their associated 'infrastructure' of roads. On the Leicestershire/Nottinghamshire border is the site of the small Roman town of Vernemetum, a name that translates as 'Great or Especially Sacred Grove', which strongly suggests a pre-Roman site. It sits alongside the Fosse Way, one of the three 'primary routes' of Roman Britain and (in this section at least) betraying all the characteristics of a prehistoric ridgeway. About 15 miles away, on the Leicestershire/Rutland border near Thistleton, an Iron Age shrine was redeveloped as a Roman temple and small town. This is located near to an east-west route that appears to be prehistoric. The roads to these shrines link them not only to local settlements, but to a national network of routes. Evidence from Ireland (where there was no Roman occupation) suggests that, not only may we reasonably expect Iron Age 'pilgrims', but such practices may go back further still.

Secular modern society substitutes tourism for pilgrimage. The superficial similarities suggest this is continuation or substitution. Indeed, tourist spectacles such as theme parks create and communicate a sense of reality, truth, and value – pretty much what might have been expected too from the best of medieval pilgrimages. The inclusion of long-established pilgrimage destinations, such as cathedrals, into the itinerary of tourists also blurs this distinction. Furthermore, in recent decades a new form of tourism has developed with pilgrimage-like aspects to it. The destinations are the battle sites and mass graves of the First World War. British and Continental tourists now tour the 'white cities' of the Somme valley in France in numbers hitherto not experienced. Australian tourists, many of the 'backpacking' generation, visit the scene of their compatriots' demise at Gallipoli, Turkey. The interest in the war graves is linked, although not always directly, with the great increase in 'ancestor worship' in Britain during recent decades – 'family history' is by far the most actively-pursued aspect of historical research in the country.

While the motives for visiting war graves are in some respects distinct from other forms of tourism, I am reluctant to regard them as pilgrimages. Indeed, contrary to a number of academic studies which see little distinction between pilgrimage and tourism, I fully support Hakim Bey's cogent observation that, in contrast to the tourist, a pilgrim is seeking a change in awareness, a shift in consciousness. In other words, pilgrimage is *experiential* to a much greater extent that tourism, which has usually satisfied with the appearances of 'otherness'.

Walking as pilgrimage

Until about 150 years ago, pilgrimage was a far more thorough-going experience. Travel by boat, although hardly a pleasant experience most of the time, was the easy option. For the rich the land journeys would be assisted by horses. But the typical pilgrims, on the move throughout medieval Europe in the hundreds of thousands every year, would be walking.

Walking itself readily becomes a spiritual activity – even through urban and suburban areas where traffic is not too obtrusive. The bodily movements generate a meditative rhythm and the surroundings 'appear' slowly enough not to intrude on streams of thought. 'Walking Zen' is a recognised meditative practice.

As will be discussed in the next sections, *all* our senses, notably sound and the kinaesthetic awareness of our own bodies, are fully involved when we are walking. This makes walking an 'immersive' experience, although not to the extent that our streams of thought are dominated by external stimuli.

While walking the rate at which we need to take account of changes in our surroundings – whether hazards in our path, flowers in the hedgerow, the opening up of a distant view, or just more subtle changes to the vista – does not usually challenge our cognitive processes, in contrast to the faster pace of cycling or motorised travel. There is something seemingly entirely natural about walking. This is hardly surprising as humans have been walking (and occasionally running) through the landscape for many hundreds of thousands of years.

By walking to sacred places several subtle physiological and mental activities combine together. Our bodies feel better because of the exercise (assuming we have not walked so far as too feel unduly tired – and even then the endorphins may be giving us a 'buzz'). The meditative state of mind induced by the rhythm of walking and immersion in our senses further improves our state of mind. Unless we have been walking through some exceptionally unattractive areas then there is at least some sense of being close to nature. More significantly, the sacred site takes its place among its surroundings, and is approached at a pace which is entirely natural.

The sense in which I am using the word 'walking' suggests more than being a pedestrian. There is a sense of purpose and awareness not associated with strolling or wandering. However a pre-ordained destination or route is not essential for such walking – the purpose is not to get somewhere else but rather a continual awareness that we are always 'here'. Such 'aware walking' provides a steadily evolving succession of 'heres'. The destination can be irrelevant – although, if the intention is to visit a sacred site, the 'aware walking' provides an appropriate sense of expectation.

Not all walking is 'aware walking', still less 'pilgrimage', for approximately the same reasons that tourism is not pilgrimage. But purposeful and aware walking sets the pace for effective pilgrimage, especially pilgrimage as defined by Hakim Bey 'an opening to other forms of cognition.' (Bey no date)

Listening to the landscape

One of the wonderful advantages of walking is that we can fully experience where we are. Most Western people are so dominated by their visual experiences that they rarely fully engage their other senses. Yet even with the limited sensitivity of the human nose a walk through woodland on a damp autumn day can offer a feast of olfactory experiences. Even when in the countryside few actively listen to the sounds around them. Only the most striking of bird songs or burbling brooks consciously register. The changes in the sounds of our footfalls as we pass from grassland to the dry soil of an arable field, over a timber footbridge, on to a gravel path, splash through a puddle, kick up some dead leaves, then swish past some undergrowth rarely break through our cognitive filtering processes into conscious awareness. We generally walk through our surroundings with the soundtrack turned off.

Vision is the dominant perception of modern culture. When we say 'I see what you mean' we do not necessarily mean this literally. Yet the dominant aim of rationalism and science is to make things visible – from graphs and flow diagrams through to telescopes, microscopes, X-rays, nuclear magnetic resonance, chromatographs and much, much else. It is as if the ultimate dream of rationalism is to see all human knowledge laid out, arranged in order – just as a landscape painting presents the scene from an idealised viewpoint (and this is not a superficial comparison but reveals how the visually-dominated metaphor of 'seeing = understanding' is *causal* in our culture).

Despite the dominance of vision, our hearing is nevertheless essential to develop a 'sense of place'. Sounds fill our surroundings (whether natural or built) and give places a specific character or 'presence'. However, unlike vision we cannot readily map sounds. Neither do we customarily record sounds in the same way photographs or drawings quite commonly 'freeze' our vision. This means that sound is typically experienced directly. And, equally importantly, if we notice sounds at all we tend to 'experience the moment' more intensely than with visual stimuli. And, unlike vision, our sense of hearing is not diminished in the darkness (indeed, in the absence of distracting visual stimulation, our hearing may appear more acute in low light).

Before the invention of writing all verbal communication was part of our sound world rather than an aspect of our visual experiences. Because we cannot 'close our ears' in the same way as we can close our eyes and because our hearing is omni-directional we always hear our complete acoustic environment, even though our cognitive processes have devised sophisticated ways of 'filtering out' non-threatening and 'background' sounds.

As briefly mentioned before, people who live in dense jungle cannot visualise the space around them. Whereas Westerners might think 'I thought I heard a monkey –

Ah, yes! I can see it over there', Amazonians would only believe there was a monkey if they *heard* the monkey, and would regard a sighting in the same way a western would respond to the sound alone. For the Amazonians 'hearing is believing', in contrast to the western 'seeing is believing' (Thorn 1997). The Suya of Brazil use the expression 'it is in my ear' where we would say 'I see what you mean'. Keen hearing is the mark of a 'fully socialised individual' and sight is considered by Suya people to be anti-social, cultivated only by witches (Classen 1993: 9). For the Songhai in central West Africa vision is often less important than taste, smell and hearing. In the Songhai language one tastes kinship, smells witches, and hears the ancestors (Stoller 1989 :5).

In such societies aural landscapes share with visual ones the concepts of landmarks and boundaries. For the Umeda of Papua New Guinea the auditory horizon is a tall ridge around the knoll where their village stands. The words used to encode these features and the traversing of the jungle create an auditory map which can only be understood dynamically, as movement (Gell 1995).

Hearing is fundamental to knowledge for Australian Aborigines in a subtly different way. They only believe the country exists when they could both see it and *sing it* by chanting the relevant 'Dreaming track' or so-called 'song line' (already discussed in Chapter 2). There must be a mental concept – the words of the song – before the landscape can be said to exist. James Cowan reports being driven along 'Dreaming tracks' accompanied by local guides, who only recognise where they are if they can 'sing up the country'. Bearing in mind that these songs were conceived for travel at walking pace, some virtuosity is needed to recite fast enough to keep up with a fast-moving 4x4 (Cowan 1989).

Acoustics and our ancestors

Early examples of the use of sound to enhance the sacredness of a place have been recognised in the caves at Ariege beneath the French Pyrénées. These contain extensive Palaeolithic wall paintings. At certain places close to significant motifs anyone singing or whistling at the correct pitch will set up dramatic resonances. This is not an isolated example; in later periods temples were designed to amplify sound as part of the ritual procedures. At Hal Saflieni on Malta a voice speaking into a certain recess resonates throughout the vaults, perhaps aweing the faithful with disembodied voices capable of a full range of tones from thunderous to whispered.

American rock art consistently occupy places which provide abnormally strong echoes or where sounds such as clapping re-echo as the sound of running animals. Similar examples have been found in Australia. (*New Scientist* 28 Nov 1992; Waller 1993a, 1993b).

In the mid-1990s more scientific investigation of the acoustic properties of prehistoric sites began (Jahn 1995; Jahn *et al* 1996; Devereux and Jahn 1996; Watson and Keating 1999, 2000). Paul Devereux has provided several accessible introductions to this research (Devereux 2001a, 2002b; 2004). Three broad acoustic responses at prehistoric sites have been investigated. The first reveals that carved or painted rock art, whether in caves or 'rock shelters', is cited at spots where the echoes are more pronounced. So chanting, singing, clapping or drumming calls forth sounds that seemingly emanate from the decorated rock surface – as if the spirits of the image are talking back.

The nearest I have come to a personal experience of such eerie effects is when a group of pagans were drumming in the nave of a high-roofed Victorian church (with a very ecumenical vicar!). The echoes formed complex sound patterns quite unrelated to the rhythm and pitch of the drums, for all the world sounding like the roof space was filled with Otherworldly spirits fluttering and chattering. Had their been even less light, or other factors had created more of an altered state of consciousness, then the illusion would have been entirely 'real'.

The second effect discovered so far is anomalous sound reflections at stone circles, especially the Scottish ones with so-called 'recumbent' stones, where the recumbent megalith acts as a 'sounding board' to help project the voice of someone standing in front. Such 'sound reinforcement' works only within the ring of stones, except for some really curious instances where the sound is also remarkably clear at a nearby prehistoric site, even though all-but inaudible *between* the two.

The third aspect of the acoustic research shows that Neolithic chambered tombs have a natural resonant frequency that falls within the range of the male voice. Experiments with setting up 'standing waves' in, say, Newgrange have resulted in decidedly odd experiences. Paul Devereux reports being inside a chamber tomb when such a standing wave was created by researchers. Moving away from the sound source the chamber would first fall silent (at the 'troughs' in the standing wave, where the 'echo' cancels out the source) then increase in loudness (at the 'crests', where the echo augments the source). 'To a people who did not understand sound in terms of waves, this would seem very mysterious indeed.' (Devereux 2002b: 29) If someone else moves within the chamber this can cause dramatic alterations in the 'distribution' of the sound and its loudness at a particular place. Other effects include 'ventriloquism', that is the sound source seems to be in an improbable place. When a standing wave is set up speech is distorted with extraordinary harmonics. These are all wonderfully impressive 'special effects' for ritual activities – as if the interior of a chamber tomb (especially while it still contained the bones of one's ancestors and other sacred objects) was not already a powerful setting for ritual activities.

These standing waves can be set up by chanting, singing or drumming. They can also arise if the wind blows across the entrance to such chambers, creating a lower-frequency version of the eerie sound created by blowing across an empty bottle. Thomas Hardy wrote in *Tess of the D'Urbervilles* of the wind blowing at Stonehenge and creating 'a booming tone, like the note of some gigantic one-stringed harp' (cited in Dickinson 2001: 98).

In recent decades first 'alternative archaeology' and then academic archaeologists have recognised that Neolithic and Bronze Age monuments incorporate complex alignments, astronomical orientations, shadow paths, etc. (see Chapter 5). Predicatably, modern minds are more likely to recognise such *visual* complexity. However, as prehistoric people probably used all their senses more equally, quite plausibly our ancestors intentionally incorporated equally sophisticated *acoustic* complexity in their monuments.

Recent work on 'archaeo-acoustics' reported at a conference in June 2003 by about twenty researchers includes studying echoes in Palaeolithic painted caves (including the recently-discovered paintings at Cresswell Crags in Derbyshire) and Swedish rock art sites. Various Neolithic chamber tombs were also found to resonate at 100 Hz, and audio frequency which significantly affects the pre-frontal and temporal cortex of the human brain (Mortimer 2003).

At a complex rock art site created by the Algonkian Indians of the Ontario region of Canada between 600 and 1,100 years ago the main group of carvings are on a deeply-fissured outcrop of marble. At certain times of the year water can be heard issuing from the fissure – and it sounds like a babble of voices. Presumably the Indians venerated the site because they thought these were the voices of *manitous* or spirits. (Devereux 2004b). Other rock art sites in the Ontario region were associated with anomalous echoes. Indeed one set of carvings is in a park known as Bon Echo. 'Had the Indians, like the ancient Greeks, believed echoes to be the sound of spirits calling, mimicking human-made noises to do so?' asks Devereux.

Interesting acoustic effects is not restricted to prehistoric sites. The acoustics of Classical Greek and Roman theatres reveal an exceptional ability to make the voices of the actors heard by a large number of people. Graeme Lawson has reported on remarkable acoustic discoveries at Wells Cathedral (Lawson 2003). Bob Dickinson has provided overviews of 'sacred resonances' in caves, mosques and even English cathedrals, such as Lincoln (Dickinson 1990a&b, 1998a, 2001). Almost certainly Anglo-Saxon plainchant could generate spectacular standing wave effects in the small cave-like stone-built churches of the time, although to my knowledge no one has attempted to replicate this experience – and there is no way of knowing if such effects were intentionally sought by early Christians. Later 'polyphonic' plainchant of the medieval era resounding through a cathedral built at the time such music was composed is a wonderful experience although modern singers typically do not attempt to pitch their voices according to the natural resonances of the building (I have been informed of a solo singer at St Ouen in Rouen who sang close to the columns; his voice caused the columns to resonate resulting in a strangely disembodied sound that had no clear place of origin).

If this sounds a little far-fetched then consider the clusters of musical stone pillars in the Nellaiyappar temple dedicated to Shiva, the Hindu 'Lord of the Dance'. Gently tapping the columns produces the seven notes of the scale used in Indian classical music. According to the temple's own chronicle these pillars were erected in the seventh century. There is a total of 161 tuned pillars, arranged in clusters with up to 48 smaller columns around a larger pillar. Each cluster is hewn out of a single piece of rock. No other temple has such an elaborate arrangement, although eight other temples in the south of India with musical pillars are known. Such musical pillars are clearly counterparts to the many Indian temples where the columns are decorated with depictions of musicians or dancers (Venkatesh 2004). Elsewhere in southern India, at Hiregudda Hill, are gong-like musical boulders associated with rock art which dates back from recent times to the Neolithic (Bolvin 2004). Other ringing rocks are known from the Kupgal district of India. But such effects may have also been known in the British Isles (Fagg 1957). In the Presceli district of south-west Wales (where the 'blue stones' at Stonehenge are believed to have originated – see

Chapters 9 and 10) there is a hamlet called Maenclochog which translates as 'ringing rocks'. The rock type is dolerite similar to that at Hiregudda Hill which makes a ringing sound when struck. The ringing rocks at Maenclochog are thought to have been destroyed by quarrying in the late eighteenth century. However it raises the possibility that the Stonehenge 'blue stones' were originally significant as 'ringing rocks', before being silenced by being stood up in the ground.

Paul Devereux also reports that in 1983 a woman was waiting for the sunrise at Stonehenge. Just before dawn 'she suddenly heard a "ringing" sound issuing from a stone close to her' (Devereux 1990: 144), although it is not clear if the stone was a bluestone or a sarsen.

In non-western societies where vision does not dominate our structuring of the world then these various acoustic phenomena could be an integral part of 'hearing is believing'. In other words, what was being heard, and where, was part of the way the culture knew about nature of knowledge. Steven Feld has written that for the Kaluli of Papua New Guinea the whole auditory domain, including natural sounds, language and song are 'cultural systems in their own right, and not just adjuncts to culture at large, but as foundations, thematic at every level of cultural experience.' (Feld 1982: 3)

Bells, gongs, rattles, whistles, fireworks, drums, shouts, foot stamping, chants, mantras and hymns are used world-wide to banish demons. The early Christian saints carried hand bells for use at key moments in the Mass, although they seem to be a continuation of pre-Christian practices for banishing unwanted otherworldly entities, as the 'bell, book and candle' of Christian exorcism clearly confirms. The larger bells of church towers were until recent times widely credited with the ability to frighten away the Devil.

Geomagnetism and dream incubation

Sight, sound, smell, taste, touch are the five senses recognised by rationalism. More subtly humans are sensitive to magnetism, specifically the weak levels of magnetism associated with the Earth's magnetic field – known as geomagnetism. Other animals have been shown to have more developed sensitivity to geomagnetism. For instance the homing instinct of pigeons can be turned off by tying small magnets to their heads, showing that their prodigious feats of navigation rely on sensitivity to geomagnetism. In the 1970s Dr Robin Baker of Manchester University showed that humans' sense of direction is also lost when magnets are placed either side of the head. He took a coach-load of blindfolded students on a circuitous journey. Most of those with non-magnetic metal bars either side of their heads could indicate roughly which direction they had come from. Those with magnets on their heads could not (Baker 1980).

Baker's research was repeated in America. This revealed that students there have a poor sense of direction even *without* magnets. Presumably this is because Americans are accustomed to finding their way around rectilinear cities and not the more chaotic European cities, so their ability to respond to their body's innate sense of direction had atrophied. In contrast, people whose lives depend on keeping their bearings over large distances have a better sense of direction than Manchester students. For example, James Cowan reports that Australian Aborigines have an 'absolute compass sense'. When transferred to hospital many hundreds of miles from their home, Aboriginal patients can readily and reliably point to the direction of home (Cowan 1992: 13).

Scientists have yet to decide which organs are sensitive to magnetism, although the main suspect is the pineal gland. This is situated in the middle of the head (but technically not part of the brain). The shape and internal structure vary greatly. Although only about the size of the nail on our little finger, only the kidneys and pituitary gland receive similar blood flow. The outside of the pineal gland hardens during adolescence and at this time becomes responsive to changes in magnetic fields (Roney-Dougal 1991; Roney-Dougal and Vogl 1993).

The influence that the pineal gland has on consciousness can only be regarded as subtle but effective. The gland is most closely associated with the production of serotonin (a neuro-transmitter) and melatonin (a neuro-hormone). The nerves to and from the pineal connect only to the autonomic nervous system. Interestingly the autonomous nervous system is implicated in various aspects of healing and 'psychic' responses. This may be because the pineal also releases beta-carboline, closely related to naturally-occurring psychoactive chemicals such as harmaline. Harmaline is one of the active ingredients in *ayahuasca*, used by the indigenous people of South America to induce an altered state of consciousness in which they contact spirit guides for various 'psychic' activities such as precognition, clairvoyance, healing and out of body travel.

Serotonin and melatonin help to control our waking and sleep cycle (Roney-Dougal 1991: Ch.4). As many people will be aware, severe stress can disrupt our sleep and this is a result of the stress interfering with the response of the pineal gland; I suspect that many readers will have experienced the disruption to sleep patterns this causes. Writing this chapter on a dull November day and fighting a feeling of lethargy reminds me that serotonin/melatonin imbalance is linked to Seasonal Affective Disorder (SAD), which can be alleviated by bright lights.

One clue that the pineal gland is sensitive to geomagnetism is revealed when people are kept in constant low light. This means that the pineal gland cannot use daylight to cue the serotonin/melatonin cycle. The body defaults to a 25 hour cycle. This is the frequency of the moon circling the earth and strongly suggests that the body is responding to subtle tides in geomagnetism.

Melatonin normally peaks about six hours after dusk. Think of how many religions regard 3 a.m. as the most powerful time to chant matins, mantras or Buddhist scriptures. Could this be the origin of the 'witching hour', the time when Cinderella must go home? Folklore frequently alludes to the intuitive states of dark and winter, but says little of the magic of sunlight.

Given these close links between sleep, stress and psychic states of consciousness, it may be no surprise that the long-standing therapeutic practice of 'dream incubation' may be linked to natural magnetic 'hot spots'. I have speculated that Greek and Roman dream incubation temples may have been associated with geomagnetic 'hot spots' (Trubshaw 1991b; 1992; 2003b&c). The starting point was recognising that there are two Roman temples in Britain where the ground plans reveal the type of buildings used for dream incubation. One is in the Forest of Dean (Gloucestershire) at Lydney. This is situated on a hill that had earlier in the Roman era been quarried for iron ore. The second is near Thistleton on the Leicestershire/Rutland border. It was revealed by aerial photography ahead of open cast iron ore extraction, although has never been excavated. Both these deposits of iron ore are especially rich in iron.

In Classical Greece and into the Roman era there were a number of temples where dream incubation took place. Many of these were dedicated to the god Aesculapius after the most famous of these temples at Epidaurus. In specially-built 'dormitories' the visitors slept and hoped for a dream in which the gods would provide guidance. Specially-trained *theraputes* helped the visitors to interpret their dreams. The practice had more in common with divination than anything we commonly think of as 'therapy'.

Presumably the Greeks acquired the practice of dream incubation from the ancient Egyptians. The Old Testament also refers to dream incubation – think of Jacob resting his head on a 'sacred stone' and dreaming of a vast ladder reaching up to heaven. The literature of ancient Chinese also makes reference to seeking divinatory dreams.

I was somewhat disappointed to find that Epidaurus is not associated with iron ore deposits. However photographs of adjacent cliffs reveal a major unconformity in the underlying rocks (limestone overlying igneous rocks), which could lead to changes in the geomagnetic field akin to those caused by iron deposits.

Curiously, one of the mystery cults with the greatest influence throughout the Greek and Roman world was based on the small and isolated island of Samothrace. Archaeologists have found a number of iron rings in the sanctuary and relevant records suggest that the initiates received an iron ring and the 'effect of some hidden, moving power was demonstrated with the phenomenon of magnetism.' (Burket 1993: 187–8) There is no indication that the Samothracian mystery rituals involved dream incubation, but instead suggest that the effects of magnetism were known and used ritually.

Seeking inspiration from dreams is known from Irish medieval literature (Drayton 1995: 11). Night vigils, dreams and 'dream explanations' recur throughout the Arthurian romances. According to these tales affairs of state in post-Roman Britain were often decided by dreams. 'They influenced Arthur's choice of Camelot instead of Cardoel for his capital city. On the occasion when he fathered his son Mordred, his murderer to be, Arthur dreamed of a terrible serpent.' (Darrah 1994: 179) Dreams are also in the forefront of the modern 'mythology' of psychoanalysis (Trubshaw 2003a: 9–12).

Divinatory dreams are part of Islamic practice. Indeed the Koran regards the study of dreams to be 'the prime science since the beginning of the world'. At the shrine of St George near Cairo both Moslem and Christian pilgrims seek cures by sleeping in or by the shrine (Heath-Stubbs 1984: 7–8). Over 1,000 Indian pilgrims go to the temple of Shiva at Tarakeswar, north of Calcutta, every day to seek dreams that will cure their illnesses (Devereaux 2002a: 195). In North America 'vision questing' is prevalent among traditional religious practices. As if to support the suggested links

The peak of Carn Ingli, Pembrokeshire.

with geomagnetism, a Montville 'prayer seat' in New England had been erected since 1950 under a high voltage electrical transmission line – as if to deliberately use the resultant changes to the electromagnetic field as part of the vision quests associated with such native sacred sites (Mavor and Dix 1989: 264). An aerial survey of geomagnetism in New England has been compared with the location of native 'praying villages' (considered to be the abodes of the spirit Hobomock). The correlation is impressive (Mavor and Dix 1989: 294). Independently of this research, James Swan reports that:

> All across the United States there are mystery spots... Two of the best known are located at Gold Hill, Oregon and Santa Cruz, California. I can find no Indian legend that says these were sacred places, but you ought to go visit them to see what you think. Strange things seem to happen there....I think they're magnetic anomalies, probably due to some geological anomalies.
> (Swan 1990: 230)

The idea that changes in geomagnetism might influence mental processes seems to have first been popularised by Janet and Colin Bord in their 1976 book *The Secret Country* (Bord and Bord 1976: 52–60). These suggestions led to experimental fieldwork in the 1980s by members of the Dragon Project, led by Paul Devereux. The preliminary results of this research were published as *Places of Power* (Devereux 1990: 62–3); see also Chapter 5. Philip Burton has followed up this research by surveying numerous prehistoric stone circles in Britain for magnetic 'anomlaies' (Burton 1993; 1995; 2002). Such anomalies include a natural stone 'seat' in a stone at Gows Fawr stone circle in the Preseli mountains of Pembrokeshire. The peak of nearby Carn Ingli has many remarkable magnetic areas; the significance of Carn Ingli and the Preseli mountains are explored in Chapter 10.

The geomagnetic field is also subtly distorted by changes in the underlying rocks, particularly at fault lines. Such fault lines are widespread and it would be overly-simplistic to suggest that sacred sites are found in proximity to such faults (that would be rather like observing that most alcoholics live within a mile of an off-licence). However some faults may have more pronounced or 'interesting' effects on humans than others. Furthermore, as has been already noted, traditional nomadic people such as Australian Aborigines are innately more sensitive to geomagnetism than contemporary city dwellers.

Dowsing and psychic responses to landscapes

If we can accept that the human body is capable of responding to magnetism – and Robin Baker's research seems to show this – and that people living in more 'traditional' cultures might have a greater sensitivity, then this opens up the possibility that humans are also 'subliminally' responsive to other external stimuli.

A surprisingly high proportion of people – probably more than half – quickly pick up the ability to dowse. Quite what these people are responding to and 'how it works' are unknown. Because so far there has been no scientific explanation so-called 'rational' people dismiss dowsing out of hand. However, there is no scientific explanation for human consciousness or even the detailed processes by which human memory operates, but these so-called rationalists do not seem quite so keen to reject the idea that they are conscious or have memories.

Much as I am unwilling to reject dowsing, much that has been written and said about dowsing sacred sites is an aggregation of gonads. How such speculative ideas came to be so widespread is discussed in Chapter 5. Some years ago I published an article called 'Dowsing: the good, the bad and the muddled' (Trubshaw 1993) which is available online. The key distinction made in this article is that dowsing for water, buried archaeological remains and other 'physical' evidence is quite distinct from so-called 'energy dowsing'.

While taking part in a number of 'field trips' organised by the East Midlands Dowsing Group (EMDG) during the 1990s I was able to observe many different dowsers. Some were very experienced and others novices, with plenty of the 'middling sort'. Some of these trips involved different dowsers working independently on different but adjoining parts of a site. For instance at Arbor Low henge in Derbyshire the leader divided up the area just *outside* the henge rather like slices of a pie. Pairs of dowsers were allocated a 'slice' and asked to mark out underground water. Only when the 'exercise' was completed was there an opportunity to compare with people in adjoining 'slices'. Even though several of the 'slices' were allocated to relatively inexperienced dowsers, the match up between 'slices' was remarkable. In almost all cases it seemed that the whole site had been dowsed in the same way.

When the EMDG organised a visit to the Rollright stone circle on the Oxfordshire/Warwickshire border, broadly the same group of people were asked to

Arbor Low, Derbyshire.

dowse for 'energy' within the circle and then sketch the results on a piece of paper. These sketches were not to be shown to anyone else until after everyone had dowsed. A number of experienced dowsers produced quite different responses, with no evidence of a common 'pattern'. The less experienced dowsers were mostly rather 'baffled' as to whether they were getting 'real' responses or not. Clearly something very different was being experienced at Rollright compared to Arbor Low.

Other field trips by the EMDG confirmed that dowsing for underground water or buried walls leads to surprisingly consistent responses, even by people with limited experience. In contrast 'energy' dowsing produces very personal responses, usually described by the dowsers using quite different metaphors to each other (e.g. the 'colour' of the energy lines, the 'number' of such lines, or the apparent width on the ground).

I am quite happy to accept that 'physical' and 'energy' dowsing use, say, the autonomous nervous system in *similar* ways to bring 'subliminal' sensations to conscious awareness. Indeed, increasing competence with 'physical' dowsing may lead to greater competence at 'energy' dowsing, and vice versa. However this does not mean that the *stimuli* are necessarily similar. If I crush my finger in a door it causes pain. If I burn my finger it also causes similar pain. Both can be looked on broadly as 'injuries' and both excite the nervous system to shout 'pain'. But their causes are distinct.

In a similar way Paul Devereux has distinguished between two types of divination. One type requires the interpretation of chance movements of objects, animals or events – whether this is reading tea leaves at the bottom of a cup, observing the flight of birds, or analysing the entrails of sacrifced animals. The other type requires the diviner to enter a trance state and then offer prophetic or oracular guidance. Devereux is not the first to make this distinction, as he also states that the Greek philosopher Cicero, who lived in the first century BCE, called the first *entechnos*, 'divination that can be taught', and the second *atechnos* or *adidactos*, a natural ability rather than one that could be learned. In practice the two types can be combined, so someone with a 'natural ability' for divination gets a more accurate response from, say, tarot cards than someone who has merely learnt the correspondences. (Devereux 2002: 156)

In a similar way a lot of people who use dowsing also have some psychic abilities, such as clairvoyance or precognition. Although it is not necessary to be psychic to be able to dowse, the two skills seemingly reinforce each other. Quite plausibly dowsing and psychic abilities are 'picked up' subliminally and brought to awareness via the autonomous nervous system, in a similar manner to the way the pineal gland 'communicates' subtle changes in geomagnetism. Some individuals could be born with greater sensitivity to such processes. However the more such processes are used, the more sensitive and, presumably, more accurate they become. Other people might not have an innate sensitivity but learn to use *some aspects* of these processes. They do not regard themselves as 'psychic' but, nevertheless, may be competent dowsers or diviners equivalent to Cicero's *entechnos*.

There is some suggestion that 'physical' dowsing is picking up exceedingly subtle variations in geomagnetism. David Taylor has reported that:

> The average reading for the Earth's magnetic field is about half a Gauss. Dr Zaboj V. Harvalik has made a considerable number of magnetometer measurements which seem to indicate that dowsers react to magnetic gradient changes as weak as one milli-microGauss or, expressed another way, 10^{-9}Gauss (0.000,000,0001 Gauss). Physicist Yves Rocard, a Professor at Ecole Normale in Paris, has similarly been able to show that human beings can detect magnetic changes down to 10^{-8} Gauss.
> (Taylor 1993: 12)

One thing we do know about the Earth's magnetic field is that it is not constant. If dowsers are, indeed, sensitive to subtle changes in geomagnetism they are not picking up some 'constant pattern' but, rather, a complex interaction affected by the moon, changes in the water content of the soil, sunspots, variations in the very pervasive man-made electromagnetic radiation, and a large number of other parameters. Clearly underground water and buried archaeology will provide dowsable responses that will outweigh any changes in the 'noise'. But any attempt to dowse more subtle 'energy' could well be picking up transitory effects rather than a persistent pattern.

Suffice to say that when experiencing sacred places we should not only step beyond our visually-dominated ways and develop a greater awareness of sound, but also accept that our bodies may be picking up subtle changes in geomagnetism. For those of us who are more 'psychic' there may be even further 'subtle processes' instigated. Such enhanced awareness is inextricably linked to the natural pace of experiencing places – walking.

Transformative experiences

In contrast to such subtleties of experience, the evidence of the prehistoric past often seems rather barren. John Keats wrote:

> ... a dismal cirque
> Of Druid stones, upon a forlorn moor,
> When the chill rain begins at shut of eve,
> In dull November, and their chancel vault,
> The Heaven itself, is blinded throughout night.
> (*Hyperion* II, i, 31)

Although Keats seems unduly despondent about the significance of megalithic monuments, he seems to be anticipating the views of Christopher Tilley, a modern day academic especially intrigued by the experience of prehistoric places:

> Considering megaliths dispassionately, they most usually consist of a few tumbled chunks of unworked stone in a field encircled with brambles, nettles and rank grass. They are frequently difficult to find and unsignposted. The hazards of getting to them may involve braving the dangers of bulls, electric or barbed wire fences, tumbling walls, barking farm dogs, farmers brandishing shot guns and so on. After a strenuous walk the stone, or stones, may, given luck, be encountered. It is almost always raining. The architectural experience of a megalith might be described as minimalist. One unhewn stone rests on another, there is little finesse. After a few minutes, and perhaps a photograph, you have seen that site... What is it that has captured the European imagination in such places, and motivated the innumerable trips of antiquaries, artists, archaeologists, tourists?
> (Tilley 1993: 49–50)

Tilley's tongue-in-cheek irony leads him to compare megalithic remains with contemporary sculpture in the landscape – so-called 'environmental art' or 'landscape art'. Although the 'meaning' will usually be sufficiently diffuse to be a matter of dispute among different viewers, such art embodies a sense of place. Is this, in essence, also how we intuitively value our prehistoric remains?

If we are to explore sacred places in a way that extends beyond mere tourism or aestheticism into the realms of pilgrimage, we need to explore them in ways that begin to make them into 'transformative experiences'. Thankfully there are some well-established words that are less cumbersome than the phrase 'transformative experiences'. Among them are 'worship' and 'ritual'. Although these are typically associated with activities at sacred places, the whole activity of pilgrimage can also be seen as a ritual, albeit one for which there is no fixed 'liturgy'. Movement, such as ritualised walking or dancing, readily assists the mind to transcend its mundane body.

Sacred places are those parts of the landscape where social and personal identities and memories are most readily constructed and transformed through re-invention and 'acting out'. 'Acting out', whether done according to revered ancient liturgies or more playfully, is of course the essence of ritual. Present day pagans often have little difficulty 'acting out' at sacred places in ways that reinforce their own social and personal identities, and help integrate the place into their world-view. The overlaps between modern day paganism and alternative approaches to archaeology are explored in Chapter 5.

However ritual, indeed worship, at sacred sites can be based on far less preordained worldviews, allowing greater potential for a more fluid and perhaps more playful relationship with the meanings of a place. In the section above on sound in the landscape I introduced some of the ideas of Bob Dickinson. His own 'relationship' to the landscape has led to a number of 'musical compositions' that he terms 'Text Music'. One of these is an appropriate way to end this chapter about experiencing places.

New Moon / Stone Voice

For one or more singers, to be performed within a stone circle (maximum number of singers to be determined by the number of stones in the circle, one singer per stone)

1. Stillness:

   - Palms resting on a stone.

   - Eyes closed.

   - Regular, slow, deep breathing.

2. Begin:

   - Your voice sounds as the stone sings through you.

3. To finish:

   - In your own time, return to silence, to the source.

(Dickinson 1998b)

Sources

Baker 1980; Bey no date; Bord and Bord 1976: 52–60; Burket 1993: 187–8; Burton 1993; 1995; 2002; Choudhury 1994: 67–8; Classen 1993: 9; Corlett 1997; Cowan 1989; Cummings and Whittle 2004: 8; Darrah 1994: 179; Devereaux 1990: 62–3; 2002a: 195; 2002b: 29, 156; 2004; Dickinson 1990a&b, 1998a&b, 2001; Dillon

1997; Drayton 1995: 11; Eade and Sallnow 1991; Feld 1982: 3; Gell 1995; Hammond and Bobo 1994; Heath-Stubbs 1984: 7–8; Klimo 1987; Lawson 2003; Mavor and Dix 1989; Mortimer 2003; *New Scientist* 28 Nov 1992; ; Raftery 1994: 104; Roney-Dougal 1991; Roney-Dougal and Vogl 1993; Sheldrake 1989; Silvermann 1994; Stoller 1989 :5; Stopford 1994; Swan 1990: 230; Taylor 1993: 12; Thorn 1997; Tilley 1993: 49–50; Turner 1974; 1979; Turner and Turner 1978; Trubshaw 1991b; 1992; 1993; 2003a: 9–12; 2003b&c; Venkatesh 2004; Waller 1993a, 1993b

4: Changing academic approaches to places

As explored at the start of Chapter 1, the significance of places comes from remembering or inventing 'narratives of meaning'. Over about the last 150 years the most inventive of such narratives about sacred places have often come from professional archaeologists. From their 'narratives of meaning' (which they term 'interpretations') we have developed our understanding of the significance of prehistoric monuments, landscapes and much else.

Archaeologists invented a great number of such interpretations and disputed them among themselves. Over the last fifteen years they have had a major rethink and greatly changed their ideas about to how we give meaning and significance to the past. This chapter presents an overview of how these archaeological interpretations of places, especially ones that might be deemed 'sacred places', have changed in recent years.

However places, sacred and otherwise, are of interest to a number of other academic disciplines as well as to archaeologists. Both geographers and anthropologists assess how people think about places. Since the late 1980s geographers have increasingly looked at issues of place and identity, and of landscapes and power – which includes gender issues. However most of these approaches, while relevant in some ways to sacred places, have a much broader scope. (For a recent survey of landscape and identity see Brace 2002; Hirsch and O'Hanlon 1995 look at the anthropology of landscape.)

Mapping space in our minds

Fundamental to all our lives is the ability to intuitively construct 'mental maps' of our surroundings. Despite the importance of such mental maps, only in recent years has there been any attempt to understand how we create and use them. And how much variation is there between different cultures, and how much variation within cultures?

Because we do not consciously think about how we form such maps they are regarded by researchers as part of our cognitive processes, who refer to them as 'cognitive maps' rather than 'mental maps'. However there is no suggestion that our minds create maps in a literal sense – 'spatial schemata' might be a better term, but 'cognitive maps' is the one that has been generally adopted. This term covers a wide range of different activities, including negotiating a familiar environment; learning a new environment; drawing a sketch map from memory; giving verbal directions; and making decisions about the best routes for a journey. Although the details of cognitive mapping research can get rather deep, thankfully Kitchin and Blades (2002) have provided an easily accessible overview.

However most of this research has been devoted to urban environments so there is a comparative lack of research about cognitive maps of rural areas, and also a lack of studies of traditional cultures. More specifically, Paul Devereux has provided some indications in his overview of how traditional cultures create 'mythic maps' of their environment (Devereux 2002a: 118–27).

Cognitive mapping is as much about routes as it is about places. Intriguingly it seems that a universal human trait is to break routes up into a series of 'vistas' (such as a specific street or country lane) which are joined together at appropriate 'transition points'. Overall, our awareness of the details of our environment are often highly selective, so long as key landmarks enable us to recognise our location with respect to these vistas and transition points. The idea of vistas, and the associated idea of impeded views, are explored further in the context of Neolithic henges (see Chapter 8).

Things ain't what they used to be

As archaeology emerged from antiquarianism during the nineteenth century it incorporated into its underlying theories the assumptions of Victorian culture. This is inevitable – the past is, in the final analysis, something we create according to our present day concerns. The antiquarians and art historians had placed artefacts – especially high-status ones – at the top of the value system. Emergent ideas about culture and evolution began to provide a 'context' for people who created the artefacts. Following nineteenth century imperialism, cultures were considered to change as a result of immigration or invasion. Ancient societies were presumed to operate by the same functionalist, materialist, economic and 'rational' ideas valued by the archaeologists of this era. Artefacts were deemed to be 'functional' or 'ritual' by projecting simplistic nineteenth century notions of 'secular' and 'sacred' back into prehistory.

The main objective of early archaeology was to recover high-status artefacts, which required excavating at locations most likely to yield such 'treasure'. The archetypal Victorian archaeologist – Indiana Jones in all but name – was someone who excavated at an archaeological 'site' and, thanks to televised archaeology, this is still the popular conception of an archaeologist. Until recent decades archaeological sites were seemingly self-evident locations and the spaces in between were simply regarded as the territory of a ruling culture, rather than as part of an archaeological landscape.

Just as artefacts were polarised according to modern day distinctions between secular and sacred, so too sites were designated as either secular (such as settlements) or sacred (for example sites unlike present day secular places) with little or no overlap. Thus was formed the idea of 'sacred sites', largely as exceptions to what was deemed secular. Although the idea of 'sacred sites' is now ubiquitous, the phrase refers to a rather mixed basket of ideas, all of which are at best misleading and mostly quite illusory.

To understand better these muddled ideas we need to explore just how much academic archaeology has changed in recent decades. During the first fifty years of the twentieth century, archaeologists developed better excavation techniques, which

Neolithic stone circles were deemed to be religious temples by the pioneering antiquarians John Aubrey (1627–97) and William Stukeley (1687–1765). This is Stukeley's view of Stonehenge published in 1740 with the title 'A peep into the Sanctum Sanctorum, 6 June 1724'.

enabled a more detailed understanding of what they might expect to find as the layers of earth were scraped away, and increasingly comprehensive theories about the societies and cultures who created the artefacts and 'sites'.

Key to the more recent decades are the archaeologists of the 1920s and 30s who self-consciously created a professional élite and strongly asserted their dominance over those they considered amateurs. Important stages in this campaign included the establishment of *Antiquity* in 1927 by O.G.S. Crawford, the take-over of the Society of Antiquities by Mortimer Wheeler and fellow professionals in 1930, and the coup d'état against the amateur-based Prehistoric Society of East Anglia and its transformation into a national society in 1935 (Morris 1992: 423).

In the 1950s the application of scientific tools of analysis – notable radiocarbon dating – began to give archaeology the appearance not just of a profession but a science. By the 1960s western society was in the grip of an excess of modernism, where materialism and scientific rationalism were the increasingly dominant world views and archaeologists whole-heartedly followed this fashion. They adopted the attitude that if the evidence did not provide a clear answer then the question was not relevant and should not be asked. So out went ritual, a great deal of the social activities of prehistory and, indeed, mostly any sense that we were looking at the clues to peoples' lives. (See Halsall 1997 for a useful summary of the changes in archaeological theories during the twentieth century.)

Little surprise that the successful archaeologists in the 1960s and 80s were those who fitted best into this world view. The finds that were being recovered from digs seemingly fitted into the established chronology of cultures, with the implicit assumption that changes came about as a result of immigration, peaceful or otherwise. The recognition that radiocarbon dating needs to be 'calibrated' threw a big spanner in the works in the late 60s by showing that everything was considerably older than previously thought, so that the Neolithic now started in Britain around 5,000 BCE rather than 3,000 BCE. But in other respects the theories were not seriously challenged.

The emphasis of mid-twentieth century archaeologists on typologies of artefacts and the distribution of their locations confirmed that, as with the antiquarians of a hundred or more years before, they were still focussed on objects rather than the people who created them. Indeed the leading archaeologists of the mid-twentieth century generally regarded the idea that we could ever recover any appreciation of prehistoric people, other than as nebulous 'societies', as mumbo jumbo verging on mysticism.

Inventing landscape archaeology

But changes were afoot. Initially an interest in landscape arose from among historians. In an attempt to understand the historical records about 'lost' medieval villages, W.G. Hoskins did something decidedly heretical for an historian in the 1950s – he put down his old documents, put on a pair of comfortable boots, and went out to look at the present day fields and lanes which overlaid the abandoned medieval villages he was reading about. And the results were far more exciting than he had expected. To his expert eye the modern landscape preserved evidence of not just the immediately previous field systems but, at least in some places, evidence for a whole sequence of changes. Ancient boundaries, field systems, and the 'humps and bumps' of long-since abandoned medieval houses could all be discerned if you knew where to look. However, Hoskins restricted his interests to rural landscapes and ignored the landscapes of industrialised areas of Britain. As such he was consistent with the 'rural idyll' myth explored in Chapter 1.

As Hoskins was no longer merely reading documentary accounts of these changes he could not describe what he was doing as history. He had invented 'landscape archaeology'. The publication of his book *The Making of the English Landscape* in 1955 alerted both specialists and the public to this exciting new development. Map-like aerial photographs of much of England taken by the RAF in the late 1940s, plus others taken specially, provided a novel and seductive way of experiencing these new approaches to past landscapes.

Hoskins famously observed that in the English landscape everything is much older than we think it is, as (apart from the field boundaries created during eighteenth century enclosure) much else dates back to the medieval era, in most cases to the formation of nucleated settlements and their associated 'great field' systems in the ninth or tenth centuries. About twenty years later it was becoming clear that in some places aspects of the landscape were much older than even Hoskins thought, as Iron Age and even Bronze Age boundaries and field systems seem to have persisted for over two thousand years.

By the mid-1980s landscape archaeology had moved on and become concerned with physical evidence for changes in population, climate, land use, technology of farming, settlement patterns, and the organisation of space. There was no attempt to see the land through the eyes of the people who once lived there, still less about how social practices and customs influenced the use of the land or brought about changes. This approach was given the text book treatment by Michael Aston (later to don stripey jumpers and become the kingpin of *Time Team*) with his text book on *Interpreting the Landscape* (Aston 1985). Christopher Taylor brought Hoskins' *The Making of the English Landscape* up to date with a heavily annotated edition (Hoskins and Taylor 1988). Most recently the topic has been brought fully up to date by Stephen Rippon (Rippon 2004).

Expanding landscape archaeology

With 20:20 hindsight we can now see that much was being missed by the 1980s proponents of landscape archaeology. Margaret Gelling's pioneering study of place-names to find clues about how people used to think about landscapes (Gelling 1984; 1988; Gelling and Cole 2000) was largely ignored. Their use of the word 'landscape' was vague and undefined, with seemingly no recognition of the work of Raymond Williams (1972, 1973, 1980) and other writers about the culturally-specific ideas underlying ideas about landscapes. Alien to landscape archaeology at this time were notions that the landscape was as much how people *thought* about their surroundings as much as how they physically changed it. Only by the late 1990s were archaeologists beginning to grapple with the idea that the meaning of landscape can be transformed without changes in the topography (Bender *et al* 1997: 150; Johnston 1998: 56; Knapp and Ashmore 1999: 10–12).

Because archaeological approaches to past landscapes were initially focussed on the evidence for medieval villages and fields, there was little impact on the activities of prehistorians until the 1980s. Unpredictably, a deepening understanding of archaeoastronomy (especially the New World approach instigated by A.F. Aveni (Aveni 1980)), opened up new ways of thinking about past landscapes that were not simplistically about 'territory'.

A much broader approach to past landscapes commenced with the publication of various essays on landscape and culture (Wagstaff 1987) and Andrew Fleming's pioneering study of Dartmoor (Fleming 1988). During the 1990s surveying landscapes was becoming more sophisticated, both technically and in terms of how the terrain could be 'read' to reveal evidence (see Bowden 1999). This broader approach has manifested in an ongoing series of detailed regional surveys by the Royal Commission on the Historical Monuments of England (RCHME). Surveys completed so far have revealed considerable evidence of prehistoric sites that had been overlooked by previous, less intensive, surveys. Likewise environmental archaeology is also beginning to shed light on how human activities have modified the immediate surroundings (see Evans 1999 for an accessible overview combined with insightful case studies).

However, during the early 1990s developments in landscape archaeology were somewhat overshadowed by far more fundamental debates that were beginning to take the attention of archaeologists.

Rethinking archaeology

Inspired by twentieth century Continental philosophers such as Edmund Husserl, Pierre Bourdieu, Michel Foucault, Jacques Derrida and others, in the 1980s a small group of British academics began to deconstruct the assumptions which acted as the foundations of British archaeological interpretations. Such debates came to the fore in 1986 when Ian Hodder published *Reading the Past: Current approaches to interpretation in archaeology;* the following year saw Michael Shanks and Christopher Tilley's equally influential book *Re-constructing Archaeology*. The dense theoretical writing attempted to critique – in many cases quite profoundly – underlying beliefs about prehistoric society and culture. Widely accepted previous theories were shown to reveal more about the ethnocentric perspectives of the archaeological community than to offer any reliable interpretation of the evidence. Artefacts were shown to be less important for their functional characteristics than for the whole range of meanings that might have been attributed to them. Most relevant to the present book, 'sites' could only be properly understood by considering them in the context of the landscapes they originally occupied, no matter how difficult it may be to establish a detailed understanding of the landscape, especially the meanings and significance of different aspects.

These critiques were far removed from the logical positivism (a desiccated philosophical outlook developed in the 1930s and still fashionable in the 1950s) that was implicit in the materialist, functionalist and reductionist archaeological

Intentional concealment: the surviving remains of the Cove at Avebury.

establishment of the 1960s to 1980s. The challenges made by these 'new kids on the block' threatened to entirely undermine established archaeological interpretation and, unsurprisingly, bitter arguments ensued. Nevertheless some of the new generation of academics began to apply these theories to more specific aspects of British prehistory. In 1991 Julian Thomas published *Rethinking the Neolithic*. For Thomas, monuments could now be 'read' as complex architecture, with their intervisibility and other spatial aspects being as important as the details of their design and construction. As an example, he attempts to show how the Neolithic monuments at Avebury cannot be understood completely from maps but only by considering the position of people in relation to the natural topography and constructed earthworks. By 'being there' and moving from place to place we experience an intriguing interplay of visibility and visual obstruction. This helps cast light on Neolithic attitudes to sacred places and rituals. This is explored further in Chapter 8.

During the 1990s an increasing number of books and academic articles appeared which applied the new-style theory to specific periods and archaeological landscapes. A number of these will be discussed in the course of the rest of this book (for a 'fun' summary of the rethinking of archaeology see Bender 1998:13–23).

By the mid-1990s the interpretation of archaeological evidence had been radically changed. Not only had this new generation of academics brought down the façade of established archaeological ideas, they had thoroughly demolished much of the foundations too.

Problems with the popular appreciation of archaeology

There was only one problem. Archaeologists who spend their lives excavating – this was the time of massive developer-funded 'rescue' digs – have little contact with academic archaeologists and, understandably, had been alienated by the densely written philosophical approaches of these writers. No one convinced a large number of excavating archaeologists that they needed to take an interest in the new approaches to interpretation, and no one thought that the public might need to be re-educated too.

So present day British archaeology is characterised on one hand by academics who have increasingly sophisticated and nuanced approaches to interpreting the past – whether that be objects and landscapes, or the cultures, societies and people who created them. On the other hand are the 'diggers' who have little time to grapple with such complexities and so risk peeling back the layers of dirt according to expectations rooted in ideas that may be twenty years past their sell-by date.

And, if not all professional archaeologists are up to speed with current theories, what hope for those who, for want of a better term, are considered to be the 'general public'? 'Not a lot', is the short answer.

For the last ten years Channel 4's *Time Team* programmes have shown that there is a substantial popular interest in archaeology. These programmes present dramatically what can be achieved during an intense three-day evaluation. As well as making 'geofizz' (geophysical surveying) a household word, they have used computer graphics and aerial photography to show how sites exist in the context of a wider landscape. But the emphasis is nevertheless on trenches and artefacts. While the professional archaeologists refer to features and finds, the presenter and production team clearly sustain an old style 'holes' and 'goodies' mentality. What a three-day evaluation cannot do is challenge accepted interpretations. Whatever is found by *Time Team* is excavated and interpreted according to ideas developed by an invisible and unacknowledged 'greater authority', channelled through the on-camera professionals.

The BBC's now defunct attempt to appeal to this audience was called *Meet the Ancestors*. The format was equally consistent. Julian Richards visited sites where human remains had been recovered and facilitated post-excavation analyses; each programme culminated with a facial reconstruction of the deceased. While vastly different in approach from *Time Team*, its scope was restricted to the very small proportion of archaeological excavations where human remains were discovered. We were presented with highly specific details about one individual, but little or no debate about how accurate such interpretations may or may not be. Indeed, the assumptions underlying the emerging art of facial reconstruction were also conveniently ignored. Apart from some one-off programmes, television producers have found it difficult to promote the complexities of understanding the past.

The popularity of archaeology in Britain is shown not only by audience rating figures for *Time Team* but also by the number of people who subscribe to the magazine

Current Archaeology. Its attractive appearance and reasonably accessible style of writing disguises the anachronism of the editorial approach. Archaeology is reduced to 'holes' and 'goodies', fetishised in full colour photographs. Interpretation is reduced to insights gained by scientific techniques. The long-standing editor was actively opposed to anything that resembled 'theory'. So an issue of *Current Archaeology* with a cover date of, say, 2005, sustains the materialistic, functionalist and science-dominated model of archaeology that was current twenty or more years ago but is far from current in academe or among the majority of excavators.

Current Archaeology deceives its readers about what is current among archaeologists by ignoring a huge proportion of British archaeological activities, notably the ones that are needed to make sense of the 'holes' and 'goodies', and failing to recognise that archaeological interpretation is about what questions that can be asked of the evidence, not establishing some imagined 'truth' about the past. This deceptive bias is mitigated in part because the authors of major articles are typically professional archaeologists but who are clearly asked to write according the expectations of the editors.

As *Time Team* and *Current Archaeology* are the main ways that non-experts consider themselves to be keeping up with archaeology, the deficiencies in their approaches have the overall result that popular awareness is almost on a different planet to academic archaeology. Thankfully the Council for British Archaeology's periodical, *British Archaeology*, does a far better job of drawing attention to the latest thinking as well as the more exciting excavations, although the readership is smaller.

Even *British Archaeology* fails to give the flavour of the intense debates between all different parties involved in British archaeology, in contrast to *Archaeology Ireland* which give a far better impression of archaeology's sometimes contentious place among the wider issues of national heritage and culture (however, understandably, this magazine rarely deals with other parts of the British Isles).

There are a large number of academic journals, such as *Antiquity, Cambridge Archaeological Journal, World Archaeology, Public Archaeology, Archaeological Dialogues*, and the *Proceedings of the Prehistoric Society*. Individually these are quite pricey and generally beyond the financial means of most individuals. The articles generally favour an intensely jargon-ridden and inaccessible style of writing. (Most archaeologists, along with many other academics, adopt a style of writing far removed from those promoted by books on effective communication skills. How professional status is supposedly enhanced by wilfully unprofessional communication skills is lost on me.) Employment in higher education is now based around a reward system which offers no benefits to those who popularise their ideas outside the realms of peer-review journals. Indeed, there are few publishers of books or periodicals who are interested in popularising archaeological thinking.

What's the problem then?

As this book is not *Current Archaeological Theories About Sacred Places* (a topic which could hardly be done justice in a book of this size) only a small proportion of the ideas that have emerged from academe in recent years can be outlined. That small proportion will emphasise those most relevant to sacred places. The aim of the next few pages is to provided a concise summary of how these ideas have developed. However a number of the ideas will be explored in more detail in later chapters of this book.

Overall, the underlying antiquarian-based obsession with artefacts which dominated archaeology until the 1980s has been replaced with broader thinking about the social and spatial contexts in which the people of the past lived. The way objects were used and the meanings they had are now as important as their shape and the technology needed to produce them. Rather than thinking of functional artefacts, archaeology now sees the physical objects in association with what we can know about how the people who created, used and experienced them, whether we are talking about a flint tool, a ceramic vessel, or a megalithic monument. Rather than merely being objects or artefacts, they are 'material culture'.

In this more complex way of approaching the meanings we give to objects, archaeologists began to recognise the problems inherent in dividing things up into 'sacred' and 'profane', 'ritual' and 'secular'. We may have become accustomed to creating such distinctions, but they exist only as ideals which are difficult to apply to specific instances. Anthropologists had also attempted to make similar distinctions but soon realised that traditional societies do not necessarily make such demarcations.

Analysis of western cultural traditions also shows that these concepts are not clear cut or necessarily exclusive. Modern society has confused the idea of ritual with formal behaviour and symbolic activities. While a wedding is undoubtedly a ritual, what about the reception afterwards? Is attending a board meeting or a football match a ritual activity or should they be better thought of as formalised events with considerable symbolic meaning? What about all the so-called 'rituals' of social eating, such as how cutlery is used, who sits where, who serves who and in what order? If we can't clearly distinguish ritual from non-ritual activities in our own culture, what chance have we for prehistoric cultures?

The problem earlier archaeologists created came from thinking that 'secular' activities – such as farming – are always performed on a functionalist and economically-efficient basis. Anything not functional and efficient was deemed to be 'ritual'. The problem got worse when secular and ritual became regarded as mutually exclusive. And it was compounded further if archaeologists could not recognise a functional purpose and so assumed an object or site was for ritual practices. Goody (1977) and Bell (1992) were among the first to discuss problems with the idea of ritual; Brück (1999) provides a useful survey of the problems of ritual in archaeology.

The largely imaginary dualism of 'ritual' and 'secular' is closely linked to a similar dualism between 'sacred' and 'profane'. Just as places and objects can be regarded as ritualistic, so too there are clearly places that in some sense are or were sacred. However we should not be in a hurry to make a neat division between sacred and profane.

Rethinking archaeological landscapes

The rethinking of archaeology taking place in the early 1990s brought with it a series of books which presented radical new ideas about archaeological landscapes. The

Wayland's Smithy, Oxfordshire.

seeds had been sown in the mid-1980s (see Wagstaff 1987) for a collection of papers that provide a cross-section of these pioneering approaches. A major study of the prehistory of Cranborne Chase on the borders of Dorset and Wiltshire by John Barrett, Richard Bradley and Martin Green demonstrated more convincingly that there was much more to prehistoric landscapes than a distribution of 'sites' (Barrett *et al* 1991).

Richard Bradley has subsequently published four books, together with a number of articles, offering innovatory approaches to prehistoric landscapes. In 1993 he published *Altering the Earth: The origins of monuments in Britain and continental Europe.* In 1997 he published a study of how prehistoric art on rock outcrops was linked to the way prehistoric people in Atlantic Europe regarded the landscape. This was followed in 1998 by *The Significance of Monuments,* which looked at how the construction of monuments in the Neolithic and Bronze Age helped to shape human experience of landscapes. By 2000 he had widened his interests to include not just constructed monuments but also the way people had used and given significance to natural places such as rock outcrops and springs. In addition to this major contribution to archaeological approaches to landscapes, a substantial number of Bradley's post-graduate students have researched other aspects of landscape archaeology.

Bradley's approach to landscape is not to look for 'sacred sites' but to identify a wide spectrum of meanings that people attributed to their topography. Sometimes the landscape could be 'lightly modified', as with inscribing designs onto rock outcrops. Other times we are dealing with more massive modifications, such as causewayed

Bronze Age barrows on the skyline above the Neolithic Avenue at Avebury. The most prominent is to the left of the clump of trees; the trees are planted around another Bronze Age mound.

camps, chamber tombs and cursuses, which are the first constructed monuments to appear in the landscape. The sheer novelty of seeing, say, a chamber tomb on the skyline is something that we cannot now appreciate quite so fully since the landscape has become increasingly modified by various human activities, monumental or otherwise. And Neolithic monuments are monuments in the true sense – not merely physically large but also built to endure, in a way that Neolithic houses were not.

Prehistoric monuments did indeed endure. Subsequent generations, while unaware of their original significance, often 'reused' and adapted these monuments. Howard Williams has provided a detailed assessment of how the Anglo-Saxons reused Neolithic and Bronze Age monuments, such as burial mounds (Williams 1998), paralleled by independent research by Sarah Semple which also draws upon the literary evidence (Semple 1998). These papers were published as part of a collection of studies entitled *The Past in the Past* which looked at how past cultures have approached the remains of previous cultures; Richard Bradley (Bradley 2002) develops these approaches.

The early Anglo-Saxons maintained a long tradition of laying claim to tracts of land by burying their dead on the boundaries. This tradition goes back to the Bronze Age; indeed the Anglo-Saxons sometimes reused Bronze Age burial mounds, or centred their cemeteries on such pre-existing monuments. But what about the Iron Age in between? Burial was not the predominant funerary custom, and burials were not usually on the boundaries of the land. But, as John Barrett has recognised, the political structures of control in the Iron Age which supported ownership of land, with the consequent importance of boundaries, were inherited from the Bronze Age (Barrett 1999). The occupants of the Bronze Age burial mounds had long been forgotten but the presence of these monuments legitimised an inherited right to the land. This same way of thinking about the land (one still easily appreciated today) allowed for these rights to be bequeathed to future descendants. Clearly these rights could be disputed and fought over but such conflicts only make sense if these is an underlying undisputed belief that land can indeed be owned and inherited. This idea of ownership and inheritance, while taken for granted in the modern western world, is a product of Bronze Age thinking. This way of thinking was manifested in the burial mounds – we can think of the monuments being not only enduring physical statements but also powerful 'mythic' statements about how people were thinking about the land

Two collections of papers appeared in 1993 and 1994 which reveal archaeologists' emerging interest in how people thought about their landscapes. One (Bender 1993a) dealt with political aspects of landscapes, and the other (Carmichael *et al* 1994) brought together primarily anthropological approaches to sacred places. Barbara Bender has since developed her ideas further (Bender 1998, esp. Ch.1 and 2) and her ideas form an excellent 'counterpart' to the first four chapters of this book.

As previous chapters in this book have already shown, how we *think* about a landscape is deeply linked to our *experience* of the landscape. I have already noted how Julian Thomas had shown how the Neolithic monuments at Avebury need to be experienced by 'being there' and experiencing how the natural topography and the manmade monument creates an intriguing interplay of concealment and visibility.

Around the same time a non-academic, Paul Devereux had independently shown that such visual 'tricks' worked on a larger scale too, linking three of the major sites (East Kennett chamber tomb, Silbury Hill and Windmill Hill) that surround the henge at Avebury (Devereux 1991). The Avebury landscape is explored further in Chapter 8.

The insights of Devereux and Thomas are a direct result of 'being there' in a prehistoric landscape. Around the same time two of the pioneers of rethinking British archaeology, Michael Shanks and Christopher Tilley, were also taking a detailed look at past landscapes. Shanks' book, *Experiencing the Past* (1992), was wide ranging in that, as the subtitle indicates, it looked at the 'character of archaeology'

Silbury Hill photographed from the west end of West Kennett chamber tomb, with Windmill Hill (the location of a Neolithic settlement contemporary with the construction of Silbury Hill and East Kennett tomb) on the skyline, level with the 'platform' near the summit of Silbury Hill. This alignment linking the three major sites around Avebury henge was first identified by Paul Devereux.

and not just landscapes. At the time of its publication it seemed rather too 'poetical' and 'far out'. However rereading this book in 2003 reveals that Shanks anticipated many ideas that are increasingly represented in the diversity of ways of 'experiencing the past' which are now incorporated into heritage management, museum curation, and various educational projects. Unusually for books with a relatively theoretical approach to archaeology, *Experiencing the Past* seems increasingly relevant a decade after it was written.

In contrast to Shanks, Tilley took a more literal 'being there' approach to various prehistoric landscapes (Tilley 1994). He too visited the Cranborne Chase monuments and provided a narrative account of walking along the Neolithic cursus which revealed how this linear monument provides a sense of ritual passage. He also visited prehistoric remains in two areas of Wales, the Black Mountains and Pembrokeshire, taking particular interest in the way the early Neolithic monuments may have related to the significance earlier Mesolithic people may have given to natural places that later became embellished with Neolithic tombs, which in turn led to further tombs sited around this original 'focal point'. (In contrast to my limited interest in Shanks' book at the time of publication, Tilley's book inspired me to spend a week in Pembrokeshire visiting the sites he mentioned and making my own assessment of his suggestions; see Chapter 10 for further details).

'Being there' is not the only way that approaches to prehistory were changing in the 1990s. Mark Patton's study of Neolithic monuments in Brittany (Patton 1993) emphasised their social contexts to a greater extent than previous approaches to monuments of this era. A more exploratory approach to awareness of landscape, monuments and memory was offered by Mark Edmonds in his book *Ancestral Geographies of the Neolithic* (Edmonds 1999). An ambitious approach to the landscapes of Neolithic Ireland by Gabriel Cooney was published the following year (Cooney 2000). Despite the huge number of Neolithic remains in Ireland, Cooney assesses the relevance of a number of theoretical approaches to provide an imaginative yet cogent overview of Neolithic Ireland. A considerable proportion of this book is devoted to the meanings that Neolithic people may have given to their surroundings, including why – and 'how' – certain places were regarded as more sacred. Cooney's study of Ireland demonstrates just how substantially archaeological thinking about landscapes has changed in little more than a decade.

Architecture, space and place

Just as archaeologists' awareness of the way people give significance to landscapes and monuments became more sophisticated during the 1990s, so too did their awareness of the way people give meaning to their houses. Plenty of anthropological studies show that traditional cultures have complex ways of delimiting their 'social spaces'. Such ideas often reflect underlying cosmological myths, so that the construction of the house and the way it is occupied and used simultaneously reflect and reinforce the culture's deepest beliefs about the way the universe is structured (see Trubshaw 2003a: Ch.10).

Anthropologists often reveal that in traditional cultures houses are not merely secular but may contain domestic shrines. Indeed the whole house may be regarded as symbolising sacred aspects of the cosmos. For example, traditional houses are often organised around a central hearth, with a 'men's half' and a 'women's half'. The hearth, with the smoke rising to a smoke hole, may symbolise the *axis mundi*, the mythic 'centre of the world' around which the heavens turn (as already explored in Chapter 2; see also Wilson 1992). As with landscapes, so houses too are something that are as much inside our heads as we are inside them. Three books provide insights into the details of the cosmology of houses: Lawlor 1994 discusses a wide range of examples of the sacred in everyday architecture; Carsten and Hugh-Jones 1995 provide a more academic approach to the anthropology of houses; Birdwell-Pheasant and Lawence-Zúñiga 1999 take an anthropological view of traditional European houses.

Anthropologists are able to combine their understanding of how architecture helps to order 'social spaces' with observations of behaviour, rituals and recitations of myths. However archaeologists are not normally able to observe behaviour, rituals or listen to myths so the ability to discern underlying beliefs from architectural evidence, such as house foundations, offers an attractive way of augmenting other attempts to understand more about how people thought. Mike Parker Pearson and Colin Richards pioneered this cosmological approach both in their own studies and by editing a collection of papers (Parker Pearson and Richards 1994).

Clearly sacred architecture is not restricted to how we think about houses. Some architectural constructions are constructed to be sacred spaces – from small-scale shrines to large-scale temples. Indeed, early cities as far apart as China and Central America can be seen to originate as large temples, with housing for the priests and their families, then growing in size as more people are drawn to the settlement to support its activities and provide services for the inhabitants. If this sounds rather far removed from British towns and cities then N.B. Aitcheson's study of Armagh (Aitcheson 1994; summarised in Trubshaw 1996) shows how a medieval town was planned in a way that embodied complex Christian cosmologies, while drawing attention away from the nearby pre-Christian 'royal centre' at Navan (or Eamhain Mhacha).

Even before the origins of archaeology, Classical Greek and Roman temples have been of interest to scholars and were subjected to pioneering archaeological excavations. Intriguingly they were also the subject of a pioneering approach to sacred landscapes. The first edition of Vincent Scully's *The Earth, the Temple and the Gods* appeared in 1962 and showed convincingly that some Greek temples were situated so that a twin-peaked (or 'horned') mountain appeared as the back drop. Although Scully continued to add detail to his research, his ideas were picked up mostly outside academe.

In the 1980s John Lundquist began to look at temples world-wide from a number of different perspectives. His overview (Lundquist 1993) is deceptive in that the concise and accessibly-written text disguises an exceptional sophisticated approach to temples. In recent years religious scholars have been increasingly interested in aspects of sacred places, although most of this work is published throughout a vast number of specialist scholarly journals. A collection of papers on sacred architecture in India, China, Judaism and Islam (Lyle 1992) looks specifically at their cosmological aspects.

A number of interesting papers on 'sacred spaces' were compiled by Benjamin Kedar and Zwi Werblowsky (1998). Werblowsky's introduction emphasises that how we think about landscapes matters more than the physical terrain. Myths about sacred places – be they mountains, sacred centres, or the notions of a Holy Land – have dominated religions worldwide for millennia. I have explored how such aspects of landscape are mythologised in some detail in *Explore Mythology* (Trubshaw 2003a) so, although the way a culture creates myths about its landscape is quite crucial, I only want to touch lightly on such topics in this book.

For example, throughout the world caves are thought to be entrances to the underworlds or wombs for rebirth. Indeed, in Eastern world views entire mountains are thought of as analogous to the human body. More commonly mountains are the location of paradise or the home of the gods; they may be nearer to the culture's idea of 'heaven' or deities. Where there is a tradition of hermits living on a mountain, their legends and hagiographies become part of the history of the mountain. Mountains are often the preferred place for prophecies. All these different ways of thinking about mountains, of embellishing the landscape with legends and myths, make travelling through the physical landscape less important than the various narratives which enable the mental 'mindscape' to be traversed.

Rock art and shamanism

Caves and natural 'rock shelters' have a long association with human culture, dating back to the Palaeolithic. The prevailing darkness and unusual acoustics readily provide an 'otherworldly' experience. Little surprise that they should be associated with humanity's earliest known ritual activities, the figurative and symbolic paintings and engravings that have survived in some of these underground locations. Because we know so little about the people who created this prehistoric rock art, there has been a vast amount of speculation as to their purpose and meaning. With even a modicum of hindsight, much of this speculation can be seen to be telling us more about the concerns of the speculators than about prehistory. However one particular strain of speculation displaced earlier simplistic notions of 'hunting magic'.

Back in the late 1980s David Lewis-Williams and Thomas Dowson were studying the rock art of the San people of southern Africa. Ethnographical reports of this art being painted while in 'trance' were apparently confirmed by the presence of motifs in the art that neurophysiological research had shown are experienced spontaneously during so-called 'altered states of consciousness' (ASCs). They first

Top: *Motifs characteristic of catoptic imagery (often erroneously referred to as 'entoptic' imagery) associated with trance states. All these motifs have also been depicted in rock art.*

Bottom: *Motifs depicted in rock art but not associated with trance states. Both diagrams based on sketches by Jeremy Dronfield.*

published their suggestions in 1988 and went on to published a number of articles and books (see Solomon 1997 for a critical overview).

At the same time there was growing awareness of shamanism, notably with drug-induced ASCs as portrayed in the dubiously authentic but widely read writings of Carlos Castaneda. More scholarly literature available at that time tended to be based on the ideas of Mircea Eliade (especially Eliade 1964) who subtly shoehorned shamanism into his own views of religion. Eliade was not an anthropologist but took anthropological information about shamanic practices in various cultures from the more northerly parts of the world and created the impression of a more or less homogenous shamanic religion that lay at the root of the present diversity. Such a simplistic model of cultural evolution is now untenable. Indeed, in recent years shamanism is seen not as a religion but a 'magical activity' that can practised by cultures with a wide range of religious beliefs (see Stone 2003 for an accessible overview of the debates about shamanism).

In the late 1980s and early 1990s most ideas about shamanism were fairly woolly and muddy. Understandably, archaeologists were not in a position to sort out the niceties of this confusion. Because of the vagueness of thinking about shamanism it was quite easy to extend Lewis-Williams and Dowson's ideas about the San rock art (where there was good evidence to suppose that these were painted while in trance, and little connection made to wider ideas about shamanism) to rock art elsewhere. The result was a profusion of papers and articles that attempted to make links between rock art and these modern Western notions of shamanism.

Throwing away the muddied bath water of shamanism does not mean throwing away the 'baby' – ASCs. Consider the personal experiences of Gyrus:

> While experiencing dynamic visual distortions due to hallucinogenic intoxication, the rough, organic irregularities of the surface of a boulder I was gazing at gradually coalesced into shimmering lattices of regular patterns: diamond shapes, nets, webs, grids... classic entoptic patterns. But I saw this *on the rock surface*. Due to my cultural background, and the relatively low dosage of drug I had ingested, I could easily recognise this – after the experience if not during it – as the projection of my own neural patterns onto a natural surface.
> (Gyrus 2003)

Gyrus recognises that prehistoric rock art blurs 'the line separating physical and mental reality'. Back-projecting modern philosophical notions of 'reality' onto the altered states of prehistoric brains is unlikely to be helpful, and neither is projecting modern cultural concepts onto earlier ways of acculturating such experiences. (For further details of Gyrus's experiences at rock art sites see Wallis 2001: 52–3.)

Richard Bradley's study of Iberian and British rock art (Bradley 1997) shows that there are many other ways of thinking about this aspect of prehistory. Rock art is the most 'minimal' way of modifying natural places; Bradley went on to place rock art within a broader spectrum of discussion about how prehistoric people gave significance to specific parts of the natural landscape (Bradley 2000: 38–9). As a result of his studies Bradley increasingly recognised that for rock art to be studied

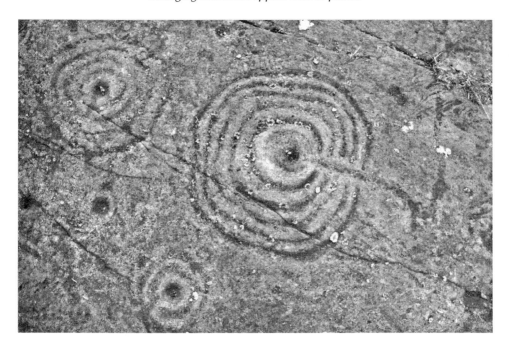

Cup and ring marks on Weetwood Moor, Northumberland.

effectively he needed to get beyond thinking about the past in terms of settlement and subsistence or ritual and ceremonial. Such distinctions are created and imposed by archaeologists but the understanding of rock art required that these categories needed to be rejected if the original meanings of the images, and the rationale behind their location, are to be appreciated.

Archaeologists and sacred places

Current archaeological thinking has moved a long way from simplistic distinctions between sacred and profane places. Instead the prehistoric landscape is recognised to be more about the 'mindscape' of the people living there than the physical terrain. Whereas not so many years ago archaeologists restricted themselves to reconstructing prehistoric landscapes as places of functionalist subsistence, they are now recognising that '... landscapes were populated with spirits... everywhere humans went they bonded with landscapes and made them culturally alive, exciting places to live.' (Taçon 1994: 135).

Archaeologists also appreciate that the significance of specific places changes over time, both in longer duration measured in lifetimes and on a day-to-day basis as different activities take place. However, although certain places were clearly regarded as more sacred than others, ritual activities do not necessarily leave clear archaeological evidence, even when they were located at surviving natural landmarks such as mountain tops, caves or springs. Indeed some sacred places, such as groves of trees, eventually disappear leaving little or no evidence at all.

If anthropologists find it difficult to fully appreciate such mindscapes for the living traditional societies they study, then understandably archaeologists have greater difficulties reconstructing the mindscapes of lost cultures. Rather than clearly differentiated 'sacred' and 'profane' locations, archaeologists now accept that such modern notions have limited relevance to pre-modern societies. 'What questions can we ask of the evidence?' is now the underlying emphasis of archaeologists, rather than trying to fit the evidence into an existing explanatory theory. However this is not to say that explanatory overviews cannot emerge from asking such questions. For example, as already noted British prehistoric monuments seem to be making powerful symbolic statements asserting the power of ancestral spirits, who gave a sense of 'ownership' to a blood line and perhaps in some way came to personify the landscape.

A very recent example of recognising the mythical significance that megalithic sites must have had for their creators can be found in Vicki Cummings and Alasdair Whittle's book, *Places of Special Virtue: Megaliths in the Neolithic landscapes of Wales*. Their book is a clear example of the way academic archaeologists are recognising some of the ideas raised in the opening chapters of this book, and as a result are providing more sophisticated interpretations of prehistoric 'sacred sites' (Cummings and Whittle 2004, esp. Ch. 7). Their title is an example of a suggestion to follow ethnographical parallels and make megalithic sites appear less familiar by referring to them collectively by such phrases as 'stones that float to the sky', 'places where the creators emerged', 'mountains raised by the ancestors' or 'places of special virtue'. They even provide translations into Welsh to increase the unfamiliarity (Cummings and Whittle 2004: 76).

However, archaeologist's current views about prehistoric sacred places are mostly restricted to the confines of academe, while popular understanding has evolved in quite different ways. The next chapter explores the greater complexities of popular perceptions of sacred places.

Sources

Aitcheson 1994; Aston 1985; Aveni 1980; Barrett 1999; Barrett *et al* 1991; Bell 1992; Bender 1993a; 1998; Bender *et al* 1997: 150; Birdwell-Pheasant and Lawence-Zúñiga 1999; Bowden 1999; Brace 2002; Bradley 1993; 1997; 1998; 2000; 2002; Brück 1999; Carmichael *et al* 1994; Carsten and Hugh-Jones 1995 ; Cooney 2000; Cummings and Whittle 2004; Devereux 1991; 2002: 118–27; Edmonds 1999; Eliade 1964; Evans 1999 ; Fleming 1988; Gelling 1984; 1988; Gelling and Cole 2000; Goody 1977; Gyrus 2003; Halsall 1997; Hirsh and O'Hanlon 1995; Hodder 1986 ; Hoskins and Taylor 1988; Johnston 1998: 56; Kitchin and Blades 2002; Knapp and Ashmore 1999: 10–12; Lawlor 1994; Lundquist 1993; Lyle 1992; Morris 1992: 423; Parker Pearson and Richards 1994; Patton 1993; Rippon 2004; Scully 1962; Semple 1998; Shanks 1992; Shanks and Tilley 1987; Solomon 1997; Stone 2003; Taçon 1994: 135; Thomas 1991; Tilley 1994; Trubshaw 1996; 2003a; Wagstaff 1987; Wallis 2001: 52–3; R. Williams 1972; 1973; 1980; H. Williams 1998; Wilson 1992.

5: Alternative archaeologies

'There is never *a* landscape, always many landscapes'
(Bender 1998: 25)

A significant proportion of popular interest in archaeology in Britain comprises viewers of *Time Team, Meet the Ancestors* and 'one off' programmes and short series. Fewer in number are viewers of the Discovery and National Geographical television channels, readers of *Current Archaeology* and *British Archaeology*, members of the Council for British Archaeology, and the great many local societies active in the country. These people would mostly regard themselves as interested in keeping up with what the professional archaeologists are discovering, although they may have active involvement through fieldwalking or taking part in 'digs'. By and large their understanding of archaeology is directly related to the way it is presented on TV and in more popular publications; they rarely have any awareness of the theoretical debates of the last decade or so.

Another level of interest in the past originates in the far more speculative ideas of Erich von Däniken, whose book *Chariots of the Gods* appeared in 1968, and more recent books of Graham Hancock and others who adopt a 'psychic questing' approach to recovering 'lost knowledge' of the past. Their highly imaginative interpretations of the past are construed as factual by selective use of evidence and various 'sleights of mind', such as using what appears to be a sceptical approach to debunk scientific theories yet, rather than considering a wide variety of alternative explanations, thereby regard their own suggestions as proven. The popularity of such books has generated intense discussion about their propositions, but in other respects had little impact on popular perceptions of the past.

The popularity of such highly speculative books has led many academics to consider that they are typical of non-academic approaches to the past. Nothing could be further from the truth as, in between these two extremes of *Current Archaeology* and *Chariots of the Gods* there are a plethora of approaches. For want of a better label these have been deemed 'alternative archaeology'. The term is unfortunate as it implicitly privileges the 'non-alternative' (i.e. academic) approaches. It is also misleading by implying some degree of homogenity. While the subtle change to the plural, 'alternative archaeologies', reflects the range of approaches, quite what fits under this umbrella term has rarely been defined. Neither has there been any attempt to look at how these approaches have evolved – often quite rapidly – since the 1970s. This chapter attempts to provide a brief historical overview of these alternative approaches to archaeology. The emphasis is very much on British 'alternatives', although some American influences have crept in and are discussed where relevant.

If the last chapter has shown that academic archaeology has changed greatly over the last fifteen years or so, and now contains a wide range of approaches, this all

An impressive standing stone on the Isle of Arran, with Goat Fell in the distance.

seems quite straightforward compared to the range of approaches (and the changes within each approach) that I am grouping together as 'alternative archaeologies'.

Situating myself in alternative archaeologies

My own involvement with alternative approaches to archaeology started in January 1974 when I bought a copy of Janet and Colin Bord's book *Mysterious Britain*. The contents list of this widely-read book effectively defines the scope of alternative approaches to archaeology at this time – standing stones, archaic crosses and carvings, hill forts, megalithic monuments, holy wells, hill figures, mazes and labyrinths, ley lines, UFOs, terrestrial zodiacs, sites connected with King Arthur and other legendary figures, and seasonal folk customs (regarded as survivals of pagan customs).

The selected bibliography at the end of this book drew my attention to the works of Alfred Watkins, T.C. Lethbridge, Guy Underwood, John Michell, Alexander Thom, Gerald Hawkins and others (all these authors will be discussed later in this chapter).

For the next ten years I had an obsessive interest in photography, especially landscapes. My holidays were spent cycling off to various places, such as Avebury and the west coast of Scotland, where there were dramatic megalithic sites. My approach to prehistoric sites at this time was essentially experiential – and visual. Only in the mid-1980s did I begin to read more fully about archaeology and folklore, and start subscribing to magazines devoted to alternative approaches to the past.

There was also an earlier 'formative phase' to my interests. In 1964, when I was ten years old, I signed and dated a copy of Geoffrey Grigson's book *Looking and Finding* (Grigson 1958) given to me as a present. In those pages I was introduced to the delights of reading maps as a way of discovering 'antiquities', leys, Green Men carvings, flints, fossils, skulls and a wide range of curiosities. Almost all of the topics introduced to me via Grigson's enthusiastic manner of writing have been of interest to me at some time in my life. Others may know Grigson's enthusiasms from *The Shell Country Alphabet* (Grigson 1966). I wonder how many other adults of a similar age to me were similarly inspired, even if they do not still have their copy of Grigson's books to pointedly remind them?

When I moved from Surrey to north Leicestershire in 1986 I began to follow up the work of previous 'alternative' researchers in the Midlands, especially seeking out examples of the sorts of topics listed by the Bords. I also joined field trips organised by an active group of like-minded enthusiasts based in northern England, led by Rob Wilson, then editor of their quarterly magazine *Northern Earth Mysteries*. On the way back from one of these Northern Earth Mysteries group meetings a friend accompanying me, Rob Midwinter, persuaded me to attempt to form a similar group for the Midlands. Rob and myself met up with four other friends of mine in June 1989 and we quickly agreed to collaborate. One of these friends, Paul Nix, offered to start a modest quarterly magazine to promote the group's activities – *Mercian Mysteries* was born. I took over editing and producing *Mercian Mysteries* after five issues and in 1994, after a further 20 issues, dropped the emphasis on the Midlands and re-launched the magazine as *At the Edge*. The subtitle-cum-manifesto stated the aims: 'Exploring new interpretations of past and place in archaeology, folklore and mythology'. The aim was as much to popularise developments in academic archaeology as to promote the best of alternative approaches. *At the Edge* also sought to intentionally step on the cracks between archaeology, folklore and mythology (an online archive of articles from *Mercian Mysteries* and *At the Edge* can be found at www.indigogroup.co.uk/edge). I developed useful contacts with a wide range of people creating the 'alternative' approaches to archaeology and, mostly as a result of attending academic archaeology conferences, also benefited from the friendship and advice of a good number of people within academe.

In 1998 *At the Edge* merged with a like-minded magazine, *3rd Stone,* and, while retaining a small involvement, I took a much-needed break from trying to keep up with developments in the academic disciplines of archaeology, folklore and mythology in my 'spare time' from a demanding day job. Only in the later part of

2001, after the demise of the day job, did I resume researching and writing about folklore, mythology and related disciplines such as cultural studies.

These brief autobiographical remarks will, I hope, help put the following remarks into perspective. As one of the 'players' who helped shape one of the alternative approaches (although there were plenty of others, some of whom were far more influential) my commentary on the mid-1980s onwards is inevitably somewhat subjective. Intriguingly, the period before I was actively involved has been described by two other authors, one of whom was a participant (Screeton 1984) and one who takes a more journalistic approach (Lachman 2001).

The birth of the ley

However, to really begin to understand alternative archaeologies in Britain we need to step back to the late 1920s. Alfred Watkins (1855–1935) was a successful Hereford businessman, running a flour milling company, with a passion for photography, archaeology and nature. He was a magistrate, county councillor and leader of public opinion. He invented a widely-used pioneering exposure meter to assist photographers. He also improved the milling of flour for brown bread. More importantly for the purposes of this book, in 1925 he published a book entitled *The Old Straight Track: Its mounds, beacons, moats, sites and mark stones*. Watkins' thesis was that a variety of landmarks, often reused over the centuries – for example a church on the site of prehistoric monument – which form exactly straight alignments over a distance of several miles. He thought that they probably marked out prehistoric trackways, as he had suggested in a more modest booklet of 1922 called *Early British Trackways, Moats, Mounds, Camps and Sites*. His ideas brought together the suggestions of a number of writers since the 1840s, as described by Nigel Pennick and Paul Devereux (1989: 30–42).

There is a practical reason why paths form straight lines between landmarks – a straight line is the shortest distance. There is essentially a 'chicken and egg' relationship between landmarks (natural or manmade) and pathways as in a landscape devoid of hedges or other such obstacles, the easiest thing way of getting about is to walk directly towards a recognised landmark. If the resultant path does not have sufficient landmarks (for example where it enters woodland along the way) then creating a new landmark (such as a standing stone) will help travellers – and simultaneously reinforce the pathway. Once pathways exist then they become the logical places to erect burial monuments and, later, churches. (See also Billingsley 2004b for a more subtle version of this argument.)

Watkins initially called these alignments of sites 'leys', although he later dropped the term. However, the word 'leys' was to become, and remains, one of the more contentious and now thoroughly confused ideas in alternative approaches to archaeology. In recent decades the word 'leys' has tended to give way to 'ley lines' and Watkins original idea of intervisible landmarks has, since the 1970s, been swallowed up by a belief in dowsable energies, as will be explored later in this chapter. So, just to reiterate, Watkins' book sets forward a definition of 'leys' that is entirely about exact (not approximate) alignments of physical sites. He was seemingly unaware of dowsing, least of all ideas that did not develop until over forty years later about dowsable 'energies' (see later in this chapter).

Three intervisible 'ley markers' – a standing stone (now leaning over), the tower of Anstey parish church, and a natural hill notch. This alignment was first proposed by Paul Devereux and continues over the hill to an Iron Age settlement site, and in the opposite direction passes through several significant sites in Leicester.

'Ley hunters' rarely propose alignments where adjoining 'ley markers' are intervisible so this Leicestershire example, with triple intervisibility, is quite unusual.

For that matter Watkins never refers to a vision of leys spreading out over the Herefordshire landscape. Although frequently repeated as fact, Watkins never makes any such remark. It is a hagiographical embellishment which originated in 1970 when John Michell added a note to the Sago Press reprint of Watkins *The Old Straight Track*.

> The revelation took place when Watkins was 65 years old. Riding across the hills near Bredwardine.... he pulled up his horse to look out over the landscape below. At that moment he became aware of a network of lines, standing out like glowing wires all over the surface of the country ...
> (Michell 1970: xv–xvi)

Michell's account introduces numerous errors (Adams 1978). Watkins was at home in Blackwardine (which is not on a hill) looking at maps and did not have a vision of 'glowing wires'. He travelled about Herefordshire in a motor car, not on a horse. But Michell's mythmaking was fully in tune with the hippy era and his romantic notion has been frequently regurgitated as fact.

What is not myth is the hostile reaction *The Old Straight Track* evoked from the academics of the time. Glyn Daniel, editor of *Antiquity*, famously refused an advertisement. Nevertheless (or perhaps because of the controversy) 'ley hunting' became a popular activity in the 1930s. As already discussed in Chapter 1, motor cars and bicycles were helping to create a greater interest in the historic aspects of the countryside, especially as urban developments were sprawling ever further into suburbia. Watkins organised the circulation of unpublished papers to members of The Straight Track Postal Portfolio Club. This was the first flowering of alternative archaeology in Britain.

The resurrection of *The Ley Hunter*

Watkins' death in 1935 and the advent of the Second World War in 1939 effectively put paid to ley hunting. In the 1950s British archaeology became increasingly obsessed with scientific approaches and professionalism. As discussed in the previous chapter, by the mid-1960s archaeology had developed quite sophisticated excavation methods but interpretation of the evidence recreated the past in terms of the present – and archaeologists of the mid-60s were still infatuated with the arid outlook of 1930s logical positivism.

This was archaeological Modernism – the soul-less equivalent of abstract minimalism in painting, twelve-tone serialism in music, or slab-sided multi-storey 'machines for living' in architecture, and the clearance of large swathes of historic city centres to make way for dual carriageways and underpasses. Not unsurprisingly, the public found few points of contact with the archaeologists' incestuous intra-academic idiom. And many of the professionals, keen to reinforce the ramparts of their ivory fortifications, excelled at providing popular books which set out the academic worldview for the public to consume in a one-way process of imposing their status. Even informed members of the public were regarded disparagingly as amateurs and expected to stay in their place (mostly as mere trowel-wielding volunteers at excavations) and not consider themselves capable of independently constructing interpretations of the past.

Glastonbury Tor.

At the opposite end of the lifestyle spectrum a group of free-thinking people, partly inspired by Alan Watts' individualistic interpretation of Buddhism and Taoism, were living decidedly bohemian lifestyles on the California coast in the late 1950s and early 1960s. These exotic Eastern-influenced ideas and experiments with drugs (notably the then-legal LSD-25) led to the San Francisco hippies' Summer of Love in

1967 and its sequel in Swinging London the following year. A fully-fledged Romantic antidote to Modernism transformed the lives of much of a whole generation of young people (Where was I in '68? Aged only 14, I was a little too young to be an active participant, although I went to art college in the early 1970s in the era before Punk provided the next major 'youth movement'.)

Out of the boiling cauldron of Sixties ideas emerged a curious work. John Michell published his book *The View Over Atlantis* in 1969. The combination of erudite information and Romantic mysticism of a lost Golden Age made Michell a cult figure almost overnight, and set the stage for the transformation of the sleepy Somerset town of Glastonbury into the spiritual heart of England for many in the hippie generation. Michell's fame brought him into frequent contact with the members of the Rolling Stones and their entourage of Sixties extreme counterculture. Michell's ideas became just one more part of emerging pop culture at the time. (See Screeton 1984: Ch.7; Schreiber and Nicholson 1987; Lachman 2001: 369–74 and Roberts 2005 for details of this era in Michell's life.)

Michell was more an elaboraor than pioneer of these ideas of a lost Golden Age and its esoteric wisdom. He picked up on the writings of Tom Lethbridge, a professional archaeologist who in later life rejected the consensus views of prehistory current in the 1950s. In a series of books published in the 1950s (notably Lethbridge 1957) he developed a view that early people needed to be more aware of their surroundings to help their struggle to survive and had thereby developed skills and a 'natural wisdom' that had subsequently been lost.

The notion of this lost wisdom was supported by Gerald S. Hawkins' controversial demonstration of the complexities of archaeoastronomy embodied in Stonehenge. His 1965 book *Stonehenge Decoded* was followed in 1967 by Alexander Thom's similar archaeoastronomical analyses in *Megalithic Sites in Britain*. The implications of these surveys were hotly contested by academic archaeologists at the time but, to the public at least, they amply demonstrated that prehistoric people may once have had a world view that had more in common with the counter culture of the Sixties than the prevailing Modernism. When Michell introduced complex numerology into *The View over Atlantis* he was following a very similar path of revealing lost erudition (indeed Michell was later to write a concise guide to what he termed 'astro-archaeology' (Michell 1977)).

The View over Atlantis also brought into the spotlight a number of ideas that had been circulating in Sixties 'underground' publications such as *International Times*. Michell was also aware that The Old Straight Track Club had been reformed in 1962 by Tony Wedd and Philip Heselton (brought together by a common interest in UFOs); they relaunched *The Ley Hunter* magazine in 1965. Wedd emigrated to Australian in 1970 and died in 1980. However Heselton, together with another early convert to the cause Jimmy Goddard, remained a key figure in the development of alternative approaches to archaeology for several decades.

Another early stalwart, Paul Screeton, took over editorship of *The Ley Hunter* in 1967 and the magazine and its associated activities thrived. In 1974 Screeton published a book, *Quicksilver Heritage*, which sought to redefine ley hunting according to the suggestive subtitle: 'The mystic leys: their legacy of ancient wisdom'. Ultimately this notion of lost wisdom is decidedly suspect, as Nigel Pennick has recognised:

> The function of much ley hunting today seems to serve the psychological need for participants to feel a sense of importance and control which is absent from the individual in the modern world. Like every other belief-system it gives us the feeling that we are special because we are members of an elite that possesses a secret knowledge hidden from lesser humans. (Pennick 1997: 3)

Before *Quicksilver Heritage* appeared Colin and Janet Bord had applied their photographic skills to ancient sites of interest to ley hunters and produced *Mysterious Britain* in 1972. Although *Quicksilver Heritage* was influential in the 70s, in many respects it was the scope of the Bords' book (already outlined at the start of this chapter) which was to prove a far better indication of where ley hunting was heading. Increasingly leys were regarded as just part of an alternative approach to the folklore and mythology of ancient sites and one among a variety of archaeological, astronomical and numerological 'insights'.

Until quite recently earth mysteries researchers have remained loyal to the suggestions of some late nineteenth century folklorists that British lore incorporates 'fossils' of pre-Christian customs and beliefs, even though such notions were (very belatedly) rejected by a new school of British folklorists in the 1970s (see Trubshaw 2002 for an overview of the changes in folklore theory).

One key source of folklore for earth mysteries researchers was a book entitled *Folklore of Prehistoric Sites in Britain* by Leslie Grinsell which appeared in 1976. Grinsell was of a much older generation of amateur archaeologists than the hippie generation (his first book, an invaluable survey of prehistoric burial mounds in England, had been published in 1936) but, in his own exemplary manner, took a somewhat maverick approach to recording British prehistory that was disdained by the post-war professional archaeologists. Indeed, in later years Grinsell himself seems to have recognised that the folklore of prehistoric sites could reveal nothing about their significance to those who constructed them. But he was a dogged compleatist and, nothing if not persistent, continued collecting the surviving lore anyway.

Janet and Colin Bord also covered similar legends in their book *The Secret Country* (1976), and the 1995 sequel *The Enchanted Land*. A large number of place-related legends were brought together, almost as an encyclopaedia, by an exponent of the new approaches to British folklore, Jennifer Westwood, in the form of a 500-plus page blockbuster called *Albion: A guide to legendary Britain* (Westwood 1987). For an insightful analysis of archaeological folklore see Jerome Voss (1987), who concludes:

> Prehistoric monuments are especially suitable focal points for [the reinforcement of dominant values and practices] precisely because they are visible and ambiguous at the same time, and may be interpreted as desired

Silbury Hill.

by a people. Although the monuments provide a link to the past, this past may be constructed in culturally appropriate terms.
(Voss 1987: 89)

Mythologising the ancient landscape

A clear manifestation of Voss's abstract remarks can be found in the books of Michael Dames. In one sense Dames shares the same interest in the lore of the prehistoric landscape as Grinsell but in almost all other respects they are situated at opposite ends of the spectrum of approach.

Dames trained as both an archaeologist and an artist. He combined an understanding of archaeological evidence with a deeply questioning approach to the 'orthodox' interpretation of the Neolithic monuments in the Avebury area. The outcome was a wonderfully imaginative and inspiring alternative interpretation that was ahead of its time. The first of his books was called *The Silbury Treasure*, which appeared in 1976, followed by *The Avebury Cycle* in the next year.

Silbury Hill is a dramatic flat-topped cone-shaped hill. Awareness that such a massive construction was made in the Neolithic adds to the sense of awe. To this Dames adds a richly detailed mythology of the shape depicting a pregnant Goddess who, at the height of the summer, 'gives birth' to the moon (reflected in the curiously-shaped 'moat' around the hill). Dames wove into this mythical narrative roles for associated Neolithic monuments in the vicinity; his ideas are explored further in Chapter 8.

My first encounter with *The Silbury Treasure* came about when I first ventured to Avebury in 1978. Dames' views inspired a number of somewhat abstract drawings of the Neolithic monuments and a large number of photographs taken during many subsequent visits. While the Bords' *Mysterious Britain* had first made me aware of this alternative approach to prehistory, it was Dames who changed my awareness into a deeper interest. Dames' approach is remarkable in its breadth and originality, but these qualities make him distinct from most of the other people active in alternative archaeology, where innovation tends to be 'evolutionary' rather than 'revolutionary'. See pages 140–2 for further details of Dames' ideas about Avebury.

Seeking a suitable name

The term 'geomancy' was adopted by Nigel Pennick to refer to this combination of archaeology, folklore, mythology, ley hunting, anomalous phenomena, and generally 'alternative' thinking. The word 'geomancy' derives from the Greek for 'earth magic'. It was coined twice, firstly to refer to divination of studying random dots (such as caused by throwing a handful of earth), and again in the nineteenth century by Sinologists to describe *feng shui,* apparently unaware of the earlier divination term. However this second sense does not appear in the *Concise Oxford Dictionary,* yet was adopted by John Michell, Nigel Pennick and others in the emerging 'earth mysteries' movement. Confusion has ensued ever since.

A retrospective and discursively nuanced definition of geomancy forms part of the preface to Jeremy Harte's bibliography *Research in Geomancy 1990–1994* (Harte 1999); as this is available on-line I will quote only a part:

> [Crucially] ... it is the sacred identity of the holy place itself which matters for geomantic researchers. The sacred presence is not to be understood as a metaphor, a consequence, or a reflection of some other factor – it is a powerful, direct image of truth.
>
> I would lay special stress on [this] factor, because it is so contrary to everything that is learnt in school and at college. In our official culture, the sciences study nature, and the humanities study people, but no provision is made for the intelligent study of the supernatural. Quite the reverse, in fact. [...]
>
> Geomancy is different, and it is worth remembering this, because at first glance it appears so similar to other work done recently within the rationalist or humanist paradigms of conventional research. There is something more to the material set out [in this bibliography] than a theoretical archaeology of ritual landscapes. It is not a geographical contribution to the anthropology of religion, either, nor should it be read as a psychology of traditional approaches to architecture and territory.
> (Harte 1999)

Despite Harte's preference for the term geomancy, the name by which these alternative approaches became known, at least to the participants, was 'earth mysteries' – hardly a self-explanatory label, and one easily misread (intentionally or otherwise) as 'earth mysticism'. The term 'earth mysteries' was apparently invented by an unknown journalist in 1974 (Pennick and Devereux 1989: 210; Heselton 1991: x) and came to the fore in 1977 when Paul Devereux took over *The Ley Hunter* and added the subtitle 'The Magazine of Earth Mysteries'.

However it was left to another magazine to attempt a tolerably concise definition. In the early 1990s the masthead of *Gloucestershire Earth Mysteries*, edited by Danny Sullivan, stated:

> *Earth Mysteries* is an holistic approach to the study of ancient sacred sites, a left and right brain synthesis, a systems based view which draws together into a coherent whole picture the seemingly disparate strands of archaeology, geographical and astronomical alignments of ancient sites, landscape lines, little-understood energy effects to do with both human consciousness and the earth, UFOs, dowsing, astrology and ancient astronomies, ancient history and folklore, the geometry of megalithic and sacred structures, virtual and symbolic landscapes, anomalous and paranormal phenomena and the art and science of 'being and seeing' at sacred sites.

Philip Heselton, who had effectively started earth mysteries when he refounded *The Ley Hunter* back in 1967, helped to define the range of the term when he co-wrote a concise overview of earth mysteries in 1985 (Larkman and Heselton 1985) and followed this with a useful book-length introduction published in 1991 as *The Elements of Earth Mysteries*.

John Billingsley, who took over as editor of *Northern Earth Mysteries* magazine in 1992 – and promptly dropped the word 'mysteries' from the title has retrospectively justified this change for several reasons, one of which is:

> The change was partly due to the popular perception of the word 'mystery'. The Earth Mysteries were originally in the Eleusinian sense of a deep and life-changing spiritual experience, which is actually the kind of experience within the land that was and remains a primary inspiration for earth mysteries and its students... More generally, however, the word 'mystery' is too often a victim of contemporary dumbing-down – the ineffable has become the vacuous....
> (Billingsley 2003b)

Similar pros and cons were behind my suggesting the title *Mercian Mysteries* for the Midlands counterpart to *Northern Earth*, and then becoming increasingly less happy with the dumbed-down sense of 'mysteries' and relaunching the magazine as *At the Edge*.

Earliest earth mysteries writers

The emphasis on 'sacred places' and the 'spirit of place' betrays close affinities between earth mysteries and the pioneering British antiquarians of the sixteenth to eighteenth centuries. Indeed, the first English person to call himself an antiquarian, John Leland (1506–62) 'paid my respects to the deity of the place' when he visited the library at Glastonbury Abbey. In his *Itinerary* (published posthumously in 1710) he set out a sacred topography (perhaps better termed 'chorography'; see Chapter 1) which influenced all subsequent English antiquarians and can still be detected, in a more secular form, in such travel writers as Arthur Mee (1875–1943).

However Leland was following a long-established precedent. As discussed in Chapter 1, the first English author said to 'speak of relics of the past, of British defences, of Roman earthworks and walls, of ruined churches, of Horsa's tomb and so forth' was Bede (c.673–735). Bede was quite possibly the first person to see the history of England as embodied in old stones and broken monuments, the most conspicuous aspects of antiquarianism.

As Peter Ackroyd has suggested

> Antiquarianism, in England, has always been compounded by a vision of Englishness itself; it is not a question of nationalism, which is often mistakenly introduced as an explanation or an easy device, but rather of the sentiment that in the relics of the past there is some inkling of what England is 'really like'.
> (Ackroyd 2002: 37)

Earth mysteries enthusiasts unwittingly maintain a tradition pioneered by Bede and revitalised by Leland. The result is an intricate intertwining of chorography and identity, both personal and national. I am well aware that these modern day ideas could not and would not exist without this long-held national preoccupation with the sacredness of places and the deeply-rooted (but rarely consciously analysed) meanings associated with ruins and 'antiquities'. I think it is not simply coincidence that the earth mysteries movement never really gained momentum in Wales, Scotland or Ireland (even though these have far more surviving megalithic monuments than England). Earth mysteries is, at least in part, an expression of implicit aspects of being English. It is very different to, say, the self-conscious expression of Irish nationalism in the mid-nineteenth century which involved (among much else) crackpot theories about round towers, Ireland as Atlantis, and the mish-mash of occultism, mysticism, revolutionary politics and literature of W.B. Yeats and his circle. Notably, little or none of this Romantic interest in the Irish landscape was reactivated as part of the resurgence of Irish nationalism in the late 1960s that was contemporary with the emergence of earth mysteries in England.

Sharing ideas

The earth mysteries 'community' shared ideas through an overlapping network of limited circulation privately-produced magazines. Jeremy Harte has provided two annotated online bibliographies covering different aspects of these magazines, *Alternative Approaches to Folklore 1969–1996* (Harte 1998) and *Research in Geomancy 1990–1994* (Harte 1999) (as already discussed, Harte uses the term 'geomancy' in the way instigated by Pennick, as a synonym for 'earth mysteries' rather than as a reference to a system of divination).

The list of sources cited by Harte for *Alternative Approaches to Folklore 1969–1996* would be unknown to most librarians – *Albion, Ancient Mysteries, At the Edge, Cambridgeshire Ancient Mysteries, Earth Giant, Earth Lines, Earthquest News, Essex Landscape Mysteries, Gloucestershire Earth Mysteries, Journal of Geomancy, Lincolnshire Dragon, Markstone, Mercian Mysteries, Meyn Mamvro, Northern Earth Mysteries, Picwinnard, Practical Geomancy, Quicksilver Messenger, The Ley Hunter, 3rd Stone, Touchstone* and *Wisht Maen.* Of these, only about half-a-dozen magazines were active at any one time, with *Northern Earth Mysteries* and *The Ley Hunter* the only two that survived from the 60s to the 90s.

Attempting to survey earth mysteries activities without delving into these elusive magazines and only reading the more easily available books is mistaking the tip of an iceberg for the complete entity (and this is a key failing of Richard Hayman's otherwise useful book comparing academic and alternative archaeologies (Hayman 1997)). Unfortunately for researchers, copies of these publications were rarely deposited with the six libraries in Britain which have the option of archiving all publications. There are probably less than ten individuals with fairly complete collections of this literature from the 1970s onwards, although a few more with a good cross-section from the mid-1980s onwards.

A number of these magazines organised conferences (called 'moots') and field trips which provided excellent opportunities for like-minded people to meet and share ideas. In many respects field trips and moots were as much a defining aspect of the earth mysteries movement as the privately-produced magazines. Such meetings were especially valuable before the Internet enabled fellow enthusiasts to be identified and contacted.

Those seeking a history of earth mysteries should also see Sandell (1988), Pennick and Devereux (1989: Ch.5) and Stout (2001). Paul Screeton provided a detailed view of his involvement in the formative first fifteen-or-so years of ley hunting, geomancy and earth mysteries in his book *Seekers of the Linear Vision* (Screeton 1984). However Screeton omits rather too much of the detail before his involvement with *The Ley Hunter* (so the formative influence of John Nicholson, Nigel Pennick, Anthony Roberts and the *Cambridge Voice* is unacknowledged) and the update in 1993 omits far too many of the activities after 1984 to be useful.

Not quite earth mysteries

Whatever badly-informed critics of alternative archaeologies might impute, earth mysteries has always considered itself far removed from the wilfully irrational romantic idealism of the New Age movement, even though the mish-mash of ideas brought together by New Agers often includes 'borrowings' (not necessarily accurate ones) from earth mysteries. Earth mysteries has also been largely dismissive of Erich von Däniken, Graham Hancock and such writers although, again critics often chose to blur all these alternative approaches into an undifferentiated 'lunatic fringe'.

However there are 'accepted overlaps' with other alternative approaches. Some aspects of earth mysteries, including anomalous phenomena such as ghosts and UFOs, are also the provenance of 'Forteans'. These people peruse the interests and approach of Charles Fort (1874–1932), who adopted a simultaneously sceptical and open-minded approach to phenomena that science explained away or ignored. The scripts of the TV series *The X Files* frequently draw upon Fortean phenomena. The magazine *Fortean Times*, founded in 1973, provides Forteans with a forum for exchanging ideas. While some earth mysteries enthusiasts read or even contribute articles to *Fortean Times*, there is little emphasis on the importance of places in Fortean studies. Certainly the anomalous events are located *somewhere* but the location is often, although not always, regarded as circumstantial and never with the sense of sacred that tends to predominate in earth mysteries studies. There is always something 'spiritual' about earth mysteries, indeed modern day pagan beliefs increasingly intermesh with earth mysteries outlooks.

Goddess worship and Wicca

There are plenty of overlaps between earth mysteries enthusiasts and modern pagans. Their various alternative ideas about prehistory and ancient sacred places can best thought of as having a common origin but a complex development of interweaving of 'evolutionary paths'. The complexities of this interweaving of ideas is hardly surprising as both earth mysteries and modern pagan 'communities' shared their ideas through an overlapping network of limited circulation privately-produced magazines. Predictably, proponents of specific paths tend to summarise these developments by concentrating on their approach to the detriment of others.

Unlike Christianity, Judaism and Islam, modern day paganism is non-hierarchical, except within specific groups. There is no higher authority to set the rules, with the result that there are almost as many different types of paganism as there are pagans (see Harvey 1997 for a useful overview of modern British paganism).

Modern paganism shares with earth mysteries the same Romantic roots which feed English culture throughout the last 120 or so years. As Jan Morris perceptively observes in her study of the 'pastoral impulse' in England between 1880 and 1914:

> For some, country walks became almost a substitute religious observance, and not only because they usually took place on Sundays. Faith in a conventional creator was on the wane, and social and geographical mobility loosened the links between church and community so that many sensed a spiritual void in their lives. Drawing on Romanticism and classical ideas of pantheism, love of Nature help to fill the gap, enabling many late Victorians to dispense with God gradually, as it were, without losing their sense of immanent divinity. Others, who continued to believe, found in Nature and Nature poetry an expression of quasi-religious feeling that fed their spiritual needs. All tended to find that transcendental terms were appropriate to this new form of worship.
>
> Most of the major poets of this time [c.1860s] – Tennyson, Arnold, Meredith, Swinburne – may be described as Nature-worshippers, and the many poetic anthologies published in this period reflected the belief in the spiritual qualities of natural beauty. But it was Richard Jefferies who above all filled the role of Nature-priest or a generation of readers...
> (Marsh 1982: 35)

However it was not just literary figures of the calibre of Tennyson or Jefferies who popularised this nature-veneration. Kenneth Grahame's *The Wind in the Willows* (1908) has been far more widely read and is, according to Marsh:

> ... a book for country lovers as well as a children's story and contains in the central seventh chapter, entitled 'The Piper at the Gates of Dawn', a sustained passage of Nature-worship. On the island, the two anthropomorphic animals come face-to-face with Pan, the spirit of Nature, before whom, 'crouching to the earth, [they] bowed their heads and did

worship.' Then, 'sudden and magnificent, the sun's broad golden disc showed itself over the horizon facing them; and the first rays, shooting across the level water-meadows, took the animals full in the eyes and dazzled them. When they were able to look once more, the Vision had vanished, and the air was full of the carol of birds that hailed the dawn.' (Marsh 1982: 38)

Like many other English children, this story was read to me many times in my formative years. Indeed, Grahame's tale has consistently been among the most popular of classic childrens' literature. While I doubt that the current interest in modern nature veneration can be attributed to this vision of Pan at sunrise, like the books of Geoffrey Grigson referred to in Chapter 1, I suspect that early exposure to such ideas can create a susceptibility to similar ideas encountered later in life.

Key to most modern paganism is a widespread belief in a 'Great Goddess' or 'Mother Goddess', sometimes regarded as 'Mother Nature'. Although rarely realised by modern pagans, the idea of Nature as a deity only arises within the Christian era (Hutton 2003: 96–7, 166–9). Regarding Nature as a singular, abstracted and personified religious being makes her a logical agent for the monotheistic Judaeo-Christian God (Williams 1980: 69). However, before nature became a goddess, there were a panoply of spirits, who individually personified the winds, the sea, the moon, forests, rivers and streams, rocks, individual trees and plants, and of course animals. These are reflected in the diversity of nature-related deities in Classical Greece and many other traditional cultures. Nevertheless, the relatively modern notion of Nature as an individual persona has become 'back projected' onto pagans of the past.

The invention of a 'Great Goddess' as a counterpart to the monotheistic Judaeo-Christian God first seems to surface in the writings of Jane Ellen Harrison around the time of the First World War. She was a Classicist inspired by writers such as Sir Edward Burnet Tylor and Sir James Frazer (see Hutton 1999: 124). In turn her ideas influenced literary figures such as T.S. Eliot and Robert Graves. In the 1970s the notion of a Great Goddess was brought to prominence by the Romanian archaeologist Marija Gimbutas. She published a book in 1974 arguing for a matrifocal, non-violent, goddess-worshipping, pan-European early Neolithic culture. In this she was following the ideas of O.G.S. Crawford (who also inspired Michael Dames' ideas about Silbury Hill personifying a Great Goddess). Although Gimbutas's ideas were deeply critiqued by fellow archaeologists, her ideas were warmly welcomed by the emerging feminist movement who, understandably, were unlikely to encounter the counter-arguments in academic archaeological journals.

The distinctly speculative ideas about a Neolithic Great Goddess became merged with an archetypal Mother Goddess, who seems to owe considerably to Catholic notions of the Blessed Virgin Mary (although pagans would argue that Catholics had appropriated pre-Christian precursors such as Isis). Add in a smattering of popular Jungian psychology and a very durable goddess 'archetype' was born. A detailed analysis of the problems with Gimbutas's thesis, and the consequent confusion among feminists, pagans and New Age enthusiasts, has been provided by Lynn Meskell (Meskell 1995; see also Trubshaw 1997b). But these dodgy 1970s fantasies of a prehistoric 'Mother Goddess' venerated by peaceable, matrifocal Neolithic peoples seem destined to live on indefinitely.

Emma Restall-Orr (in dark robe) and Mark Graham (on right) lead a Druid handfasting at Avebury. Spring equinox, 2003. Photograph by Andy Worthington.

James Lovelock's 'Gaia thesis' (Lovelock 1979) created a sophisticated concept of nature as a self-sustaining homeostatic system acting in the manner of a single organism to sustain its own life. The popular media reduced the sophistication of Lovelock's ideas to more simplistic notions which inferred that Earth was all-but a sentient being akin to 'Mother Nature'.

The increasing interest in ecology and the 'Green' movement in Britain and America meant that a nurturing Mother Goddess or Mother Nature figure was highly appropriate. This Green and feminist view of Goddess-led prehistory meshed neatly with the way Wicca (witchcraft) was developing in the early 1980s. The original magical rituals and gnostic enlightenment which characterised the form of Wicca promoted by Gerald Gardner (1884–1964) in the 1950s had become a part of 1960s pop culture through the activities of Alex Sanders (1926–1988); see Hutton 1999 for a detailed history of the origins of Wicca. During the last twenty years Wicca has become increasingly based around nature veneration, instead of being essentially magical and gnostic. Simultaneously Wiccan worship has moved out of secluded gardens and back bedroom temples and out into the landscape, sometimes using convenient local woodland groves but also more impressive Neolithic henges.

Many of the ideas that Wiccans have about prehistoric sacred places are derived from ideas that have long since been rejected by more informed archaeologists. Speculation is often presented as fact and sometimes defended passionately – bigotry

Rollright stone circle on the Oxfordshire/Warwickshire border is frequently used by modern pagans for rituals as it has remained in private ownership and is the most south-easterly henge to have survived (making it reasonably convenient for people living in London, the Home Counties and the Midlands).

is certainly not exclusive to Christianity! Indeed, in many cases, assumptions about the pre-Christian sanctity of specific 'sacred places' were part of the mythologised (and largely invented) history which some pagans accepted as the 'true' history of the past.

As an example of modern pagan approaches to sacred places here is a quote from Marian Green, a widely-respected writer and teacher:

> Find a local place with really ancient connections, be it a tumulus, quoit, fogou or hut circle, and try to visit it alone. Sit down, relax, and allow your mind to cross the vast river of time which separates that construction at its foundation from our modern, hurried world. Sink into meditation, with a

A site in the Charnwood Forest, Leicestershire said by early nineteenth century local antiquarians to be a Druidical altar.

silent request on your lips and in your heart to learn something of the wisdom which set up the structure, the powers which were handled there, the aspects of the goddess or god which were honoured.
(Green 1991: 88)

Pagans, although very much a manifestation of post-modern culture, sometimes have considerable problems with the idea that there is no 'true' view of the past but only a plurality of pasts, each of which reflect the questions asked of the evidence. However in my experience most modern day pagans are usually unaware that their beliefs are based on ideas that have been abandoned and, when challenged, are keen to widen their understanding. The problem is less a reluctance to revise their ideas and more the lack of popular and accessible overviews of recent archaeological thinking, together with the tendency of pagan writers to recycle and further distort the outmoded ideas.

The great variety of ideas within modern pagan movements has led to a corresponding variety of ideas about sacred places. In the last twenty or so years pagans have shown an increasing interest in prehistoric 'sacred sites', epitomised by stone circles and henges. At the same time the free festival movement, which had started in 1974, was bringing more and more attention to Stonehenge, especially at the time of midsummer sunrise, so Stonehenge has become the icon for younger peoples' spirituality and intense opposition to the politics of the day (see Chapter 9).

Stonehenge is also indelibly linked in the popular imagination with modern day Druidism. The revival of Druidism from the late eighteenth century onwards brought the notion of traditional Celtic spirituality to the fore as part of the anti-English political sentiment of the times (see Hutton 1991: Ch.5). As little is known about the nature of Iron Age religion, the absence of facts provides space for vast amounts of speculation. While Druids did not regard themselves as 'pagans' until at least the middle of the twentieth century, in the last fifty years there has a been a revival of Druid ideas and an increasing overlap with Wiccan ideas (although Druid rituals remain rather Protestant in character and lack much of the 'exoticism' of Wicca). However the emphasis of modern day Druidism on 'spirits of our ancestors' and 'spirits of place' makes them the pagan religion with the greatest interest in sacred places, and investing specific places with a sense of reverence. (See the extensive writings of Philip Carr-Gomm or Emma Restall Orr, who are both key figures in the Druid movement of recent years).

Common antipathy to Christianity

The emphasis of 'alternative archaeology' in the last 30 or so years has been unsympathetic to Christianity, preferring instead to draw ideas from both the archaeology of pre-Christian religions and modern day paganism. While different individuals within the alternative archaeology movement show widely-differing degrees of tolerance or antipathy to Christianity, the underlying consensus is effectively that the only good church is a ruined one, or at least one standing on the site of a prehistoric stone circle.

A tacit assumption of alternative archaeology in the 70s and 80s was that Christian sites were re-used pagan sites. This was consistent with the then widespread belief that folklore and customs were 'fossils' of pre-Christian religion. Many people involved in alternative archaeology progressively dropped both these assumptions during the later 1990s, although the ideas still linger on among some modern pagans and others who are one or two steps removed from alternative archaeology.

Mysticism, dowsing, and energy lines

As with paganism, earth mysteries underwent a diversification of views during the 1980s and 90s. One direction emphasised the mystical and more 'New Age' aspects while the other, strenuously instigated by the then editor of *The Ley Hunter*, Paul Devereux, looked to an increasingly scientific rationale.

The more mystical approach can be attributed in large part to the popularity of two books. According to the back cover blurb on Francis Hitching's book *Earth Magic* (1978) the author's

> ... search for information about the elusive 'earth magic' has led him down some strange paths: from astronomy, geometry and higher mathematics to UFOs, ESP and dragon lore, to a rich synthesis of science, folklore and speculation. This is an absorbing investigation of a central, overwhelming

Opposite: *A site in Charnwood Forest, Leicestershire, frequently used for rituals by modern day Druids*

question: *is there indeed a hidden force that our ancestors knew and used, but that we have lost?* [emphasis in original]

Speculation there certainly was, and the 'earth magic' may have been elusive because it was a figment of the author's prior assumptions. But the ideas were nevertheless influential.

The second book was Tom Graves' *Needles of Stone* (1978) which brought into this heady mysticism the notion that the path of leys could be detected by dowsing, and that there was a 'subtle energy' concentrated at standing stones and henges. He was drawing upon ideas about dowsing in the books of T.C. Lethbridge (e.g. Lethbridge 1961; 1976) and Guy Underwood (e.g. Underwood 1969); see Romano 2002 for a recent overview of Lethbridge's approach to archaeology and dowsing.

Intriguingly, such dowsable energies seem to be akin to the ideas about electrical 'lines of force' interconnecting objects which were popularised by a contemporary of Alfred Watkins, the pioneer scientific broadcaster Sir Oliver Lodge in the 1920s in BBC radio broadcasts and a book entitled *Ether and Reality: A series of discourses on the many functions of the ether of space* (Lodge 1925). Even at the time of publication the concept of 'ether' was reaching its sell-by date. However such outdated conceptual concepts have a habit of surviving long past their use-by date as Lodge's spurious speculations were seemingly the basis of Virginia Woolf's notions of filaments psychically connecting her protagonists in *Mrs Dalloway* and *The Waves* (Woolf 1929; 1931), an idea which left its fictional origins and became woven into spiritualist beliefs of that era. When the successors to these speculations were 'rediscovered' in the 1960s and 70s by writers such as Guy Underwood, Francis Hitching, Tom Lethbridge and Tom Graves they seemingly beget the modern myth of dowsable 'energies'.

Graves regarded his ideas as speculative but they were widely quoted as facts by many other writers. Havelock Fidler attempted to apply basic scientific approaches to such approaches to dowsing for such energies and published his book *Ley Lines: Their properties and properties – a dowser's investigation* in 1983. Although the results are clearly highly personal observations, the attempt at a scientific approach gives them a semblance of veracity. The adoption of Graves' and Fidler's ideas by numerous other writers led to Watkins' idea of leys as physical alignments being swamped and replaced by complex explanations of the 'ley line energy' detected by dowsers. The consequences were that, at least in the eyes of many on the 'fringe', stone circles were incontrovertibly centres of such energies, and the term 'ley lines' came to mean such dowsable 'energies'.

Graves was the first to extensively criticise this seriously muddled thinking (Graves 1991; a summary is available on the Web cf. Trubshaw 1993). Nevertheless the notion of 'ley lines' as dowsable energy lines is still prevalent. Note that neither Graves nor myself are critical of what might be termed 'physical dowsing' (such as detecting underground water or buried archaeological remains and the like, where dowsers produce results consistent with each other and the predictions – even unexpected ones – have been proven by excavation), just the so-called 'energy lines'.

Earth mysteries research

So, while earth mysteries was going off in one direction in a decidedly mystical fashion, at the same time Paul Devereux had taken over as editor of *The Ley Hunter* and was keen to develop a more rational and scientifically-based approach to leys and anecdotal evidence of various anomalous phenomena at prehistoric sites. His own interest had been instigated by seeing a UFO and, with the assistance of Andrew York, he evaluated all the published sightings of UFOs and ghosts in Leicestershire. This led him to conclude that these were closely associated with geological fault lines, notably one between Loughborough and Ashby de la Zouch. This fault is associated with two of Britain's largest earthquakes, experienced on 11th and 12th of January 1957, which registered as 5.3 and 4.2 respectively on the Richter scale and with another earthquake a year before (10th January 1956) with a magnitude of 3.6 and its epicentre at Ashby de la Zouch. (See Devereux 1982: Ch.7 for details; earthquake data taken from the British Geological Survey web site).

Devereux's theory was that the stresses built up in the rocks could create anomalous light forms. Indeed 'tadpole shaped' lights were seen in the sky before the 1957 earthquake. Geophysicists at the U.S. Bureau of Mines were able to create such lights by putting rocks under stress in the laboratory. Devereux's ideas were dubbed 'the earth lights hypothesis' (see Devereux 1982 and 1989 for details).

After Devereux's first book on earth lights was published in 1982 a large number of such anomalous 'lights in the sky' were seen in West Yorkshire by hundreds of people. These were associated with about 45 'after shocks' with epicentres in the Pennines which followed a major earthquake (Richter 5.5) on 19 July 1984 at the western end of this fault sequence at Porthmadog (Devereux 1989: 181–3). Extensive programmes of observation in places as far apart as Norway and New Mexico have provided plenty of evidence of such 'earth lights' in places where there are active faults (Devereux 1989).

Encouraged by this apparent success of the earth lights research, and assisted by the scientist Don Robins and a small army of volunteers, Devereux created the Dragon Project. This had an ambitious scope including using Geiger counters, ultrasound detectors, infra-red photography, equipment for monitoring brain rhythms of volunteers, and various other techniques to survey various prehistoric sites and a number of 'control' sites. Preliminary results were published (Robins 1985; Devereux 1990) but the project was never fully evaluated. The main result was to show that a number of stone circles in the British Isles contain stones which are strongly magnetic. This has since been followed up by Philip Burton (Burton 1993; 1995; 2002); see also the section of Chapter 3 on geomagnetism. A continuation of the Dragon Project looked specifically at how prehistoric sacred sites influenced the dreams of volunteers (details of the results have not been fully published, for partial reports see Krippner, Devereux and Fish 2003; Devereux 2004a).

Simultaneously Devereux was taking a critical look at Watkins' ideas about leys, specifically the evidence for aligned sites in traditional cultures world wide. This work was done in collaboration with another earth mysteries stalwart, Nigel Pennick. The resulting book, *Lines on the Landscape* (Pennick and Devereux 1989), remains as the definitive study of this contentious topic. Their approach is in stark contrast with Tom Williamson and Liz Bellamy's selective (and sometimes misquoted) use of evidence in their exercise in debunking published in 1983 as *Ley Lines in Question*. While Williamson and Bellamy may have succeeded in their aim of confirming to academe that leys were spurious, academics were of course unlikely to read the deep critiques of this book that appeared in the earth mysteries periodicals.

Devereux's interest in the ethnology of aligned sites developed further and took the whole concept of leys into a new direction. Picking up on the growing interest in shamanism, he proposed that leys were physical manifestations of 'spirit paths' along which shamans were believed to travel to the Otherworlds, or along which the dead travelled to the afterlife. These ideas were first published as *Shamanism and the Mystery Lines* (Devereux 1992a) and *Symbolic Landscapes* (Devereux 1992b) then developed in numerous articles in subsequent issues of *The Ley Hunter* and various books by Devereux. Some of his initial thoughts were contested (notably in Stone 1998), and the understanding of shamanism has become a good deal more nuanced in recent years, but the latest versions of his approach (e.g. Devereux 2001b: Ch. 1–3) offer a sophisticated interdisciplinary approach to 'spirit paths'.

New antiquarians

Just as earth mysteries was getting ever more studious, and academic archaeology was becoming increasingly 'speculative' in its attempts to interpret the past, along came a pop musician obsessed with megalithic sites. Julian Cope had found fame (and presumably some fortune) as the lead singer of the Teardrop Explodes. The band quite intentionally toured to places where Cope wanted to 'check out the vibes' at prehistoric sites. The result appeared in 1998 as *The Modern Antiquarian: A pre-millennial odyssey through megalithic Britain,* a lavishly produced 438 page large format tome in a day-glo orange cover that combines badly-digested versions of woefully out of date and downright fictional ideas with personal insights and responses to over 300 prehistoric sites in Britain. It has recently spawned an international successor, *Megalithic European: The 21st Century traveller in prehistoric Europe* (Cope 2004).

While all credit goes to Cope for successfully visiting so many sites while at the peak of his pop career, his enthusiasm for sightseeing is in inverse proportion to his ability to assess sources or check facts. The result is a curious mix of many of the muddled ideas which had emerged among earth mysteries enthusiasts and modern pagans over the previous three decades. Interestingly Cope does *not* include leys or 'earth magic'. As an example of his approach, he are his thoughts on the Neolithic long barrow at Bryn yr Hen Bobl:

> I'm sitting on the forecourt entrance to the enormous mound, the wind blowing up a storm and thick constant towers of fast-moving low cloud bales overhead from the south-west. It was on these shores that the Druids made their final stand against the onslaught of the approaching Roman Legions almost 2,000 years ago. For most of the battle, wailing women stood on these shores, their tradition already over 3,000 years old even then. They were not willing to easily give up this magical kingdom, forced

as it were into the very last corner of the Brythonic lands by shaven robots
run by a technocratic death system. To sit in this wind on this demented
ridge is to feel the millennia peel away in easy stages, and Bryn-yr-Hen-
Bobl opens up before me in one trumpet blast from our distant past.
(Cope 1998: 309)

Understandably, given the book's high profile, academics regard such idiosyncratic
and sloppy writing as characteristic of the 'fringe', although it is not. So remote is
Cope's approach from that of traditional archaeologists it would be reasonable to
expect that the review of *The Modern Antiquarian* in *Antiquity* (the most august of
the academic archaeological journals, whose founder editor had derided leys and
early earth mysteries) would simply trash such a book. But so far had academic
archaeology changed by the late 1990s that Tim Darvill's review (Darvill 1999) is
open-minded and perceptive. Darvill recognised that Cope had provided an
excellent example of a 'holistic, humanistic, polymathic approach' to prehistoric
landscapes, that is akin to recent academics' phenomenological approaches
(although Cope seems quite unaware of these developments) and blamed Cope's
ignorance of current thinking on the inability of academics to present their ideas
effectively to a wider public.

But, overall, in the late 1990s the earth mysteries 'movement' was drawing to a
natural conclusion. Leys were declared 'dead' by the final editor of *The Ley Hunter,*
Danny Sullivan, who understandably wound the magazine up in 1999 (although this
led to the formation of the Society of Ley Hunters to act as a forum for those
interested in aligned sites). To many who had been actively involved with earth
mysteries over the years, the new interpretations and approaches coming from
academic archaeologists in the mid-1990s were more exciting than most of what had
come from the 'fringe'. And the Internet was opening up new opportunities for
sharing ideas, 'fringe' and otherwise.

Shorn of mysticism, ley hunting, and – apart from the spirit lines theory – any new
hypotheses to test, all that was left of the original scope of earth mysteries was the
inter-disciplinary interest in archaeology, folklore and mythology, especially as they
related to places. This was almost going full circle back to the interests of the early
antiquarians such as Leland, Stukeley and Aubrey. Indeed an 'earth mysteries'
magazine with a national scope, *3rd Stone*, was launched in 1994 with the subtitle
'The magazine for the new antiquarian', which it retained until being wound up in
2003, by when it had become the last-surviving of such national magazines.

However three of the regional earth mysteries magazines have continued publishing,
Meyn Mamvro (concerned with sites in Cornwall); *Touchstone* (the newsletter of the
Surrey Earth Mysteries Group, edited by one of the founders of earth mysteries
researcher, Jimmy Goddard); and the pioneer of all such regional 'zines, *Northern
Earth*. However many of the ideas originally developed among the earth mysteries
activities of the 1970s and 1980s had been adopted enthusiastically by modern
pagans and become uncritically absorbed into their belief systems (this overlap is
especially conspicuous in *Meyn Mamvro*).

*'Thirty-eight Long leaves'.
A homage to Richard Long
created and photographed by
the author in a Sussex wood,
November 1989.*

Earth mysteries and art

At the same time as earth mysteries was flourishing, a small number of British artists were exploring new ways of integrating art and the landscape, such as Hamish Fulton and Richard Long. John Billingsley has provided an essay looking at artists such as Long from an earth mysteries perspective, and asking why we do not think of prehistoric stone circles as art, and noting that both Long and earth mysteries researchers are 'responding to the subtlety of place (Billingsley 2003a).

Although for several years in the 1980s and 90s Brian Larkin compiled an annual 'art supplement' for *The Ley Hunter* magazine, there were no overlaps between earth mysteries and avant garde art. The apparent separation between earth mysteries and art is all the more surprising given that a number of the earth mysteries magazine editors and other key players were art school graduates (e.g. Paul Devereux, Brian Larkin, myself) or accomplished artists (e.g. Nigel Pennick). And this is not anomalous, as a significant proportion of subscribers to *Mercian Mysteries* and *At the Edge* were amateur artists or professional graphic designers.

And yet, and yet... On the fringes of earth mysteries was an interest in sacred geometry, labyrinths and so-called 'terrestrial zodiacs' (attempts to use topographical features and place-names to define the twelve constellations in the landscape). All

---

The Ancient Sacred Landscape Network (ASLaN) charter

+ Please take care when visiting sacred sites to leave them as the next visitor would like to find them. Respect the land and all its inhabitants, people, animals, and plants.

+ Digging holes for any purpose will damage plants and probably insects and archaeological remains. Damaging archaeology makes it harder for us, and future generations, to understand the history of the site. Damaging any aspect of the site will damage the spirit of the place.

+ Lighting fires can cause similar damage to digging. A fire can damage standing stones. If they get too hot, they split. Fires can spread quickly in summer, killing wildlife, and it can be very difficult to make sure a fire is truly out. Fires also cause archaeological damage by preventing geophysical surveys and contaminating archaeological layers with ash and charcoal. Heat, candle wax, and graffiti damage moss and lichens, which can take decades to recover. Damage caused by fires will damage the spirit of the place.

+ If an offering seems appropriate please think about all its effects. Don't leave artificial materials. Choose your offerings carefully so that they can't be mistaken for litter. Please don't bury things. Biodegradable offerings decay, please bear this in mind if you leave them. If there are already offerings at the site, consider the effects of adding more.

+ Please don't take anything, except litter, from a site. Much of the vegetation around sacred sites is unusual or rare so don't pick flowers. Don't take stones -- they may be an important part of the site in ways that aren't obvious.

+ In times past, it was traditional to leave no traces of any ritual because of persecution. This tradition is worth reviving because it shows reverence to nature and the spirit of the place.

+ Don't change the site; let the site change you.

---

these are intensely visual ways of creating meaning and significance, so perhaps the apparent distinction between 'art' and 'earth mysteries' is because of the restricted boundaries of these categories, whereas the reality of what was being imagined and researched unselfconsciously straddled such boundaries.

The folk doth protest too much

From the mid-1980s the pagan community was becoming more actively involved in eco-protest and the protection of prehistoric monuments. Understandably much of writing by eco-pagans aims to counter specific threats, although Graham Harvey (1997: Ch.8) Jenny Blain and Robert Wallis (Blain and Wallis 2002a) have provided

Waiting for the sunrise – summer solstice and Stonehenge in 2001.
Photograph by Andy Worthington.

overviews. Much of the originally energy of such protests were directed towards the road-building programmes of the late 1980s and early 1990s (see Letcher 2000; 2001).

Intriguingly this protest movement generated its own mythology and folklore of pixies, trolls and fairies, as recorded and deftly analysed by Andy Letcher (2001). For example, fairies came to symbolise the forces of nature while 'pixieing' became a euphemism for sabotaging construction equipment and other defiance of authority.

When government funding for such developments was suddenly cut drastically, the pagan community's awareness began to more actively embrace threats to prehistoric sites such as stone circles threatened by quarrying or what were considered to be unacceptable 'heritage management' policies. Pagans and earth mysteries enthusiasts combined to form groups such as Save Our Sacred Stones, the Cornish Sacred Sites Protection Network, and the Ancient Sacred Landscape Network (or ASLaN; the conscious link to C.S. Lewis's bestial analogue for Jesus is indicated by ASLaN's letterhead depicting a lion).

ASLaN has proved to be the most active of these groups, engaging in dialogue with, among others, English Heritage and representatives of the Church of England regarding approaches to sacred places. Their activities can be explored on their Web site (at the time of writing to be found at www. symbolstone.org/archaeology/aslan).

ASLaN's 'charter' offers quite specific advice to pagans and other visitors to prehistoric sacred sites (see previous page).

However, as always, diversity of opinion is inevitable. How much should prehistoric sites be preserved or be allowed to transform according to activities resulting from how they are given significance in the present day? For surprisingly similar views by an academic archaeologist and a long-standing pagan see Cornelius Holtorf (2003) and Julian Vayne (2003). For other debates about conservation see Blain and Wallis (2002a esp. page 24) and Worthington (2002a; 2002b; 2002c; 2004).

So, on the one hand the threat from quarrying to Nine Ladies stone circle on Stanton Moor in Derbyshire has led to recent co-operation between the landowners and protesters regarding repairs to the site, while on the other hand English Heritage's public relations fiasco regarding the removal of 'Sea Henge' from the north Norfolk coast in 1999 revealed just how differently the significance of a 'sacred site' is regarded by English Heritage and pagans, with the local community also having a range of disparate views.

Chris Wood has written a very useful overview of these debates (Wood 2002), and includes a critique of the academic view of these debates offered by Robin Skeates (Skeates 2000). Wood considers Skeates' book to be 'important as much for what it omits as for what it includes, reflecting thereby the attitude of archaeology as a profession' (Wood 2002: 53). Wood's own views were critiqued by Ian Brown (2002). However the general consensus is that one lesson needs to be learnt from Sea Henge – that consultation with interested parties is a far better strategy than over-hasty 'we know best' intervention.

Demise and tentative resurrection

The demise of most of the earth mysteries magazines (especially the 'flagship' of the movement, *The Ley Hunter*) in recent years could be regarded as the demise of the ideas associated with the movement. However this would be very misleading as many of the ideas that originated with earth mysteries researchers live on in the belief systems of modern pagans and, in grotesquely distorted forms, the mish-mash of New Age ideas. Furthermore a 'hard core' of earth mysteries enthusiasts have retrenched. Some of these have formed the Society of Ley Hunters, with its emphasis on the physical alignment of sites as originally proposed by Alfred Watkins. The editor of the only earth mysteries magazine to have spanned the rise and fall of the approach, *Northern Earth*, recently provoked readers by asking if 'it's time for a fond farewell' or whether 'It is time to move our ideas forward.' (Billingsley 2004a: 22, 25). At the time of going to press this article had provoked a lively response from three earth mysteries stalwarts who put forward three quite contrasting futures for earth mysteries

- a 'fundamentalist' Watkinsian approach (Heaword 2004)

- a reconsideration of dowsing and earth mysteries (Lonegren 2004)

- a decidedly philosophical approach to the 'interface' between people, places and phenomena (Kimmis 2004).

With articles such as these then earth mysteries seems far from dead and the debates are likely to continue.

Sources

Ackroyd 2002; Adams 1978; Bender 1998; Blain and Wallis 2002a; Billingsley 2003a; 2003b; 2004a; 2004b; Bord and Bord 1972; 1976; 1995; Brown 2002; Burton 1993; 1995; 2002; Cope 1998; 2004; Dames 1976; 1977; Darvill 1999;

Devereux 1990; 1992a; 1992b; 2001b; Fidler 1983; Graves 1978; 1991; Grigson 1958; 1966; Grinsell 1972; Harte 1998; 1999; Harvey 1997; Hawkins 1965; Hayman 1997; Heaword 2004; Heselton 1991; Hitching 1976; Holtorf 2003; Hutton 1991; 1999; 2003; Kimmis 2004; Lachman 2001: 369–74; Larkman and Heselton 1985; Letcher 2000; 2001; Lethbridge 1957; 1976; Lodge 1925; Lonegren 2004; Lovelock 1979; Marsh 1982; Meskell 1995; Michell 1970; 1977; Pennick 1997; Pennick and Devereux 1989; Robins 1985; Romano 2002; Sandell 1988; Schreiber and Nicholson 1987; Screeton 1974; 1984; Skeates 2000; Stone 1998; Stout 2001; Trubshaw 1993; 1997b; Underwood 1969; Vayne 2003; Voss 1987; Wallis and Blain 2003; Watkins 1925; Westwood 1987; Whitworth 2003: 210; Williams 1980; Williamson and Bellamy 1983; Wood 2002; Worthington 2002a; 2002b; 2002c; 2004.

6: The middle way

Academic archaeologists are well aware of multiple approaches within their discipline but are often blind to the diversity of alternative approaches. In addition, they tend to simplistically oppose (unacceptable) alternative approaches with (acceptable) academic approaches. Such dualist polemics are well-loved by politicians but do little to reflect the complexities of reality.

Why do academics demonise alternative approaches? In large part it arises with the 'professionalisation' and increasingly scientific approach which characterised archaeology in the 1920s to 1980s. But why does similar antagonism appear in the books of academes' own 'heretics', the post-modernist revisionists of the late 1980s and 90s? Michael Shanks is one of the key figures in this movement and back in 1992 made a bad job of summarising 'alternative' approaches in his book *Experiencing the Past* (Shanks 1992: 59–63). The problem with this summary is less factual errors but rather serious omissions, presumably based on Shanks' limited (apparently non-existent) contact with proponents of the ideas he attempts to outline.

However his post-modern pluralism leads him to write:

> I do not think that fringe archaeologists should be dismissed out of hand as cranks, weirdos and hippies. I have tried to show that the impulse to think and mine the subjective and affective, holistic and meaningful aspects of the past is a reasonable one. What is perhaps more unreasonable is a social science [i.e. archaeology] which is not very able to deal with these aspects of the past, creating a gap filled by popular, media and fringe archaeologies.
> (Shanks 1992: 114–5)

So far, so good. But the passage then continues with a highly opinionated view of the fringe:

> … the problem with fringe archaeologies, with their mysterious powers in the past, spacemen and catastrophes, is the overwhelming tendency to mysticism and irrationalism. Intuition, inspiration, extra-sensory perception, initiated wisdoms, mystic energies are fertile ground for nonsense. They can certainly lead to a past-as-wished-for rather than as past as it is.
> (Shanks 1992: 115)

In fairness to Michael Shanks he expressed more nuanced views about the fringe five years later (Shanks 1997) and may no longer agree with his comments written over twelve years ago. I quote these remarks only as a clear example of how alternative archaeologies were viewed in the early 1990s.

Whenever academe wants to deride fringe or alternative archaeology, Erich von Däniken's *Chariots of the Gods* (1968) is invoked, as if in some way his ideas and beliefs are typical. Clearly they are neither. Rather von Däniken can be thought of as

> ... the most important and brilliant satirist in German literature for at least a century... This master literary spoofer and creator of a new genre of cosmicomic books is merely carrying to the extreme a method that has been pursued by eminent archaeologists...
> (Wunderlich 1975: 170)

Unfortunately the punchline has never hit home and his books do no more than trigger the academics' knee jerk reaction to 'fringe' archaeology. This is even odder as von Däniken's main aim seems to have been theological – disproving the existence of God – rather than archaeological.

Shanks' impression of the fringe is at odds in almost every respect with how the 'fringe' sees itself. He, and others, created a phantom demon that effectively existed only in their imaginations, and then felt in some way threatened by its unreal presence.

Yet, faulty as such statements are, they are the basis for other archaeologists' 'understanding' of alternative archaeologies, even if there is acknowledgement that the 'fringe' has arisen because archaeologists have not been good at popularising their ideas. For example Francis Prior observed: '... regrettably weird, 'New Age' versions of antiquity are now coming into prominence – largely as a result of our own reluctance to communicate.' (Prior 1996) Similar self-castigation of professional archaeologists inability to promulgate their recent thinking also forms a key part of Timothy Darvill's review of Julian Cope's *The Modern Antiquarian* (Darvill 1999: 237–8).

The mirror image of this castigation is fervent 'sermonising', as Cornelius Holtorf has observed:

> Some archaeologists have suggested that nothing is more important than proving such alternative archaeologies and their results wrong. In this vein, Francis McManamon, Chief Archaeologist of the United States National Park Service, recently [2000] stated that 'the distortion of archaeological interpretation by looters, misdirected hobbyists, some developers and different kinds of charlatans is a great concern to all in the field.' He argued that 'pseudo-archaeologists, or individuals perceived by an under-informed public as carrying out archaeological investigations' and their 'misguided interpretations' must be challenged, and with almost religious fervour demands that professional archaeologists 'must develop effective means of spreading accurate interpretations of the ancient, historic and recent past based upon scientific archaeology'. For McManamon and others, it is only the scientific discourse followed by professional archaeologists which leads to valid insights about the past.... Others are welcome to assist the professionals but need to learn first the 'proper' ways (and beliefs) of science generally and of archaeology specifically.

McManamon is therefore asking archaeologists, especially those teaching introductory or general survey courses, 'to inculcate in their audiences an appreciation and understanding of archaeology' by which he means scientific archaeology.
(Holtorf 2004 citing McManamon 2000: 5, 6, 16)

Colin Renfrew has expressed concerns that post-modern approaches to archaeology (such as Shanks') imply that one person's view of the past is as good as the next person's and 'there is nothing to distinguish the research which [such theories] would produce from the most fantastical assertions of the lunatic fringe about flying saucers, earth magic and corn circles.' (Renfrew 1994: 9)

As Michel Foucault famously observed, 'knowledge is power'. Challenges to knowledge are challenges to power – so 'alternative' views about the past are a direct challenge to the controlling narratives of society. Renfrew and McManamon are clearly among those who expect their authority to be respected rather than challenged.

Shanks' himself came up with an unusual version of the demonisation of feminist-inspired archaeologies, under the surprising subheading 'The castrated archaeologist: subjectivism and relativism':

> Subjectivism refers to a position which would celebrate those elements which are conventionally identified with the feminine...; it is this matriarchal order which would castrate the archaeological self. The archaeologist who follows the conventional order of knowledge gendered masculine fears the Father who disciplines his self with the authority of reason. There is the fear of disappointing and of succumbing to the other, the bestial, mythical, magical whose penalty is the castrating loss of reason and security...
> (Shanks 1992: 132–3)

While my initial reaction was to say 'There, there, be careful to take more water with your Freud in future', it remains a remarkable 'confession' of the fears non-academic approaches to the past can invoke.

The universal 'normative strategy'

Thankfully there is no need to pursue further the demonisation and fears born of 'oppositional' ways of viewing different approaches to the past. Far more interesting than polemical 'them' versus 'us' stances is a widely-adopted strategy for promoting one's ideas as 'normal' – offering them as a 'middle way'. Although this might be thought of as an essentially British way of seeking conciliation and consensus, it is also one that is deeply rooted in Buddhism and Taoism. The 'middle way' was also part of Aristotle's philosophy. The north European and Scandinavian cosmological model of the physical Earth being between an upper-world and an under-world was transformed by medieval Christianity into the now-familiar topography of the Earth betwixt Heaven and Hell. Such cultural cosmologies are so 'taken for granted' that we are usually unaware that ideas seem to be 'normal' when we make three-fold distinctions and reject the two extremes.

Yggdrasil, the world tree of Scandinavian mythology.
From Eddalaeren *by Finnur Magnusson (published 1824).*

In the realms of archaeology three distinct approaches can be recognised. One is the 'objective' approach based on science, where 'the past' comprised of objects and material culture and where causality shared modern-day rational and positivistic reasons.

The antithesis to this approach is the subjective and, at times, mystical and artistic approach, where 'the past' comprised of people and social functions, and causality is based on modern romanticism and fictional rationales.

The third approach falling between these two extremes sees 'the past' as the interaction of social groups with their material culture, and adopts a post-modern pluralism to approaches, causality and reasoning.

In practice regarding this as simply a homogenous 'third approach' is difficult as there is a spectrum of approaches which includes, among others:

- various post-modern academic approaches (including those exploring the past based on 'agendas' related to ethnic minorities or gender)

- well-informed amateur archaeologists

- earth mysteries enthusiasts

- modern pagans.

Rather than attempt the thankless task of distinguishing this ever-shifting spectrum of approaches, I am content to refer to this 'middle way' without making any assumptions of homogeneity.

Convergence

In reality there has always been a degree of overlap between the fringe and academe, although from the mid-1970s until about 1990 it might be thought that just one person was single-handedly walking in what must have seemed like a wilderness. Aubrey Burl took an interest in megalithic sites in a way that did not fit neatly with either academic or alternative approaches of the day. He is reputed to have observed that 'The gap between the professional and the alternative is only wide at the far ends. In the centre conclusions are often almost the same.' However such common ground was not recognised by either professionals or 'alternatives' until the 1990s. A useful summary of the way in which Burl has explored – indeed pioneered might be the better term – this middle way has been written by Alex Gibson (Gibson 1998); see also Hayman 1997: 264–8, 275–8.

In the 1980s the middle ground was jumped rather than occupied by a number of academic archaeologists who were drawn to the discipline from earth mysteries. One cut his teeth as an amateur with a very useful survey of Derbyshire stone circles, which included data obtained by dowsing, but after his academic career took off seems to have disowned this 'alternative' approach. Sometimes the proponents temporarily swapped sides, as in 1991 when the then editor of *The Ley Hunter* had a short paper published in *Antiquity* (Devereux 1991) about his observations in the Avebury area (discussed further in Chapter 8).

Convergence of fringe and academe came to the fore in 1995. Julian Thomas previewed a paper he later gave at the Theoretical Archaeological Group Conference in December 1995 when he spoke at *The Ley Hunter* Moot in October 1995. Michael Moore's 1995 paper in the *Proceedings of the Prehistoric Society* contains a full-page map of leys (referred to in academic-speak as 'alignments') between Bronze Age sites in Co. Waterford (although clearly he was not aware of the debates between statisticians in *The Ley Hunter* which concluded that three-point alignments are probably mere chance). This was also the year when a number of people in the earth mysteries movement began to openly recognise this 'convergence' – for example it was when I was planning the relaunch of the 'old school' regional earth mysteries magazine *Mercian Mysteries* as *At the Edge,* with the primary aim of popularising the latest developments in academe. Simultaneously but quite independently, similar changes in editorial direction took place with *3rd Stone* magazine.

My own contributions to exploring this overlap also included an article in a 1994 issue of *The Ley Hunter* offering a concise summary of the latest theories in academic archaeology (Trubshaw 1994c), and an intentionally provocative article in *Assemblage* (an e-zine run by University of Sheffield post-graduate archaeology students) asking 'Who's fringe now?' (Trubshaw 1996a). As if to confirm the accusations in this article, Richard Hayman independently noted that Richard Bradley's description of alignments at Temple Wood stone circle in Kilmartin 'could have been written by Paul Devereux' (Hayman 1997: 266, re Bradley 1993: 45).

Cornelius Holtorf, an academic archaeologist, has independently approached the convergence of professional and alternative archaeologies and discerned that:

> Many professional archaeologists, who are perhaps not sufficiently familiar with these more theoretical discussions in other disciplines, seem to think that people will by default benefit from agreeing with the current academic version about what happened in the past. They will not question this basic belief, even though it has been argued that archaeological interpretations follow fashions and change according to larger political and ideological trends (Wilk 1985), that academic papers which are peer-reviewed might as well be chosen by chance to achieve similar standards (Rothwell and Martyn 2000), the link between the sciences and the state is fundamentally undemocratic (as argued by Paul Feyerabend, see Holtorf 2000) and that the existing interest in the past may have less to do with genuine interest and more with a need of people to distinguish themselves by expressing certain social values and attitudes (Schulze 1993: 142–50). There is a danger that academics, who see the status of their own work threatened, resort to ideological fundamentalism and verbal violence against those alternatives they are seemingly competing with. This is unfortunate since professional and alternative archaeologies ultimately resemble each other more than some might like to think, and occasionally they are difficult to keep apart (see also Meskell 1999 and Denning 1999b). A case in point is archaeoastronomy which was once considered a playing field of alternative archaeology par excellence and is now taught at a major British university by Clive Ruggles, Professor of Archaeoastronomy.
>
> Scientific archaeology is in itself the manifestation of various mythic quests which often resemble those represented by alternative archaeologies. There are mythological overtones to the entire scientific enterprise, and especially so to scientific archaeology (Williams 1990; Zintzen 1998).
> (Holtorf 2004)

Each of us has developed specific ideas, ideologies and belief systems about the past. Our understanding of the past depends on the present-day ideas and beliefs. Simultaneously we make sense of the present in terms of the past – ranging from large-scale 'lessons of history' through to more fragmentary narratives (such as those which sustain our sense of self-identity and which sustain a sense of belonging to specific social groups – see Danser 2005 for a wide-ranging overview of the role of narrative in the construction of social reality). The consequence is that the meanings we give to the past and the present intimately co-exist or – more accurately – co-create each other. And creation of meanings is part of a dialectical process which also requires the consumption of meanings. Ongoing processes of construction and consumption of meanings reflect back the past and present as if in some infinitely complex kaleidoscope.

Within this complexity some meanings are regarded as 'orthodox' and others as 'alternative'. But the standpoint for making such judgements as 'orthodox' and 'alternative' is always relative, always shifting, an interim opinion that is neither true for all people at any one time nor for any substantial period of time. Claims to 'scientific truth' and the like simply betray naivety about the philosophical understanding of the nature of knowledge – not least that all 'scientific truths' were once challenges to the previously-understood truth. Too often 'alternative' archaeologists are not totally ignorant of academic archaeology but rather are not aware of how frequently academics have changed their minds about the 'truth' of the past and are basing their ideas on ideas that have been dropped by academe.

Accepting that opinions are always relative and shifting does not mean that all opinions and beliefs are equally valid. Opinions and beliefs are tools for achieving further insights and practical outcomes – and some convictions are more insightful than others, just as there are a few occasions when a quickly sharpened stick is an effective tool but many more occasions when either Swiss army knife or an electric power tool will be more appropriate. While I do not wish to extend the metaphor to suggest that specific opinions about the past equate to either sharpened sticks or power tools, nevertheless there is a sense in which the past is best reconstructed with the benefit of a wide array of suitable mental tools. Without ever-improving intellectual equipment the past will cease to be significant and meaningful.

Sacred places as common ground

The convergence of academic and alternative approaches to archaeology is best seen in relation to ideas about sacred places. This is not too surprising, as sacred places have always been at the core of earth mysteries and modern pagan approaches to the past. The common ground might be summarised as a recognition that sacred places are significant not for their practical significance but what they signify. The more academically-inclined (and this certainly includes some of the earth mysteries community) would develop this approach further, along the lines that while sacred places originally signified access to deities and the Otherworld, they now they signify a nostalgically-viewed past when people accessed deities and/or the Otherworld there.

Professional archaeologists – especially those closest to the 'heritage management' end of the spectrum – are beginning to acknowledge pluralism of approaches to the past, but nevertheless many find it difficult to shake off the privileged stance of academe. Even when this hurdle is recognised there is understandable difficulty in coming to terms with the great diversity of 'alternative' approaches, not helped by the mass media's well-known tendencies to grossly simplify or intentionally subvert such distinctions. For example, academic archaeologists cited elsewhere in this chapter have used terms such as 'New Age' and 'neo-shamanism' as umbrella terms when it seems they are referring to people who would not consider themselves to fit into such categories.

Kathryn Denning was the first academic archaeologist to attempt to survey the range of 'alternative archaeologies' in Britain and to provide academic archaeologists with a broader theoretic perspective about the different ways people from different backgrounds construct their knowledge of the past (Denning 1999a).

Convergence also came about when, as explored in Chapter 4, in the mid-1990s academic archaeologists interested in rock art picked up on shamanism. Subsequently Robert Wallis has looked in some detail at neo-shamanic approaches to archaeology (Wallis 2000; 2001; 2003; Wallis and Lymer 2001; Blain and Wallis 2002a; Wallis and Blain 2003).

The most recent of Robert Wallis's publications, co-authored with Jenny Blain, looks in detail at the way contemporary paganisms are increasingly engaging with archaeological sites and constructing their own narratives and knowledge of such places. They emphasise that 'paganism... encompasses several recognised and coherent sets of beliefs and practices... (Wallis and Blain 2003: 308). They observe that the diversity of interactions between pagans and prehistoric sites sometimes challenges and sometimes encourages the 'preservation ethic' of heritage management. Pagans' narratives likewise sometimes derive from academic interpretations and sometimes from concepts alien to academe, such as spirit beings, Neolithic shamans, prehistoric goddesses and dowsing. As Wallis and Blain are fully aware, such pagan interpretations are a form of modern folklore – one which 'appears to be eclipsing the old "folklore" – dare we say I! – of traditional archaeology.' (Wallis and Blain 2003: 314).

Wallis and Blain conclude that 'sacredness' of prehistoric places is not defined by modern pagans but instead 'made evident' by narratives which have meaning within the mythologies or meta-narratives by which different groups construct their identity. The plurality of meanings of 'sacredness' which result means that simplistic sacred:profane dualisms have been superseded by multiple 'folklores' of pagans' 'sacred sites' (Wallis and Blain 2003: 318).

The most surprising convergence of ideas between academe and 'fringe' is perhaps a book called *Sacred Earth, Sacred Stones* written by two notable academics, Brian Leigh Molyneaux and Piers Vitebsky. Although published in 2002 the scope of the contents closely matches that of books by Janet and Colin Bord, Nigel Pennick, Paul Devereux and a number of others published at various times since the early 1970s, although there is no acknowledgement of such precedents. Stunning colour photographs provide an immediate appeal for *Sacred Earth, Sacred Stones,* but even more interesting is the text, which provides an accessibly-written overview of sacred places from an anthropological perspective, putting archaeological evidence into the wider context of shared traditions. The seamless way in which these ideas fit together provides confirmation that the pioneering efforts of the earth mysteries movement were neither as 'lunatic' nor 'fringe' as academics of a previous generation often alleged.

Looking back over the last thirty or forty years of academic approaches to alternative ideas to the past I find myself sympathetic to both the irony and the arrogance lurking within a witty remark encountered in the writings of Idries Shah, which suggests that criticism has to go through three stages:

- It is impossible.

- It is possible, but it is useless.

- It is useful, but I knew about it all the time.

Situating myself in between

As previously mentioned, my own involvement over the last twenty years has been exploring the overlaps between academic and alternative approaches to archaeology, folklore and mythology, especially as they relate to places. At times my activities might be deemed almost shamanic, such as my first ventures into the 'Otherworlds' of dowsing workshops and pagan discussion groups, and the different Otherworlds of academic archaeological conferences. While such encounters all seemed far less Otherworldly as they became more familiar to me, such events remained very much 'other' to my then 9-to-5 persona, a suit-wearing sales and marketing representative in the plastics industry (although, now three years have passed since dropping that persona, it too seems decidedly Otherworldy). Is this a present day counterpart to shamanic shape shifting?

A personal predilection for liminality has made me comfortable with being betwixt and between, neither 'really' an academic, yet not entirely comfortable with many aspects of the 'fringe'. As author, editor and publisher I have repeatedly attempted to popularise recent developments in academe and also to promote the more interesting alternative approaches. The magazine I founded and edited, *At the Edge,* attempted to capture this aspect of liminality and 'walking on the cracks' in its title. My activities with Heart of Albion Press continues this approach in the form of books (including this one) rather than magazine articles.

Looking back with 20:20 hindsight it seems my contribution to the events described in the previous two chapters has been largely about the recognition and promotion of the 'middle way'. However it is not always appropriate to drive into the future while being concerned only with what can be seen in the rear-view mirror.

The future of the middle way – the blurring of 'fact' and 'fiction'

The 'middle way' seems to me now, in early 2005, less about a convergence of 'academic' and 'alternative' approaches than recognising more clearly the processes by which ideas about the past are produced and consumed. This process is emphatically *not* a simplistic situation of the academics and heritage managers *producing* and 'the public' merely *consuming*. Increasingly consumption is interwoven with production.

The notion that consumption of ideas has become more important than human interaction with the natural environment can be traced back to Jean Baudrillard

(1981; 1983) and more fully developed in his 1990 book, *Revenge of the Crystal*. We do not have to think of Disneyworld (or even the more limited UK theme parks such as the American Adventure in Derbyshire and Camelot in Lancashire) to see how consumption of the past becomes a major aspect of the *production* of how 'the public' think about the past. Visitor centres and museums at major archaeological sites – such as Newgrange in Ireland and Avebury in Wiltshire – can also be regarded as influential producers of the ideas that 'consumers' are encouraged to adopt about the past.

Visitors' centres, museum displays, guide books, interpretation boards and the like might be thought of as essentially factual accounts, very much part of the production of 'orthodox' ideas about the past, suitably enlivened for popular consumption. Yet not only is the style of writing of such interpretative material a long way from the dense and arid style of, say, an excavation report, there are enormous underlying ideologies inherent in the typical chronological account. Almost without exception interpretation proceeds from 'earliest known' information about a place, then proceeds to an indeterminate cut off date. For many prehistoric sites there may be little reference to the last 2,000 years, apart from any major activities by archaeologists. Even for medieval sites, such as castles, their post-medieval usage may be given scant attention. So the whole process of survival, partial restoration, consolidation of ruins, and the like – i.e. all the activities, intentional and accidental that have determined the physical form of what the visitor is actually seeing – are swept aside.

Even the act of writing historical accounts along a time line of 'oldest first' is a fictional approach. Self-evidently, it is the most recent changes that are the most conspicuous and, in the case of buried archaeology, the past is usually revealed in reverse chronology. The 'and then' and 'after that' narratives imposed on the interpretation of history are so ubiquitous, so 'transparent', that we forget that this is a narrative device inherent in human cognitive processes (and based on presuppositions about causality) and not something inherent in the nature of the reality (see Danser 2005: Ch.9 and Ch.13 for a summary of the construction of narrative and the 'myths' of causality). At its most fully developed this narrative device flowers as the romance of 'discovery'. The past becomes something that is in some way distinct from the present moment, even though the past exists only as it is recreated in the present, which means that past and present are deeply interwoven.

Indeed, the more one looks at the way authors of guide books and interpretation panels present their ideas, the more one sees affinities to historical novels and Hollywood epics. Archaeological narratives emphasise spectacle, the 'romance of the past' and discovery. There is a spectrum of genres that overlap without clear boundaries between excavation reports, academic overviews, tourist guides, quests for 'lost wisdom', adventure stories, historical novels and fantasy fiction. And the spectacle, 'romance' and sense of discovery are present – explicitly or otherwise – in all these genres.

Michael Shanks (Shanks 1992: 54) suggests the metaphor underlying the 'production' of these archaeological narratives is judicial – finds and other evidence enable the past to be 'accused', even though the accusations are Kafkaesque in their ambiguity, and the past never knows what charges the present day is pressing. A plethora of self-appointed judges arbitrate and pass sentence, only for the processes of appeal to review all such decisions.

There is not a 'past' that is objectively 'out there', to be discovered, still less a 'truth' that can be discovered, reminiscent of the One True Way of bigoted religions. Rather there is a constant 'conversation' between the past and the present. By 'conversation' I mean the type of discussions where ideas are exchanged in a manner that results in what might be regarded as the 'whole' at the end being greater than the 'sum of the parts' at the beginning. This conversational interaction with the past changes the emphasis from clearly defined producers and consumers to an ongoing interaction where all consumers are also producers (albeit in some cases unwittingly quite naïve and ill-informed) and those who might be traditionally considered as producers could more usefully be thought of as better-informed consumers.

The past has no author and no referee

These metaphors about the processes of archaeology lead to the notion that the past is akin to a book that has no author but only readers. Rather, the past is less like a book than a game, so the past has not so much readers as players (but no referee, and even the rules are the same as those created by the cartoonist Bill Watterson for the 'Calvin Ball' game in the Calvin and Hobbes cartoon strip – First rule: The only rule is there are no rules; Second rule: Each game has its own rules).

Recreations of the past are differentiated from the present by a range of notions that broadly come together as 'nostalgia'. Unlike more academic approaches to the past, where production and consumption of such recreations can be more clearly differentiated, the consumption of nostalgia is all but inseparable from its production. The middle way of approaching sacred places is neither the 'pure production' of academe or the more blatant consumption of, say, Disneyland. But the middle way is where consumers of the past can also be producers of approaches to the past, whether the rose-tinted perceptions of middle class tourists visiting medieval cathedrals, or the activities of pagans at stone circles.

In these middle ways, sacred places are best thought of as having purely mythological references to the past. Their physical presence is far less important than what the places signify. Their 'true' age and the changes that led to their present day presence are rarely grasped in any meaningful way, rather they signify a vaguely defined past era, a soft focus blur of 'oldness', and are meaningful simply because of person feels 'empowered' in some way by relating to that 'oldness'.

The physical evidence of the past – whether an artefact or a place – is more about what it is *not* than what it *is*. A flint arrow head is clearly not a mass-produced item, neither does it have any useful purpose for most present day people, so it is an icon for a previous era. A stone circle is not a field, nor a church, still less a housing estate or shopping precinct (even though many stone circles have, knowingly or otherwise, once stood where all that can be seen now is fields, churches, houses or shops). The reasons for the survival of megalithic sites into the twenty-first century have usually more to do with the 'marginal' nature of land for farming, which in turn often means settings which the modern mind regards as picturesque. The romantic notions of countryside and nature (explored in Chapter 1) create the sense of 'otherness' of such locations which contrasts with most people's everyday lives.

Beliefs are tools

We are accustomed to thinking of archaeology as materialistic, with the emphasis on objects and places. But the 'middle way' is essentially about *idealistic* approaches to the past – how we think about the past, how we intentionally or otherwise recreate the past based on present day concepts and concerns. The middle way recognises that what we *know* about the past is of far less significance than what we *believe* about the past. Our beliefs about the past – and our beliefs about appropriate approaches – are akin to a tool box. Just as different tools help us achieve different tasks, so a 'tool box' of different beliefs allows us to access different pasts. A mix-and-match attitude to beliefs (and, indeed, entire belief systems) enables one person to recreate the past in a greater variety of different ways. Some of these ways will be more relevant than others, depending on what objectives the person has at the time, just as a hammer is not the best tool for putting in screws.

The remainder of this book is about taking different 'tools' to a variety of sacred places in the British Isles. At the risk of mixing metaphors to excess, these different tools/beliefs about the past can be explored as 'conversations' with the past so, just as we might imagine a number of people with different approaches to the past gathered together and sharing ideas and beliefs in a manner that might be thought to be greater than the 'sum of the parts', so the remainder of this books brings together several different beliefs to create imaginary conversations about aspects of the past.

Sources

Baudrillard 1981; 1983; 1990; Blain and Wallis 2002a; Blain and Wallis 2003; Bradley 1993: 45; Cavallaro 2001: 52–4, 208–10; Danser 2005; Darvill 1999: 237–8; Denning 1999a; 1999b; Devereux 1991; Gibson 1998; Hayman 1997; Holtorf 2000; 2004; McManamon 2000; Meskell 1999; Molyneaux and Vitebsky 2002; Moore 1995; Renfrew 1994: 9; Rothwell and Martyn 2000; Schulze 1993: 142–50; Shanks 1992: 59–63, 132–3; Trubshaw 1994c; 1996a; Wallis 2000; 2001; 2003; Wallis and Blain 2003; Wallis and Lymer 2001; Wilk 1985; Wunderlich 1975: 170

7: Landscapes of Neolithic Britain

> The voyage of discovery is not in seeking new landscapes but in having new eyes.
> Marcel Proust

As suggested in the last section of the previous chapter, the remainder of this book will look at ideas about sacred places, exploring a range of ideas from recent academic and alternative approaches. While not wishing to take the metaphor too literally, think of this as a 'conversation' between the different approaches. As with real-life conversations, ideas and approaches are not necessarily fully developed before moving on to a different aspect,

This conversational metaphor is however less about the informal interplay of different approaches to the past and more about a conversation between the present and the past. In other words, how present day ideas influence how we recreate and reinvent the past, and how new ways of thinking about the past reflect back on how we think about the present.

These decidedly discarnate 'conversations' took place in the middle of England in Spring 2003 and were revised at the end of 2004. The past they refer to is, in objective chronological times, often around four thousand years ago. Yet, subjectively, this is a past that only exists (if it can be thought to exist at all) in one person's mind at the start of the twenty-first century. A different version of the past will be recreated and reinvented by each person reading these chapters, depending on their own prior knowledge of archaeology in general and their experience and attitudes towards sacred places. The interplay of ideas between this book and each reader represents yet another level of the conversation metaphor. Or would it be better to adopt the metaphor of the past as a game, and think of ourselves as players?

Rather than weave further complexity into these metaphors, let us discuss first the context in which megalithic monuments began to be constructed in Britain, the early Neolithic of around 4,000 BCE.

A conversation with the landscapes of Neolithic Britain

Popular use of the term 'sacred places' usually refers either to churches, mosques and the like or to stone circles, henges, chamber tombs and other Neolithic monuments. Indeed the Neolithic era left us with some of the most impressive monuments from prehistory. But trying to establish the significance of these monuments at the time of their creation requires a sophisticated appreciation of the Neolithic and, more especially, the key changes and transformations that were taking place.

KEY DATES IN BRITISH PREHISTORY

(all approximate and subject to regional variations)

Early Neolithic c.5,000 to 3,500 BCE

Middle Neolithic   3,500 to 3,100 BCE

Later Neolithic 3,100 to 2,500 BCE

Early Bronze Age   2,500 to 1,800 BCE

Middle Bronze Age   1,800 to 1,100 BCE

Late Bronze Age   1,100 to 800 BCE
    long barrows   3,800 to 3,000 BCE
    West Kennet   3,800 to 3,100 BCE
    cursuses   3,600 to 3,000 BCE
    henges   3,000 to 1,800 BCE
    Stonehenge   3,000 to 1,700 BCE
    Avebury   2,900 to 2,500 BCE
    round barrows   2,300 to 1,700 BCE

While the popular appreciation of prehistoric monuments places them in a somewhat indefinite sense of 'oldness', as discussed in previous chapters, in recent decades academic archaeologists have been able to establish quite detailed chronologies of their use. While the details of these researches are beyond the scope of an overview such as this, suffice to say that the insights gained are sophisticated and subtly nuanced. Gabriel Cooney in his study of *Landscapes of Neolithic Ireland* includes a summary of academic archaeologists' ideas about the different ways in which Neolithic people would have thought about landscape:

> Today we tend to see the landscape as the mute background for economic and social activity. In Ireland up until quite recently however it would have been viewed as alive... embodying history and myth and giving people a recognisable frame of reference to explain their place in the world. (Cooney 2000: 20)

Cooney also notes that 'sacred' or 'ritual' landscapes are not separate from 'secular' ones 'but rather as interwoven aspects of life' (Cooney 2000: 21). Ritual sustains a society's structure, mostly by conserving time-honoured traditions but also by legitimising any changes of practice or meaning. One of the key ways of sustaining links with the past is to perform rituals in defined, special places (Cooney 2000: 89). And, seemingly for the first time in human history, places of burial are among the key places of ritual from the start of the Neolithic. However there seems to be a blurring between respect for specific individuals and a more generalised 'ancestor worship'. This infers that the rituals of death sustain social identity and provide bonds with both the past and the locality. Our modern mentality prevents us fully appreciating how the Neolithic mindscape would have regarded the land as imbued with the spiritual presence of dead ancestors.

And yet the nature of monuments such as chamber tombs is that they do not simply provide links to the past. They are constructed in such a manner that they will endure long beyond the lifetimes of the people who constructed them – they intentionally cast a shadow into the future.

To help better understand Neolithic monuments and mindscapes we need to look at a number of social developments at the time that were radically changing how people thought about landscape.

Hunting and farming

The Early Neolithic era is, by definition, when humans begin to cultivate crops for the first time rather than rely on a hunting and gathering lifestyle (although livestock such as cattle and sheep may have been herded by this time). Farming requires a less nomadic way of living than hunting, gathering or herding, and brings about closer association between a group of people and the land that sustains them.

Because farming has been the normal way of existence for so many millennia it seems to us a 'better' way of life. Indeed, efficient farming can support denser populations. But ethnographic studies quickly reveal that farming is not the 'easy option'. Firstly, cultivating crops requires far more effort than hunting, gathering and herding. Secondly, there is a great risk associated with farming – if the crops fail through drought or pestilence then the survival of the whole group is put at risk. The Anglo-Saxon Chronicles reveal just how often the crops failed in Britain – rarely did five years pass without at least one year of severe problems. When problems arose on successive years the results could have major consequences.

Rather than thinking of the Neolithic as a time when everyone switched from hunting and gathering to farming, the archaeological evidence suggests that farming first took place in areas which were especially suited to cultivating crops; the major transition to farming did not take place until the middle Bronze Age (around 1,500 BCE). The areas most suitable for the earliest farming seem to have been islands such as the Orkneys and Shetland – bear in mind the climate was significantly less hostile at the time. Such maritime communities strongly suggest that boat-building and navigation skills were highly developed. And these pioneer farmers were also the first people in the British Isles to live in substantial stone-built houses and villages. This was where revolutionary new ways of farming and living were being explored (Noble 2003). Locations which we now regard as peripheral and backward were, in the Neolithic, the trendiest places to be living. Recent research suggests that the largest prehistoric settlement or ceremonial site in Britain may have been at the Ness of Brodgar in Stenness, Orkney. Geophysical surveys reveal a large area of the landscape with archaeological anomalies, with a clearly-defined limit that suggests a now-invisible boundary.

In contrast to the northern islands, evidence for early farming in mainland Britain is patchy and most of the evidence has come from Wiltshire. Clearly the well-drained downland soils are not typical of much of England so care must be taken before generalising. The main evidence of food is prodigious quantities of cattle bones. This implies something akin to 'ranching' which in turn fits in well with the evidence for substantial clearance of woodland (presumably by fire) during the Neolithic. Sheep bones are found in quantities that also suggest domestication. The sheep of this era are not the short-legged and meaty breeds that resulted from eighteenth century breeding but are more goat-like animals. Nevertheless the teeth show that, like modern sheep, they thrived on grassland that had been fairly intensively grazed by cattle.

Evidence for cultivation is more tentative but suggests that cereal crops were grown. We think of these being processed into flour to make bread but the effort required to grind flour is substantial. The easiest way to extract the nutrition from grain is to brew beer-like beverages. (Both leaven bread and beer are yeast-based processes so it reasonable to assume that their origins are closely contemporary.) Indeed, the advent of pottery implies new ways of preparing food and eating.

People living in areas less suitable for farming, such as the upland areas of Britain, presumably maintained a predominately hunting and gathering way of life. (An approximate analogy is the way European farming displaced native America lifestyles in eighteenth and nineteenth century America, leaving the indigenous population with only the rockiest and most arid regions.)

To what extent these different groups of people intermingled or exchanged produce is difficult to establish but, based on the distribution of specific types of pottery and stone axes, the Neolithic seems to be a time of widespread exchange of goods. However we need to leave open whether this is evidence for trade (in the modern sense) or the consequence of ritual gift giving.

Party time

Cattle, sheep and grain are all foods that can be both stored and transported. This enables comparatively large populations to survive even if drought or other natural disasters affect the resources available to hunting and gathering peoples. But the ability to store and transport foods enables an even bigger social development. It means that substantial numbers of people can gather together in one place for more than a few days. This brings us back to the Neolithic monuments. Whatever other significance they have, their construction requires substantial numbers of people to work over extended periods, and such a workforce would rapidly exhaust immediately available natural food resources.

Both the scale of the resulting monuments and the labour required to create them strongly suggest that substantial numbers of people gathered together for ritual events. Did the development of farming enable such large gatherings? Or, as ethnographical parallels suggest, was necessity the mother of invention and the ability to produce storable foodstuffs came about as a way to support such events?

Above all, if 'wealth' could be transported in the form of livestock then it enabled a privileged leadership to receive tribute from a dispersed subservient population. Ethnographical parallels suggest that some of this wealth might be redistributed as food for feasts and the like. The more one looks at the Neolithic in detail the more one sees a series of social developments which, while seeming quite 'normal' now, were quite innovatory at the time. Farming was just one aspect of these social

Wayland's Smithy, Oxfordshire. A well-known example of the Neolithic 'technology of memory' – a chamber tomb constructed to intentionally endure, to connect the past with the present, to connect the dead with the landscape, and to cast a shadow into the indefinite future.

changes. Its widespread adoption and the consequent improvements in techniques were more probably in *response* to demands created by other social changes.

The invention of the domestic and the monumental

Just as farming enabled significant social changes so too it brought about a profound psychological one too. Settlements and cultivation plots (and maybe also woodland cleared to optimise grazing) began to be distinguished from the rest of the landscape. As already explored in Chapter 1, ideas about the natural world being benign are very much a modern innovation. The natural world was until recent times generally regarded as threatening and chaotic. However Neolithic settlements increasingly represent a more ordered and safer zone. We more or less take for granted the idea of this sense of domestic security and comfort, yet it is a concept that dates back no more than 6,000 years.

Just as the home was beginning to be thought of as distinct from the rest of the world, so too monuments began to create a distinction between the 'untouched' natural world and places of ritual significance. As the landscape of Britain has been modified by human activities for some many millennia we have difficulty imaging what it would have been like to intentionally create monuments, such as chamber tombs or causewayed camps, for the very first time.

Clearly early Neolithic people in Britain had been modifying the land in more-or-less subtle ways, such as burning woodland to improve grazing, or by building timber and thatch houses. But these activities were essentially transient – woodland regrows rapidly and houses such as these would survive for no more than a few generations at best.

We can assume that hunting-gathering people also had a sophisticated knowledge of the landscape, and quite probably natural landmarks acquired mythic significance in ways akin to the Australian 'song lines' and Irish *dindshenchas* (see Chapter 2). But chamber tombs are neither transient modifications nor the mythologising of natural landmarks. For the first time the intention is to create something which will *endure* – the very definition of a monument. Such monuments are an intentional 'technology of memory' to connect the past with the present (Thomas 1993: 32).

Identity and belonging

Why was there a need to connect the past and the present with monuments? Why were they placed in prominent positions so that they were usually visible over a wide area? Why specifically chamber tombs? Why did they contain the bones of some of the people but certainly were not the predominant way of disposing of the dead? Why did the exteriors look somewhat like houses of the time? Why, why, why… ? The interrogation of the past is seemingly endless but we have lost the evidence and the memories that would have once provided detailed answers. The best we can do is assume that in some way, probably evoking a symbolism more complex than we can now recognise, these tombs and their occupants signified a sense of 'ownership' of an area of land with a group of people. They were investing time and effort into a sense of 'security'.

To what extent the groups of people who created chamber tombs represent a 'blood line' is not yet known. Whether such a blood line was passed down through the mothers or through the fathers could only be established if suitable evidence was found for sophisticated DNA testing. Whether the men of the group 'stayed put' and required their wives to move to their land, or the other way about (or possibly, but much less probably, a mixture of both) we also do not know. But what is clear is that the links between genetics and geography tightened considerably with the onset of farming in the Neolithic and intensified in the Bronze Age. Such links evolved into the land units of Iron Age and Roman Britain, and further evolved (in some places with little change) into the parishes and villages of later Anglo-Saxon England, which have survived to the present day. The intervening 5,000 years or so have seen changes but the main ones have been to 'scale up' this sense of belonging into regional and, in the last few hundred years, national identity.

We know now that early Neolithic monuments such as chamber tombs were not a 'passing fad' but rather the start of a long-sustained practice of building monuments, culminating in prehistoric Britain with the sophistication and seemingly unique architecture of the later phases of Stonehenge (and, internationally, with an unbroken sequence that encompasses the monumental architecture of Egypt, Classical Greece, the Roman Empire, medieval cathedrals, stately homes, Victorian town halls, and modern corporate offices).

The earliest monuments were 'respected' by later Neolithic people, even if only to close off the chambers and restrict ritual activities to the 'forecourts' in front of the blocking stones. This suggests some complex changes in significance and meaning, quite possibly a long series of such changes over the centuries. Whatever Neolithic monuments may have meant to their creators, we cannot assume that the significance remained unchanged for very long. Oral cultures are much more suited to repeatedly but subtly 'redefining' the past in terms of present day concerns than literate cultures (Ong 1982).

There is sufficient evidence to suggest that early Neolithic monuments remained significant *in some way* for very extended periods, but we cannot assume that this significance was unchanging. Indeed, we cannot assume that all people who were aware of the significance of a given monument at a given time shared the same beliefs. Modern people do not share exactly the same attitudes to, say, mosques so we should not assume that prehistoric people had homogenous attitudes to their 'sacred places' either. Neither can we assume that modern ideas about sacred or significant places are neatly matched by Neolithic ideas.

Where did you get that axe?

A teasing glimpse into the complexity and 'otherness' of Neolithic thinking and culture can be discerned from studying the large numbers of beautifully polished stone axes created during this era. These are aesthetically impressive and immediately suggest that they are 'high status' rather than merely functional. Note that such Neolithic stone axes are quite distinct from Palaeolithic and Mesolithic tools made from flint and flint-like rocks. Indeed these high status implements are also distinct from contemporary functional tools.

Axe-like flint tools, whether used for butchering, tree-felling or woodworking, are among the earliest tools used by humans so had been in use for many hundreds of millennia. By the time of the Neolithic the designs had evolved into efficient use of flint for robust tools. Alongside these everyday tools however polished axes were also in circulation. And I use the word 'circulation' rather than 'use' intentionally. Some do indeed show evidence of having been used. But most do not. The effort required to produce such a beautiful looking object goes way beyond any functional requirements. This is clear evidence of conspicuous consumption (or, perhaps more accurately, 'prodigious production'). These high status stone axes, while quite capable of functioning as chopping tools, were clearly not destined for everyday use and the consequent risk of damage. Using such a prestigious item for felling or butchering would be rather like using a Rolls Royce to pop out to collect a takeaway – it would do the job but runs counter to the significance that its high status conveys.

127

Four Neolithic polished stone axes. All were found in Leicestershire; the top two are made of rock from Great Langdale in the Lake District. The one to the bottom right is made of millstone grit, probably from Derbyshire. Reproduced by kind permission of Leicestershire County Council Heritage Services.

These polished stone axes are mostly produced from fine-grained igneous rocks such as granites, although some are from less durable metamorphic shales, or hard sedimentary rocks such as quartzite and millstone grit. By careful examination of the minerals making up these rocks, combined with painstaking analysis of the natural outcrops where they occur, researchers have created distribution maps of the origins of these stone axes. A large number come from the Lake District, although examples can be found from many regions where suitable rocks outcrop, including the Preseli mountains where the bluestones of Stonehenge originate from (see Chapters 9 and 10).

What gets really interesting is that these stone axes are commonly found many tens, even hundreds, of miles from their place of origin. The widespread distribution of these labour-intensive polished stone axes implies something else – a widespread network of exchange. These exchanges might have been purely 'commercial' transactions, for example the bartering of livestock or food for axes. Or they might be evidence of a more complex network of gift-giving, with all the implications of status between donor and recipient (perhaps with obligations for reciprocal gift-giving in the short- or longer-term).

It was *where* the stone axes come from that in some way conveyed their significance. The distinctive colours and textures of the different rock types would make identification of origins as easy for those 'in the know' as, say, teenagers today recognise models of mobile phones in an instant, with the concomitant recognition of which are 'cool' and which are not, and the conferred status on the owner. Indeed a key reason for all the effort required to polish the axes may have been to make the rock type more visible, or even to 'bring out the best' in the rock (either for aesthetic reasons or, perhaps, because by enhancing the 'essence' of the physical rock in this way then the non-physical significance of the rock was also being enhanced; see Cooney 2002: 95).

Once these axes were traded outside their place of origin then they would become increasingly 'exotic'. For example, the greenstone characteristic of axes made in Cornwall would be commonplace in Cornwall – but exotic in Wiltshire. Likewise a flint axe would be commonplace in Wiltshire but exotic in Cornwall.

However it may not simply be the type of rock which gave significance. Intriguingly, the outcrops chosen to make the Lake District stone axes are *not* the most accessible ones, but those on wind-blown and perilous ledges above vast scree slopes. Were these locations of mythological importance *prior* to the quarrying? Whether they were functionally better as axes seems almost irrelevant compared to the conspicuous effort to produce them, and their 'exotic' origin.

Ethnographical parallels suggest that quarrying was not only physically onerous and dangerous, but also ritually dangerous. When quarrying the Tungei of Papua New Guinea considered it was important to keep on good terms with the spiritual guardians of the stone by maintaining ritual purity and enacting the correct axe-making magic (Burton 1984: 240). Other New Guineans deliberately buried such axes if they were broken in use (Toth *et al* 1992: 70).

Given the propensity for a good proportion of present day people to flaunt their status with, say, a big Merc or BMW, perhaps only the nature of the status object has changed over the last four millennia, not the nature of human preoccupations. Or has it? Were polished stone axes 'merely' Neolithic power dressing, a statement of worldly status? Or 'merely' gaudier-than-thou tail feathers (or even highly-polished phallic symbols) that enhanced the sex appeal of the bearer? Or could these impressive artefacts be seeking Otherworldly high status, seeking the favourable attention of the deities? Or are such distinctions between profane and numinous status-seeking simply too modern?

Today we rarely think of stone quarries as sacred places. But the parallels drawn in the previous paragraphs suggest that modern preconceptions are not necessarily a reliable guide to prehistoric thinking. Stone axes seem to provide clear evidence that the specialness of a place could be transported, at least symbolically. Other researchers have looked to how – and where – these high status axes are deposited, which also suggests essentially ritualistic practices rather than the accidental loss or causal disposal associated with more utilitarian stone tools. Whether such deposition sites were already 'sacred', or acquired their sanctity from the presence of the axes is a trickier question to resolve.

Similar questions arise about Neolithic pottery from Orkney. In a similar way microscopic analysis has suggested that the clay and, more especially, the 'grog' (used to temper the clay and make it more resistant to changes in temperature) are sourced from specific locations that may have special significance. Some of these grogs are from rocks which are rich in quartz, which may have had a special significance because of its striking whiteness (quartz also glows in the dark when struck). Elsewhere materials used as grogs – such as shell or bone – are also bright white, and this may be as much an allusion to the brightness of quartz as their suitability as grog.

Likewise the stones used for megalithic monuments may have been brought from significant sources rather than merely the nearest suitable ones. Again rocks with quartz veins seem to be preferred, when available. Famously the bluestones at Stonehenge create symbolic links with the Preseli mountains of South Wales (see Chapter 9).

The ethnographical parallels are clear enough. Victor Turner (1969: 39) describes how the Ndembu of central southern Africa bring specific items into their ritual meeting place, saying that these objects bring to the ceremony the specific powers and virtues they are believed to possess. Similarly, British folklore recounts how early modern administrative meetings required the representatives of different places to bring with them a turf. Only when all the turves were placed together was the meeting able to start – an example of this lore from Leicestershire required the turves to be placed on top of a standing stone near Queniborough, known as the Moody Bush Stone (probably a corruption of the 'moot [meeting] bush' stone).

Polished axes tantalisingly suggest some of the complexity of Neolithic culture. Their place of origin is clearly important, suggesting that the quarries themselves were of mythical significance, even if not necessarily 'sacred' in a modern sense. If we do not see quarries as sacred or even spiritually dangerous places, what other 'natural' assumptions in the Neolithic are we also overlooking?

Watch the skies

The complex culture intimated by polished axes is only one of many ways in which archaeologists have steadily begun to accept that Neolithic thinking was far more sophisticated than hitherto accepted. One of the key triggers to this rethinking was the recognition that some of the Neolithic monuments are orientated towards significant celestial events. As already explored in Chapter 5, when this research started in the 1960s it generated considerable controversy, not least because key proponents came from outside academic archaeology. By the mid-1990s archaeoastronomy was an accepted aspect of prehistory and being taught at a leading UK university.

Whether the prehistoric monuments are aligned to the midwinter sunrise (as at Newgrange, Ireland) or the midwinter sunset (as at Maes Howe, Orkney), or the rising of the midwinter moon (as at Bryn Celli Ddu, Anglesey), the axis of the chamber tomb is symbolically linked to the whole cosmos.

*Bryn Celli Ddu, Anglesey. Symbolically aligned with the whole cosmos –
specifically the rising of the midwinter moon.*

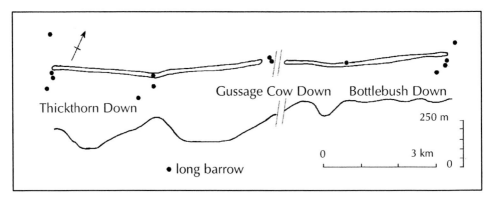

Sketch plan of Dorset cursus and exaggerated vertical section.
(Based on Barrett et al 1991: 48).

Dead straight – monuments, solar alignments and burials

If the astronomical orientation of chamber tombs suggests an invisible alignment, then linearity is an even more conspicuous aspect of the more or less contemporary 'cursus' monuments.

One of the best studied of these cursuses is in Dorset, running about six miles across rolling country which contains a wealth of evidence for other Neolithic activity. The cursus and associated barrows form clear alignments directed at the midwinter sunset (Penny and Wood 1973; Pennick and Devereux 1989). Even though little of the Dorset cursus is now visible, by working through the detailed information provided by a number of excavations, it is possible to reveal in surprising detail how the cursus and its associated monuments developed (Barrett *et ai* 1991; Bradley 1993; Tilley 1994). In particular:

> The line of the Cursus may either have been established between a series
> of existing long barrows, or some of the barrows themselves may have
> been aligned on prominent features of the Cursus. Where both earthworks
> share the same axis no sequence can be established, but where one
> appears to be aligned directly on the other, either the relationship is
> fortuitous or an obvious sequence is involved.
> (Barret *et ai* 1991: 49)

The Dorset cursus appears to have been aligned on three earlier barrows, although a number of barrows appear to have been created *after* the cursus and share its alignment. Indeed, no less than half the long barrows within under a mile of the cursus closely imitate features of the cursus.

What is surprising about the Dorset cursus is that its overall design makes little sense except to someone inside it. From a distance, despite its great length, it would not have been particularly visible – indeed, some sections may have been dug through wooded areas. The same is true of the curses at Stonehenge and Rudston. The concept of a cursus seems to be essentially about exclusion. This is also indicated by the lack of recognisable entrances through the ditches and banks.

However, to those who did stand within it, the Dorset cursus makes 'its most impressive visual impact between the Bottlebush terminal and the long barrow on Gussage Cow Down, if only because this includes the longest stretch which can be seen from one vantage point.' (Barret *et ai* 1991: 56) And this alignment is the midwinter sunset sight line. In fact, there seem to be five astronomical sight lines between the cursus and particular mounds, or between mounds.

Other cursuses seem to have been built with similar intentions. The Dorchester on Thames cursus aligns on the midsummer sunset, while Aubrey Burl has suggested that the Stonehenge cursus could have marked the equinoctial sunrises (see Chapter 9).

So, John Barrett and his colleagues conclude, 'Ritual is sometimes described as employing a different concept of time from everyday affairs; surely it was the nature of this great monument [the Dorset cursus] to deny the attrition of time altogether. More importantly, it made the dead seem part of the unchanging world of nature and appeared to confirm their status in perpetuity.' (Barret *et ai* 1991: 56)

So, we have a long linear monument aligned to the setting sun in a manner intended to honour the dead 'in perpetuity' and link them directly with the landscape.

Otherworldly straightness

What did straightness and linear alignment mean to Neolithic people? Why is straightness frequently associated with funerary monuments? We are all familiar with the phrase 'dead straight', but why should straightness be linked to death? As ever we can never be sure but some clues may be found in mythology. Around the world the 'Otherworld' is depicted as being exactly the opposite of everyday life. So daytime here is night-time there, and other such dualistic inversions.

So what about straightness and its 'inversion', curviness? In a pre-technological society exact straight lines are so rare as to be all but non-existent. There are few natural forms which are exactly straight. One of the more dramatic is rays of sunlight bursting from behind a cloud – a transient and itself almost Otherworldly experience. Furthermore, it seems that Neolithic thinking made close links between the sun and death.

Other examples of straightness in early societies seem only to be based on human artefacts – a thin thread drawn tight, the flight of an arrow, or the shaft of a spear. But each of these has Otherworldly overtones. For example in Classical Greek and north European myths the three Fates (a.k.a. the Norns or Wyrd sisters) measure the span of a human life in thread which is then cut off. The supernatural flight of an arrow arises in various legends – where the landing place becomes, say, the site of a grave, as with Robin Hood. In anthropological literature, shamanistic healing rituals also involve arrows. And a spear – even a simple shaft with a fire-hardened wooden tip – is the weapon which would be most commonly used for dispatching hunted animals, or human adversaries in battle, to the Otherworld.

However we need to be careful when associating the Otherworld solely with death. Shamanic and some other traditional worldviews recognise a variety of Otherworldly spirits, not simply spirits of the dead. Simply because we use the words 'spirits' and

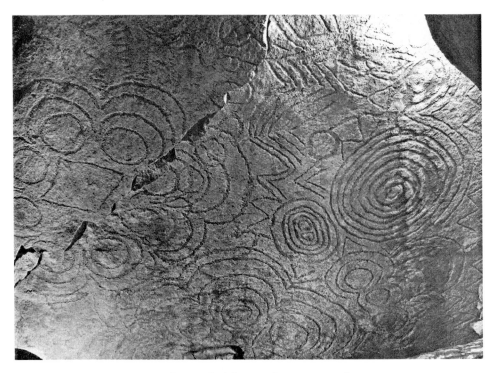

Curvilinear carvings on the roof of the north recess inside Newgrange passage tomb. Photograph by Anthony Weir.

'Otherworld' as catch-all terms to refer to a wide variety of categories of being does not mean that other cultures do not have more sophisticated distinctions. However, even accepting that the Otherworld need not be exclusively a realm of the dead, the nature of the Otherworld is usually depicted in myths as the opposite of the physical world.

As the living world is made up of curves, so any worldview where the Otherworld is the contrary of this world, straightness would be inherently Otherworldy. Indeed travel to the Otherworlds – either after death or during shamanic experiences – commonly involves either travel in a straight line, or one that is *intentionally crooked* to deceive evil spirits (Devereux 1992; Stone 1998). This idea also transferred to the folklore of medieval labyrinths which, according to some sources, were run to ward off the Devil (who, it is confidently stated, can only travel in straight lines). The Rösaring 'dead road' at Uppland, Sweden is a straight track ending at burial mounds and a labyrinth. Scrambled threads were a common content for witch bottles buried until recent times with the intention of trapping ill-doing entities. Speculatively extrapolating these modern and medieval examples of straightness and 'spirit traps' back in time, could the labyrinthine patterns carved outside Neolithic chamber tombs such as Newgrange and Bryn Celli Ddu also have served a similar function?

How Neolithic people actually thought about straightness may of course bear little or no resemblance to these speculations. But we should allow the possibility that their thinking – perhaps expressed through mythical stories and ritual activities – did incorporate a sophisticated appreciation of the significance of straightness, and such significance might be counter-intuitive for modern day thinking.

The complex significance of places in the Neolithic

Our understanding of the Neolithic period and the changes to the landscape associated with that era are derived from substantial excavations, often part of well-defined academic research strategies. Within the last fifteen years archaeologists' theoretical assumptions have been thoroughly reconsidered. We no longer think of our ancestors of around four thousand years ago as ignorant savages but rather as a sophisticated culture developing novel technological and cultural solutions to the challenges of living in the British Isles. In particular, specific aspects of Neolithic archaeology (such as archaeoastronomy, cursuses and polished stone axes) provide useful clues as to the complex significance given to places and the landscape. The next three 'conversations' will develop this general understanding of the Neolithic to explore some specific places in greater detail.

8: Avebury

Such generalised thoughts about the nature of Neolithic culture are important for putting 'sacred places' such as megalithic monuments into a richer context, rather than merely a indefinite sense of 'oldness' and 'otherness'. But how do such thoughts influence how we think about specific sites? The Neolithic site that first 'turned me on' in a big way, and which I know most about (and I assume readers may well have visited too) is Avebury in north Wiltshire. Because Avebury is so interwoven with my own interest in archaeology and the mythology of places, what follows is a reprint of an autobiographical 'confession' first published in a pagan magazine in 1991; the walking holiday in Wiltshire described in the article took place in 1978. Some of the ideas and ways of writing differ from my current preferences, but the account is interesting on a 'warts and all' basis. The original title was 'Losing my innocence in Wiltshire' (Trubshaw 1991c).

Losing my innocence in Wiltshire

Innocence is invaluable. It is like being barefoot in a forest, every detail makes its presence felt. So, when I was young and fit enough to think that walking twenty miles every day for a week was what holidays were all about, I took myself off to Wiltshire. My pocket guide to archaeological sites had photos of hill forts and details of a few barrows and wasn't there supposed to be a ley running up from a hill fort through Salisbury cathedral to Old Sarum?

Such holidays were solitary events where my only companions were a brace of cameras and a large supply of film. The rhythm of a few days walking soon cleansed the mind of complicated thoughts. The pace of the human gait allows a closeness with the particulars of every place that is blurred on a bicycle and unimaginable when driving. Internal streams of thought can be followed along their courses until they merge with the Big Ideas of Life that occupy wide rivers or even entire oceans.

'Walking Zen', I knew it as then, for at this time my tutors were books about eastern religions. My local 'born-again' librarian clearly considered my appetite for Hindu Goddesses and the like to be very peculiar. It would be many years before I was to discover that there were even a few others in Britain who felt that feminine deities were still alive, and later still to find that practising pagans almost abounded, if one knew where to look!

About half way into my week's walking in Wiltshire, having already 'done' Salisbury and Stonehenge, I found a farmhouse doing B&B. The

Megalithic portraits: the Avenue, Avebury.

next morning was Wednesday (Woden's Day) and it seemed auspicious to
walk Wansdyke (Woden's Dyke) which is the remains of a long earthwork
running over a ridge of downs. The horizon seemed so far away as to
have all of southern England spread around, the solitude was nearly total,
the weather was hot and almost sultry and the sense of self slipped away
to be replaced by a one-ness with the land.

Avebury through the eyes of innocence: personable stones and transient people.

So it was the day after this rapturous experience that I made my first encounter with a place that has called me back on many occasions since. The enormous grey sarsen stones along the avenue and within the vast space enclosed by the gargantuan ditches have a presence unlike that at any other stone circle. At Avebury, for this is where I am describing, each stone had its own personality and to photograph them was as if taking a portrait of a human face – from different angles the character changed but was always distinct.

Perhaps because of the spaciousness of this monument other visitors rarely disturb your thoughts. They seem almost Otherworldly, like ghosts that can be seen but not felt. The sheep and cows which graze there have a greater presence but they too seem transient. In several photographs that I took people dissolve away in the light, and sheep blur at the edges. To say that this is 'caused by' effects of focus and flare, or from slow shutter speeds is to miss the *reality* of these images.

From the circle it is an easy walk along the side of a stream to reach the most enigmatic of all prehistoric sites, Silbury Hill. The writings of Michael Dames (*The Silbury Treasure*, 1976, and *The Avebury Cycle*, 1977) had been like throwing a handful of pebbles into a lake; in this case the ripples resonated with all my feelings for the Earth as Mother. Although I was unable to connect the reality of the monument with the

138

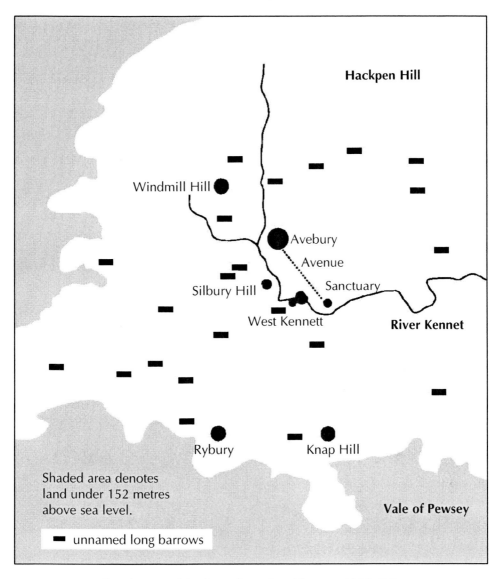

Sketch map of Avebury (based on Thomas 1993: 31).

complex ideas which I associated with it the scale of the construction and perfection of its shape were surprising.

On the crest of the next hill is the chambered long barrow at West Kennett. Irresponsibly restored, with a glass-block roof, it has still succeeded in retaining its sense of sacredness. Like a human figure laid down there are five recesses corresponding to the head, arms and legs. That this is intended to be recognised as a Goddess, the Great Mother, is left in no doubt - the entrance is between the legs and to enter that tomb/womb for the first time aroused the same intensity of emotion as, say, the moment of conquest of a lover. But this was no sensual emotion but a primeval resonance with both Her life-giving and dark aspects.

The mixed excitements that this cluster of sites aroused in me led me to read avidly about them and to visit the many other sites in the area. On subsequent trips I waited patiently for dusk and dawn, sleeping rough through the short summer nights. But the innocence was gone. I now knew too much, my head was full of knowledge and it left no space for words of wisdom to speak across the millennia. My preoccupations became more concerned with 'getting a good photo' and whether the light was right.

There is a moral here. My interest in Earth mysteries is such that I co-edit a magazine devoted to the subject (*Mercian Mysteries*); my understanding of the Goddess and other aspects of neo-paganism has developed so that I feel able to discuss my ideas openly. However, someone recently wrote to me wanting to come along on a *Mercian Mysteries* field-trip as she was 'only just scratching the surface as far as knowledge of earth mysteries etc. goes'. She felt in some way inferior because of her ignorance but my reaction was entirely opposite and my heart goes out to her as this is an experience I can no longer regain. Too often we know too much; far better to allow places to tell their own tale and wrap you with their wisdom.

Even by the time I wrote this reminiscence in 1991 I already felt I was one of those who 'know too much', and in the intervening years I have come to know considerably more, making it even more difficult for me to allow prehistoric places to 'tell their own tale'.

Allowing places to tell their own tale

While I still feel that places should be 'allowed to tell their own tale', the main change in my ideas since 1991 has been to increasingly recognise that the tale gets more interesting when the 'teller' – each person visiting the place – is aware of the many different tales (and resulting 'conversations' – whether convergent or controversial) that the place has 'told' before.

The 'tales' that Avebury inspired Michael Dames to tell remain, in my opinion, among the most remarkable examples of alternative archaeology of the 1970s. This 'remythologising' of a Neolithic sacred landscape in terms which resonate readily with late twentieth century aspirations may or may not be 'true' in any objective sense, but their 'truth' (or otherwise) is largely irrelevant when the ideas of professional archaeologists of the 1970s era are also now rejected as largely false by present day academics.

While I would strongly recommend reading Dames' books in their entirety to get the full flavour, his key ideas are that Silbury Hill (the largest prehistoric earthwork in Europe) was intended to symbolise the body of a Great Goddess, specifically her pregnant womb and her eye. This concept of the Neolithic 'Great Goddess' was proposed by the archaeologist O.G.S. Crawford in his 1957 book *The Eye Goddess*, and developed by Gordon Childe (1958) and Glyn Daniel (1958). However, such

Inside West Kennet chamber tomb, with the entrance partly visible bottom left. The light source at the top was inserted after the monument was excavated.

speculations about a 'universal' Neolithic goddess were almost entirely rejected by academic archaeologists in the 1980s (although belief in a goddess-led Neolithic culture lives on among some feminists and pagans).

Dames suggests that the 'moat' or quarry from which earth was taken to raise the mound of Silbury Hill provides the shape of the rest of the goddess's body. He then develops a whole series of associations which bring together the following ideas:

1. The pregnant seated goddess.

2. The goddess half buried in the ground.

3. The eye goddess, supreme intelligence.

4. The White Mountain in the primordial water.

5. The cosmic egg.

6. Sickle, grain and cornstook.

7. The throne.

8. The stag.

9. The umbilical snakes.

10. Mother and child.

11. Women with phallus – the androgynous being.

12. The spinning and weaving goddess.

(Dames 1976: 83)

Unlikely as these appear when listed 'cold', Dames provides resourceful (if not always convincing) arguments to support these symbolic associations. In his sequel, *The Avebury Cycle*, Dames argues that this complex goddess symbolism manifests in the Avebury monuments, which

> ... were created as a coherent ensemble to stage a religious drama which took one year to perform, with each edifice offering in turn a special setting for the celebration of a particular event in the farming year.
> (Dames 1977: 9)

Indeed within a year of the publication of *The Avebury Cycle* modern pagans were celebrating such rituals. Women dance on Silbury Hill at the August full moon in response to Dames's suggested rituals, and West Kennett chamber tomb is also the focus of numerous pagan celebrations. Twenty years later the Goddess-focussed mythology which Dames created for the Avebury monuments was merged with far more idiosyncratic ideas and misunderstandings when Julian Cope's *The Modern Antiquarian* appeared in 1998.

I am well aware that Dames bases much of his evidence on ideas that subsequently have been deeply critiqued by academic archaeologists. On the other hand his rich imagination and ability to weave his ideas into a seductive story stand as one of the most powerful examples of late twentieth century mythmaking. The importance of these two books is not whether or not they are 'true' but the re-animation of a prehistoric landscape. They are a remarkable example of 'alternative' approaches to sacred places producing meaning and significance in a manner that has not been matched for any other British prehistoric location.

A year after my visit to Avebury Aubrey Burl's monumental guide to the archaeology of Avebury appeared (Burl 1979). Had his book been my first introduction to this

Some of the concrete markers denoting the original timbers at the Sanctuary. East Kennett chamber tomb is concealed by the tree clump in the far distance.

prehistoric site I suspect my attitude to Avebury and, perhaps megalithic sites in general, would have been quite different. Burl presents his information quite enthusiastically and with a literary flair but his thinking lies within quite a different, and far more conventional, context of 'production' and 'consumption' of facts and interpretation than Dames. A revised edition of Burl's book appeared in 2002; a must-have work for anyone interested in the prehistory of Avebury.

Subtle obstructions to sacred spaces

I am not alone in using Avebury as a key 'case study'. Julian Thomas discussed the Avebury area to illustrate what he referred to as his 'rather abstract' ideas about the Neolithic (Thomas 1991: 162–77; 1993: 29–43). Akin to Dames, although starting from very different presuppositions, he considers 'the monuments of the Avebury area were intended to be seen in sequence rather than simultaneously, forming a kind of spatial narrative... ' (Thomas 1993: 38)

We have become so accustomed to seeing map-like site plans of archaeological sites that it is easy to forget that this 'God's eye view' was not available in the Neolithic. Instead a far more complex *experience* of visibility (and wilfully hindered sight lines) was designed into their construction.

One aspect of Thomas's approach to Avebury was to show how the Neolithic monuments cannot be understood completely from maps but only when we *experience* the relationship between the natural topography and man-made earthworks. By 'being there' and moving from place to place we become part of an intriguing interplay of visibility and concealment which sheds light on Neolithic attitudes to sacred places and rituals.

Silbury Hill seems designed to catch the eye of the onlooker from a distance. Yet it is not visible from much of the north and west (the area where the Avebury henge is situated), being hidden by Waden Hill. Only the very top of Silbury Hill is visible from the site of the so-called 'Obelisk' (a massive but now-lost megalith in one of the inner circles at Avebury), raising the tantalising suggestion that activities on the top of Silbury could be observed during simultaneous rituals at the Obelisk.

The bank of the henge itself serves to restrict visibility of the interior from the distance, while providing a natural amphitheatre for those inside the bank – who are still excluded from the interior by the intervening ditch. The interplay of visual or physical obstruction with visibility and access seems to be intrinsic to the design of these monuments. Likewise the tightly spaced tree trunks of broadly contemporary timber henges and palisaded enclosures also suggest they were intended to act as hindrances to visibility. Stonehenge provides a unique example of a stone circle with similarly obscured views of the interior.

In contrast, to the south-east of Avebury is a smaller site made up of circles of timber and stone, known as the Sanctuary. Unlike the main henge, this has no ditch, and Thomas speculates that 'its unbounded character suggests that its role was to admit rather than exclude.' From here, the Avenue prescribes a path through the valley towards the henge, 'insinuating rather than forcing a particular passage.' It is as if 'the Avenue served as a guide to the correct way to act for those submitting themselves to approved rules of order, rather than forcing particular acts upon the unwilling.' (Thomas 1993: 41)

Walking along the Avenue from the Sanctuary the henge is invisible (just as the Avenue is invisible from the inner circles of the henge). Only about 400 yards from the henge, where there is a rise in the ground, does the henge 'peep' into view. At precisely this point the Avenue abruptly changes direction. Yet the protrusion of the eastern bank and two especially large stones in the outer circle mean that the stone circle is still obscured. Even after entering between the massive 'portal stones', further subtle arrangements of stones partially impede vision. This means that the central stone, the Obelisk, was at the centre of a series of nested spaces, 'separated by barriers which impede rather than totally closed off access.' (Thomas 1993: 43)

Thomas takes this to infer that in Neolithic society knowledge was 'graded' rather than there being a binary division. The architecture of the ceremonial complex at Avebury is able to accommodate a large number of people and also to segregate their movements and thereby subtlety 'grade' their access to ritual activities.

Seclusion and exclusion is even more pronounced at chambered tombs, such as West Kennett. Thomas suggests that if there was 'graded' access (seen only from a distance; access to the forecourt; access to the interior) and access to the inside was restricted to a privileged élite, then the significance of such monuments may have evolved, so that the monument became something to be *seen* rather than entered, with the consequence that the interiors were eventually blocked off although rituals continued in the 'forecourt' area (Thomas 1993: 34).

Sleight of eye at Avebury: the Avenue looking towards the henge, which is invisible because of the slightly rising ground

Sleight of eye surprises

At the same time Julian Thomas was visiting Avebury to prepare this case study on subtle sight lines, Paul Devereux was making extended visits to Avebury which would inspire him to prepare a quite different case study about the same monument. These ideas appeared in his *Symbolic Landscapes* (Devereux 1992), published a year after Thomas's *Rethinking the Neolithic*.

Paul Devereux devoted a chapter of this book to several carefully crafted 'sleight of eye' surprises at the Avebury group of monuments. These include a double sunrise around the time of the Celtic festivals of Beltane (1st May) and Lammas (1st August). When standing on the top of Silbury the sun is first seen to rise over the distant horizon. Then, if you move down to the 'platform' near the summit, the sun rises again a few minutes later over the intervening Waden Hill.

Standing on the top of Silbury at sunrise with your back to the sun can produce a startling effect if there is dew on the grass. Your head creates a 'huge golden glow of light' within the shadow cast by Silbury itself (Devereux 1992: 149). This dramatic refraction effect is normally only seen from mountain tops and is known as a 'glory'.

The earthern bank at the western end of the West Kennet chamber tomb was lengthened long after the rest of the monument was constructed, perhaps at the time the interior was blocked. Standing or sitting at the far end of this extension and looking at Silbury Hill to the north reveals a curious alignment – on the far horizon is Windmill Hill, a causewayed camp and probably used as a settlement site since

145

before any of the major monuments were constructed – and it appears to be 'sitting' on the shelf-like platform just below the summit of Silbury Hill (Devereux 1991). (See photograph page 72.)

Shamanic spirit paths

However these sublte lines of sight were only a small part of Devereux's interest in Avebury. The main idea explored in *Symbolic Landscapes* was the idea of shamanic spirit paths. These can be thought of as the intersection of Otherworldly concepts of place with the physical landscape. At the time Devereux was editor of *The Ley Hunter* magazine and this spirit paths hypothesis opened up ways of thinking about straight alignments between prehistoric sites which were quite distinct from either Watkinsian trackways or dowsable energies.

In the subsequent twelve years Devereux has continued to develop his ideas about such spirit paths and some of the opinions expressed in *Symbolic Landscapes* have been superseded. Although the subsequent work looked at the concept of spirit paths from an international perspective, interestingly this novel approach was inspired by the prehistoric sites around Avebury.

Intriguingly, the English Heritage archaeologist responsible for the recent detailed survey of Silbury Hill, David Field, has noted that the water in the ditches would have been 'mirror-like' and have had 'symbolic implications', noting the parallel with shamanic mirrors (Field 2003: 17) – although Field seems unaware that these ideas were pioneered by Dames in the late 1970s and Devereux in the early 1990s. Field also makes the interesting observation that Silbury is 'also at a geologically liminal position', where the chalk meets the flood plain of the River Kennett (Field 2003: 17).

A richness of approaches

As David Field – perhaps unwittingly – reveals, bringing the current ideas of professional archaeologists into the same imaginary conversation with ideas pioneered by Dames, Burl, Thomas and Devereux (all of whom at some time or another have been regarded as somewhat maverick by established academic archaeologists) enables a richness of approaches to Avebury.

Further insights are gained by looking not just at the magnificent monuments but the whole of the archaeology of the area. And the Neolithic monuments need to be put into the wider context of evidence from earlier in prehistory, through the Roman and medieval period, into the early modern era when the significance of the henge was recognised. Joshua Pollard and Andrew Reynolds' book *Avebury: The biography of a landscape* (Pollard and Reynolds 2002) provides an accessible but scholarly overview of exactly this wider context, and the metaphor in the subtitle reveals that they too, if not quite having a 'conversation' with the past, are well aware of the literary fiction that underlies all narratives of the past (even those written in dull pseudo-objective 'official-speak').

However, despite the importance of the Neolithic monuments in the Avebury area, we still know next to nothing about where and how the people who built and used them lived.

Experiencing Avebury today

What we see today at Avebury is the result of complex processes of survival, destruction and modern site management. Many of the stones survived right through the Iron Age, Roman eras and, despite the creation of the village in their midst, well into the medieval era. In the fourteenth century the clergy encouraged the villagers to bury the stones. This was followed in the eighteenth century by enthusiastic stone breaking for road repairs and constructing buildings. Meanwhile the village houses and fences continued to encroach on the prehistoric remains.

Alexander Keiller bought the village in the 1930s and paid for the excavation of the henge. Subsequently he re-erected some of the stones, set up concrete markers on the site of lost stones, and removed trees, fences and buildings to make the prehistory more visible among the modern day settlement and farming. The Avebury we see today is largely the result of Keiller's restoration. With the increasing number of visitors in recent decades there have been controversial plans to change the post-medieval aspects of Avebury, to provide further visitor attractions and facilities. The present museum, visitor centre, restaurant, pub and car parking arrangements provide a reasonably satisfactory compromise between the demands created by visitors and preserving a seemingly unspoilt (although, in reality, carefully planned and managed) sense of place. While not quite as artificial as, say, Alton Towers, what we see today at Avebury reflects the prejudices of each era – from the destruction caused by eighteenth century zealots, to the reconstruction of the 1930s, and the principles of late twentieth century heritage management. Present day visitors' views are determined by hedges, trees, buildings and controlled access that have nothing to do with the prehistory of the site. These generate their own subtleties of sight lines and exclusion which have little or nothing to do with the equivalent subtleties experienced in prehistory.

To many visitors the picturesque cottages in the main street, the sixteenth century manor house, the medieval church with its twelfth century Romanesque font, all merge with the henge and the megaliths into a 'heritage soup' of vaguely appreciated oldness and quaintness. Other visitors, such as pagans, focus on the prehistoric stones and earthworks to the exclusion of the more recent developments, but rarely appreciate the extent to which what they take to be 'prehistoric remains' are in large part the result of deliberate changes and restorations made in the 1930s.

There is no 'real' Avebury. Like any other prehistoric site or sacred place, Avebury reflects back the meaning and significance we are seeking from it. Do you see the heritage soup of dumbed-down tourism? Or reflections of a more spiritual quest? Or responses to the quizzical approaches of archaeology? Or something even more individual? Whichever, you are seeing your own reflection…

Sources:

Burl 1979 (2002); Dames 1976; 1977; Devereux 1992; Field 2003; Harding 2003; Pollard and Reynolds 2002; Thomas 1991; Wallis 2001: 150–1

9: Stonehenge

Neolithic henges were clearly places where large numbers of people gathered for seasonal celebrations based around astronomically significant events. Despite the large numbers of people needed to construct Stonehenge, which suggests that equally substantial gatherings came together for the celebrations, the key characteristics of Stonehenge are restricted sight lines and 'nested' access, akin to those explored at Avebury.

The successive rebuilding of the stones has created a central area largely blocked from the sight of anyone standing outside the trilithons. The bank of the henge, although not a formidable physical barrier now, would have been a significant symbolic boundary, at least as significant as the fencing which today keeps tourists away from the stones. Modern day access is also nested, as a further boundary prevents access except via the official entrance and ticket booth, an exclusion zone which modern secular political leaders recently sought to extend to four miles (at least at the time of midsummer) with a show of force that the Neolithic rulers and their priests would never have been able to manifest.

Stonehenge signifies

The importance of Stonehenge goes well beyond being the grandest, most monumental, of the Neolithic monuments. Stonehenge is iconic. It is the crowning achievement of British prehistory. It is an essential ingredient in the heritage soup served up to American tourists 'doing the old country' (simmered down to Edinburgh, Stratford, Stonehenge and London). It is an icon for a lost golden age, one where astronomer-priests displayed their knowledge of the intricacies of the sun's cycle. This aura of mystery and esoteric knowledge has been appropriated by numerous writers of fantasy fiction and films (see Jones 2001 for details), linking Stonehenge with swords and sorcery, a place where Tolkien's hobbits would seem at home. And, for reasons that will be explored later in this chapter, Stonehenge has an iconic status for those seeking an 'alternative Albion'.

Stonehenge evolves

As with Avebury, what now exists at Stonehenge is the result of a long process of prehistoric construction and repeated reconstruction, followed by neglect, preservation, partial reconstruction, and the neo-brutalist visitors' facilities of the 1960s. Our understanding has also undergone repeated reconstruction too, as archaeologists have devoted increasing attention to Stonehenge and its surroundings. The Royal Commission on the Historic Monuments in England and the archaeologist Julian Richards looked in detail at the surrounding landscape (RCHME 1979; Richards 1990, 1991). The detailed and critical analysis of twentieth century excavations by Rosamund Cleal, K.E. Walker and R. Montague enabled a

Stonehenge seen looking south from the mid-point of the cursus. Only at this point do the stones appear to sit on the horizon – a few paces further east, west, north or south and the stones are hidden by the subtle slopes of the ground. A 'sleight of eye' missed by most modern visitors yet probably an intentional aspect of the approach to the henge from the cursus, matched by similar subtly obscured sight lines along the approaches to other henges.

reassessment of Stonehenge's development (Cleal *et al* 1995). An accessible summary has been compiled by Barbara Bender (Bender 1998: Ch.2).

Stonehenge was in use as a ritual site for about 1,700 years between about 2,800 and 1,100 BCE. This is much less than half its life, but longer than any of the churches in Britain have been in use. Like many churches, several phases of partial rebuilding resulted in major changes in the architecture at Stonehenge.

The area where the stones were to be erected was settled by Mesolithic people, as there is evidence for both hunting and occupation dating back to about 8,500 BCE. During the construction of the car park at Stonehenge an alignment of three large post holes was excavated. These perhaps originally supported something akin to North American 'totem poles'. Although radiocarbon dating has not enabled a precise date to be established, they were dug sometime between 8,800 and 6,600 BCE, making them rare examples of Mesolithic ritual activities. The row of pits for the 'totem poles' aligned on a further pit, believed to have been caused naturally by the roots of a tree that had already grown very large before the posts were erected. Presumably this 'world tree' was venerated by the Mesolithic people and became the focus for the various rituals. Although this tree died perhaps ten thousand years ago, as the ancestor of all subsequent rituals and monuments it has cast a long shadow through time.

At the start of the Neolithic (about 2,800 BCE, i.e. around 5,000 years after the 'world tree' and the totem poles), the first monuments had begun to appear in Britain, in the shape of long barrows. People were living in the area that would later become Stonehenge. Around this time, long before stone circles had been dreamed up, a simple ditch and bank was dug amid the various settlement sites. Just inside the bank a ring of timber posts was erected (in the so-called Aubrey holes). This phase of the monument might have incorporated alignments to significant lunar events. The skyline to the north was emphasised by parallel banks and ditches of freshly excavated white chalk which ran for about a mile to the west and a mile to the east; these are known today as the Cursus (other Neolithic cursus monuments are discussed in Chapter 7).

About 300 years later ritual activity all-but ceased in the whole of the Stonehenge area. Many books suggest that the site was effectively abandoned, but archaeologists now think that, although it was neglected long enough for scrub to grow, the timber posts would still have been visible when the first stones were erected about 2,550 BCE. At least three subsequent phases of construction have been identified during the next thousand years. The famous bluestones, which show evidence of having been previously used somewhere else in a lintelled arrangement, were the most frequently moved stones, suggesting that they had the greatest symbolic significance. About 1,600 BCE, in the early Bronze Age, two more rings of pits (the so-called Y and Z holes) were dug, perhaps to take yet more stones, but abandoned instead. Notably, the astronomical alignments evolved from being primarily lunar to primarily solar, suggesting some significant changes in the cosmological beliefs of the time.

All these changes are assumed to be the result of different groups of people having different ideas about what was appropriate, and having the authority and resources to implement their ideas. Clearly the reconstructions of Stonehenge increasingly embody a society with hierarchical élites. Visibility into the centre of the circle was increasingly obscured. The effort and grandeur of the construction increased too. Those at the top of a hierarchy of power were keen to both show off their status and to exclude, at least visually and symbolically, those they deemed lesser mortals. But these changes are not necessarily an expression of conflicts between competing élites, although our modern day mentality makes this an obvious analogy. The lengthy period over which the changes to Stonehenge took place – about one thousand years – is similar to the time that major European churches and cathedrals have been in use. These also undergo successive rebuilding and modification, reflecting changes in liturgical and architectural fashion rather than deeply contested power struggles. For example, the most controversial political change in English ecclesiastical history – the Reformation – does not directly result in major rebuilding or modification of existing churches (although it does result in the destruction of most of the monastic buildings).

Certainly at least some of the early Bronze Age people had considerable wealth and status, as was revealed in 2002 with the discovery of the remains of the so-called 'Amesbury archer' a few miles from Stonehenge. Isotope analysis suggests that he had grown up in Europe, so perhaps was part of an élite social group with wide-ranging influence. Since the 1970s archaeologists had speculated that during the Bronze Age the area we now know as Wiltshire was at the centre of a potentially highly profitable trade route, with the many magnificent monuments an expression of this wealth. If this is accurate then the distant connections of the 'archer' are less surprising.

Stonehenge embodies

While there are only tantalising clues about trade and travel, clearly the source of construction materials for the later phases of Stonehenge was important. Stone available locally was ignored and instead the massive sarsen stones were transported over twenty miles from near Avebury; indeed the two henges share the same geological 'genes'.

The smaller (although still weighing three to four tons each) bluestones came from the Preseli mountains in south-west Wales. In the twelfth century legend has it that they were brought by giants from Africa to Ireland, from whence Merlin brought them to Wiltshire. A twentieth century version of this legend was provided in 1923 by the geologist H.H. Thomas, who argued that they came from the Preseli mountains in Pembrokeshire, with the so-called Altar Stone from deposits on the shore of nearby Milford Haven. The less romantically-inclined argue that glaciers might have assisted the stones on their way, without being able to offer convincing evidence. There is sufficient evidence on the bluestones of reuse for it to be probable they once formed a monument elsewhere, although that elsewhere could be anywhere from Wiltshire to Pembrokeshire.

Presumably such movement of stones – whether over relatively short distances or much longer ones – enacted a symbolic transfer of political or spiritual power. At a time when cars made in Germany have more kudos than locally-made ones, the trendiest electronic devices are made in the Far East, and fresh produce is transported by air from southern Africa or South America to satisfy our cravings for out-of-season produce, then floating spiritually-charged four ton stones on rafts for a few hundred miles seems entirely reasonable.

Stonehenge: the last 3,500 years

After the stones had stopped being rearranged around 1,600 BCE, the Avenue was extended for a further 1½ miles to the River Avon. The area remained important for about five hundred years, as shown by the many early Bronze Age barrows ringing the horizon. Later in the Bronze Age (from about 1,600 BCE) Stonehenge seems to have lost its significance and the remains of field systems suggest that the area was important only for agriculture. Yet the field systems 'respect' the monument and do not encroach on it. Did people still think of it as sacred, or were they simply scared of it?

Stonehenge began its long career as a mysterious ruin, with natural dilapidation and wilful vandalism taking its toll. There is plenty of evidence for Romans visiting Stonehenge, suggesting some vestiges of residual sacredness. However, the Druids almost certainly did not have any interest in the monument, preferring groves in more woody and watery settings. Indeed, if Stonehenge had been associated with the Druids then the Romans presumably would have demolished it as part of their ruthless suppression of this priestly caste who they considered acted as a focus of opposition.

The recent rediscovery of an Anglo-Saxon skeleton excavated at Stonehenge in 1923 reveals that he was beheaded, probably while in a kneeling position. However there is no way of knowing whether he was a victim of ritual sacrifice or simply a condemned criminal done away with at a prominent place. Archaeology so often teases rather than reveals…

Stonehenge resurrected

There is nothing written about Stonehenge until the twelfth century when both Henry of Huntington and Geoffrey of Monmouth make reference to the monument. Not until the seventeenth century do documentary references become more frequent, largely as a result of the visits and writings of the pioneer antiquarians John Aubrey and William Stukeley.

In 1680 the right was granted to hold a two day fair at Stonehenge every September. At some later date the fair shifted to midsummer, perhaps as a result of William Stukeley's writings about the significance of the solstice becoming well known, leading to considerable crowds gathering to see the sunrise. The fascination with Stonehenge at this time went as far as King James I demanding that it be made to give up its secrets. Inigo Jones, the royal architect, made the assumption (entirely

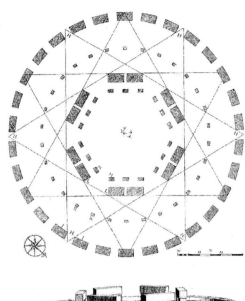

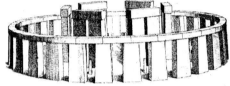

*Inigo Jones' idea of Stonehenge
as a neat-and-tidy Roman
temple.*

reasonable at the time) that it had been built by the Romans and so created an idealised plan based on Vitruvian geometry. This plan in turn was the inspiration for John Wood's Circus at Bath, adjoining the Assembly Rooms.

Stonehenge as celestial temple

Stukeley was the first to speculate about Stonehenge being a temple to the sun, moon and stars. His ideas were widely read so we should not be too surprised that in the late eighteenth century John Smith of Boscombe noted that Stonehenge was built 'to show the steady, uniform and orderly motions of the heavenly bodies' (cited in Olivier 1951: 36). Around 1900 the Astronomer Royal, Sir Norman Lockyer, surveyed Stonehenge and thought he could see similarities to the astronomical orientations of Egyptian temples. His ideas were widely publicised in the influential journal *Nature* (Lockyer just happened to be the founding editor). However his knowledge of archaeology was rudimentary and he linked together sites of different dates. But the underlying suggestions had captured the popular imagination, in a similar way to Stonehenge already being indelibly connected with Druids. In 1965 the American-based astronomer Gerald Hawkins published his provocatively titled book *Stonehenge Decoded*, with Alexander Thom following two years later with his detailed astronomical analysis in *Megalithic Sites in Britain*.

At the time most professional archaeologists vigorously opposed this intrusion into their domain, but by the 1990s a steady stream of articles about astronomical

153

alignments at ancient sites throughout the world appeared in the pages of *Antiquity* and other academic journals. One of the more fascinating insights to emerge in recent years is a study of Mediterranean tombs and temples by Michael Hoskin (Hoskin 2001). The vast amount of field work undertaken by the author shows that prehistoric tombs in southern Iberia, south-eastern France, the Balearic islands, Tunisia, Algeria and Morocco were orientated towards sunrises at the equinoxes, midsummer or midwinter. In contrast, temples on Menorca, Mallorca, Malta and Gozo seem to have been aligned to stellar events.

A similar variety of celestial events are represented in the alignments recognised at British prehistoric sites, suggesting these alignments had a complex significance. Gerald Hawkins, who pioneered the archaeo-astronomy of Stonehenge in 1965 had, by the time of his death in 2003, backed up the mathematics with quotations from Classical Greek authors which suggest that the Britons of the time understood the 56-year cycle of lunar eclipses, seemingly embodied in the ring of 56 so-called 'Aubrey Holes' which predate the trilithons and bluestones at Stonehenge (Hawkins and Tiede 2004).

In addition, a variety of astronomical alignments are incorporated in Stonehenge (assuming none are merely accidental). Indeed the famous midsummer sunrise alignment over the Heel Stone is so inaccurate as to perhaps be 'chance', whereas the midwinter sunset alignment, in more or less the opposite direction, is much more exact (Prendergast 2003); there is also an alignment towards the midwinter sunrise (North 1996: 458–65). But midwinter on Salisbury Plain is far less inspiring to the modern mentality than midsummer, so the popular association with midsummer sunrise gatherings is likely to persist.

While modern thinking is apt to think of Stonehenge and other megalithic sites with celestial orientations as 'observatories', this is more than a little deceptive. Prehistoric people did not have our scientific mentality; their interest in the sun, moon and stars had a significance quite different to ours. Meticulous astronomical observation does not require any of the sophisticated architecture of Stonehenge. Instead Stonehenge and other megalithic monuments with celestial alignments might be thought of as a way of 'reflecting' the heavens, a way of ostentatiously 'showing off' complex knowledge of the solar and lunar cycles, a permanent record of painstaking study over many previous decades. In other words, more akin to a planetarium than an observatory.

Stonehenge and the Druids

The combination of Welsh nationalism and Methodism which had fuelled the reinvention of Druidry earlier in the eighteenth century was increasingly tempered by antiquarian interests in megalithic monuments, notably the writings of William Stukeley, and by the onset of the Romantic movement. Despite its anti-English origins, Stukeley managed to appropriate Druidry as an adjunct to the Church of England, and Druids became icons of freedom rather than revolt. Druidry was adapted sufficiently to be adopted by English establishment figures – at least, by the more eccentric ones. However there has never been a single Druidic order – the movement has always been characterised by splinter groups and inter-group rivalries.

While the Druid orders have always celebrated the summer solstice, they only began using Stonehenge in 1905, when the Ancient Order of Druids (founded in 1781) assembled for a mass initiation of 256 novices on 24th August. A more radical and fractious Druid order, An Druidk Uileach Braithreachas (known in English as the Church of the Universal Bond, and led by Dr Macgregor Reid until his death in 1946), were caught illegally burying the ashes of one of their deceased members at Stonehenge the same year, but no charges were brought. In 1925 the Universal Bond led a protest against the admission charges at Stonehenge and at the summer solstice they rushed the turnstyles and encouraged about 1,000 other people to enter without paying.

During the 1920s and 30s the summer solstice at Stonehenge and the activities of the Druids were watched by up to 3,000 people. In anticipation of the free festivals of the 1970s and 80s, they spent the night partying and using portable gramophones to dance to the latest 'rebel music' – jazz – by the light of car headlights. More respectably, according to the *Salisbury Journal*, in 1929 '… minstrels enlivened the vigil with mandolin selections.' (cited in Stout 2003: 39). Such spontaneous gatherings of the lower classes enjoying themselves tend to make the establishment twitchy. However the Ancient Order of Druids stopped using Stonehenge after 1932 (Reid was now over 80) and the numbers of other people attending steadily declined. By 1939 only 400 people were there, entertained by the Wiltshire Folk Dancers.

However Reid's son Robert resumed the Druidic rituals in the late 1940s and by 1960 the associated solstice crowds had resumed their pre-war numbers, with a great many from the nearby military bases intent on a good party. Their drunken antics disrupted the activities of morris dancers in 1952. In 1956 thunder flashes were thrown at the Druids, and the two thousand strong crowd closed in on them scornfully. There was less trouble for the Druids the following year but two skiffle groups appeared and attempted to drown out the sound of each other, although they reportedly only had a repertoire of four songs, endlessly repeated (Stout 2003: 41). In 1964 access to the stones at midsummer sunrise was restricted to the Druids and journalists. In 1969 the attempts to exclude the crowds failed and about 2,000 people – many of them 'hippies' – tried to join the Druids' activities.

Until the 1950s the Druids' rituals had fallen within the British establishment's ability to accommodate harmless eccentricity and were tolerated as they helped boost tourism. However their antics greatly offended the then editor of *Antiquity*, Glyn Daniel, who referred to them as 'horrid' and 'bogus'. However his wish to ban them from the monument did not prevail. In the 1970s the Druids were joined by an increasingly heterogeneous mix of hippies, punks, bikers, Hell's Angels, travellers, peace activists, anarchists, musicians, jugglers, mystics, dreamers, New Agers, Hare Krishna devotees, Quakers, and any number of independently-minded people who considered themselves excluded from the government's Thatcherite policies. To the establishment and the mass media they were homogenised as undesirable weirdos.

The mid-1970s was also the era of free festivals bringing together this disparate alternative community. These festivals were an example of what Peter Lamborn Wilson (a.k.a. Hakim Bey) was to call 'temporary autonomous zones' (Bey 1985). A field next to Stonehenge became the venue for the biggest of the annual cycle of such events. The first such festival at Stonehenge was in 1974. The numbers attending grew year by year and by 1985 probably exceeded fifty thousand. During the early 1980s Thatcher-right policies had become increasingly intolerant of those critical of the establishment, especially the peace protestors and those dubbed as 'New Age travellers'. In the 1985 the National Trust and English Heritage took out an injunction against the Stonehenge festival organisers. The police provoked violent confrontations in an attempt to prevent the festival proceeding, notably the 'Battle of the Beanfield' which took place just outside Cholderton on the Wiltshire border on 1st June 1985. Police dressed in riot gear attacked a convoy of 150 travellers' vehicles on their way to the Stonehenge festival. They truncheoned people holding babies, arrested 420 of them (although few were formally charged) and severely damaged many of the vehicles. This was the onset of provocative policing strategies to be repeated with the printers at Wapping, the miners at Orgreave, and the Poll Tax protests. (See Worthington 2004 for a full account of the Stonehenge free festivals, and Stone 1996: 153–60 for a detailed discussion of the Battle of the Beanfield. Wallis has also summarised modern pagan approaches to Stonehenge; Wallis 2003 153–67)

For fifteen years after the Battle of the Beanfield at the summer solstice Stonehenge was the epicentre of a four mile exclusion zone, policed at vast expense. When English Heritage unexpectedly relented in 2000 a peaceful gathering of 6,000 people ensued. The following year 14,000 people were present, rising to around 20,000 in 2002 and the following years; despite the growing numbers there has been minimal trouble.

While not directly related to the archaeology of Stonehenge, the Battle of the Beanfield and the annual exclusion zone all intensified the iconic link between Stonehenge and a variety of alternative and counter-culture groups. This iconic significance continues to provide another level of meaning for the monument among present day counter cultures.

The conservation of Stonehenge

What a visitor to Stonehenge sees today is the more or less the final phase of the prehistoric changes, subjected to the intermingled processes of natural decay, deliberate vandalism, restoration and heritage management. While not ideal, things could have been a lot worse. By 1822 there were so many tourists (and rather too many of whom wanted to break off pieces to take back as souvenirs) that a warden was appointed to live nearby.

In the late nineteenth and early nineteenth centuries the dogged individualism of then landowners, Sir Edmund Antrobus and his son, also Sir Edmund, thankfully preserved Stonehenge against the 'good intentions' of archaeologists and Ministry of Works officials. In an effort to keep out the 'riff raff' Sir Edmund junior erected a fence around the monument in 1901 and charged an entrance fee of one shilling (about £5 in modern value). Considerable protest ensued but Sir Edmund was certainly not the sort of chap to be easily swayed by other peoples' opinions. After his death Stonehenge succumbed to state ownership in 1918.

The archaeologist William Hawley was appointed to undertake a major excavation between 1919 and 1926. Although he cleared half the site, the longer he worked the less he felt he knew about the place. His efforts have been deemed a disaster (Chippindale 1983: 183) although the circles of pits known as the Aubrey holes and the Y and Z holes were revealed.

Major archaeological excavation and restoration did not resume until the 1950s. In 1952 Richard Atkinson claimed to have found the image of a Mycenean dagger carved into one of the uprights. Here was a link to the glamour of Mediterranean and the Classical cultures considered to be at the core of the evolution of Western society. Stonehenge was not the work of a dubious Druid but of a Mycenaean architect. When the recalibration of radiocarbon dates in the late 1960s put the construction of Stonehenge back long before Mycenaean culture then Atkinson's putative architect quietly departed. Characteristically for the time, there was no serious attempt to write up and publish details of the 1950s and 60s excavations. Barbara Bender makes a dismal assessment of the activities of the relevant archaeologists:

> When finally…all the excavation material of [the twentieth] century was laboriously assembled, there was an agreement not to dwell on the ineptitude of the excavators. But anyone reading the five hundred page volume [Cleal *et al* 1995] will catch glimpses of barely-suppressed outrage at the amount of evidence lost, fudged or (almost wilfully) misinterpreted. Given a prehistoric landscape central to our sense of national identity, we have astonishingly little evidence.
> (Bender 1998: 8)

With similar ineptitude, in 1968 the visitors' facilities were rebuilt in an underground 'bunker' using the then *de rigueur* concrete. In 1993 a House of Commons Select Committee declared them a 'national disgrace'; twelve years on they still grace the place. Equally insensitive was the decision to cover the ground surface inside the circle of megaliths with orange gravel, thankfully replaced with turf in 1978, although this was at the expense of the public being able to walk among the stones – a policy based on decidedly dubious arguments for conservation. Should Westminster Abbey or other major cathedrals be closed to visitors because the stone floors are being worn away by visitors' feet? The ground surface at Stonehenge is mostly backfill from archaeological digs and of negligible 'conservation value' compared to a cathedral floor. In 1998 English Heritage relented slightly by allowing small groups of visitors to apply in advance for access inside the main circle at times when the monument is not open to the public.

Stonehenge continues to be one of the leading tourist destinations in the country. A survey in 1990 established there were 700,000 paying visitors a year, and about 250,000 who 'chose not pay'. At peak times they arrived at the rate of two thousand an hour. Americans made up about forty percent of these visitors; indeed Britons were outnumbered three-to-one by overseas tourists. The average duration of these visits is under thirty minutes, of which half is typically spent in the loos or the shop. Not surprisingly only one in six of those interviewed thought they got 'good value' from their visit.

Who speaks for Stonehenge?

English Heritage owns Stonehenge on behalf of the nation, and the National Trust holds about 2,100 acres surrounding the henge (and has plans to acquire several times more), also on behalf of the nation and its public. Around this are the vast tracts of Salisbury Plain colonised by the Ministry of Defence whose ultimate rationale is to act in the national interest, even if their track record of defending archaeological features has mostly been limited to trashing them with tank tracks. (This is a long-standing military tradition – the eastern end of the Cursus near Stonehenge was destroyed when it was overrun by the Larkhill camp during the First World War, and a road heavily used at this time by military lorries and early tanks ran just five yards from Stonehenge itself.)

The French intellectual Michel Foucault wrote 'A whole history remains to be written about *spaces* – which would at the same time be a history of *powers*... ' (Foucault 1980: 149). He is also famous for arguing that those who have and create knowledge are also in a position of power. So who has power over sacred places such as Stonehenge? Who really 'owns' the heritage? Who is really entitled to speak for the monument and its environs? Who makes the final decisions about who has access, optimum conservation strategies, and all the rest? While the anonymous grey suits at English Heritage headquarters continue to exert the powers they have either been bequeathed or appropriated, two substantial books have devoted to bringing to wider attention the largely unrepresented (and frequently *mis*represented) alternative attitudes towards Stonehenge (Chippindale *et al* 1990; Bender 1998).

Since Stonehenge became a United Nations World Heritage Site in 1986 there has been widespread agreement that the 1960s neo-brutalist concrete structures which control access are highly inappropriate, and that the local road system impinges too severely on the surrounding landscape, although the political will to fund an effective solution was seriously elusive. The Council for British Archaeology has been the focus of vociferous objections to earlier under-funded schemes for 'improving' Stonehenge. However at the time of writing, while billions of pounds were being devoted to the destruction of Iraq, the necessary millions of pounds were finally allocated to the improvement of the Stonehenge area in a manner that is seemingly acceptable to interested parties (although certainly not optimum). Completion date is planned for 2008.

The once and future Stonehenge

As already noted in Chapter 3, in *Tess of the D'Urbervilles* Thomas Hardy wrote of the wind blowing at Stonehenge and creating 'a booming tone, like the note of some gigantic one-stringed harp'. More metaphorically, the meaning of the monument readily resonates with a wide range of ideas, echoing the evolution of modern day thinking.

How we think about Stonehenge, the significance we give to it, is a reflection both of how the heritage industry prefers to recreate the past and of wider society's concerns. For all that the heritage industry seeks to package a notion of Stonehenge with a deep-rooted and stable past, an icon of the nation's identity, the reality is that Stonehenge is the prehistoric site where present day visitors and the attendant facilities, fencing and guards make more impact than the prehistory, making it redolent of a run-down theme park.

For the present day alternative community Stonehenge has become simultaneously an icon of Thatcher-era intolerance and a focus of their search for ancestral spirituality. But the complexity of the diverse alternative attitudes have been reduced by the dominant discourse of the heritage industry and mass media to concepts that can be easily parodied and dismissed.

Stonehenge has for over a hundred years been both the most contemporary and most contested of British megalithic sites. The repeated rebuilding revealed by detailed study of the archaeological evidence suggests there must have been ever-changing conflicting ideas about the monument in the Bronze Age too. Or is this just another example of simply seeking and recreating a past that is a reflection of our own times and anxieties?

Jacquetta Hawkes once famously declared that every age has the Stonehenge it deserves – or desires (Hawkes 1967: 174). So far the desires and 'deserves' include a Druidical temple; an outpost of Mycenaean civilisation; a key to lost wisdom of the heavens; a site of major archaeological significance; an icon for the national heritage; a badly designed tourist spectacle; the location of a major free festival; the site of confrontational policing; an icon for an alternative Britain; a focus of ancestral spirituality; plus any number of personal agendas. And of course we can now add the explicitly 'multivocal' approaches initiated by Chippindale and Bender and outlined here.

Sources

RCHME 1979; Chippindale 1983; Richards 1984; Chippindale *et al* 1990; Shanks 1992: 59; Bender 1993b&c, 1998; Jones 2001; Stout 2001, 2003; Pitts 2001; Worthington 2002a; 2004; Kaiser 2003; Pitts and Richards 2003.

10: Pembrokeshire and south-west Scotland

Going to prehistoric sites and purposefully 'looking around', seeing how they are intervisible, how they are obscured by the lie of the land when walking towards them, how they appear on the skyline when viewed from specific places, and such like was part of the alternative 'earth mysteries' approaches of the 1970s and 80s. When academics caught up with this idea and realised that the God's eye view of maps, plans and aerial photos gave very little idea of the *experience* of the landscape they gave this 'looking around' an all but unpronounceable name – 'phenomenology'. It kicked off in 1994 with Christopher Tilley's book *A Phenomenology of Landscape: Places, paths and monuments*. Although his opening chapters are a fairly daunting philosophical analysis, he sums up in a more down to earth way. Phenomenology for Tilley is, in practice, a considered way of experiencing prehistoric monuments, approaching them on foot not merely from the nearest place to park the car but, where relevant, from other prehistoric sites. By approaching the same place from different directions he is able 'to observe in a much more subtle manner the way in which it is related to its physical surroundings, the lie of the land.' (Tilley 1994: 74) He realises that not only are all places in their landscapes, but the 'landscapes constitute the place.' (Tilley 1994: 74)

> Walk from one place to another or approach it from a different direction and everything will change. Things that loomed large in your visual field may become small, or look different. What was at the centre may now be on the periphery; what could be seen has now disappeared, and new horizons come into view.
> (Tilley 1994: 74)

In the last two chapters I have already summarised aspects of Tilley's approach at Avebury and Stonehenge. One of his first 'case studies' was devoted to the Neolithic tombs in Pembrokeshire and the western part of Carmarthenshire, at the south-western tip of Wales. Unlike Avebury and Stonehenge where a group of Neolithic monuments developed within easy walking distance of a focal place, in south-west Wales the megalithic sites are scattered around the landscape. However this scatter is certainly not random. Detailed surveys of the area have identified about thirty-one Neolithic burial chambers, often in a poor state of preservation (indeed a couple are rather doubtful) and, although some must have been lost without trace, these thirty-one survivors probably represent a good proportion of all such monuments erected in the region. All were once covered by earth mounds or stone cairns, usually round or oval in plan but sometimes rectangular. These have since been removed, exposing the characteristic and rather sculptural arrangement of a massive cap stone supported by various upright megaliths.

The Devil's Quoit now sits amid sand dunes with Milford Haven oil refinery conspicuous out of shot on the northern skyline. However both the refinery and the dunes were absent in the Neolithic. Despite its coastal location the sea is barely visible. Instead the Preseli mountains are the main natural feature of the skyline.
(Cummings and Whittle 2004: 164)

The surviving tombs provide a good indication of how the Neolithic people intended them to be visible from different places in the landscape. While most of these tombs fall into recognisable groups, the construction of the burial chambers reveals remarkable variety. Guesswork is often needed to provide details of the original architecture, but enough survives to confirm that none of them were identical. Indeed the variety has defied archaeologists' attempts at classification. Tilley considers that this difference was intentional, 'perhaps one of their most characteristic and important features.' (Tilley 1994: 90) In contrast:

> '... their relation to topographical features of the landscape is highly structured and repetitive. The relationship to the coastline, especially in relation to bays, inlets and peninsulas, of many of the monuments is obvious... '
> (Tilley 1994: 93)

Nearly half of the tombs are less than three-quarters of a mile from the coast. Yet at only half of these can the sea actually be seen, and even then it may be a distant coastline rather than the nearest part. The location of the tombs seems instead to be determined by how there were seen from *inland*, where the people were presumably living. And even then they could only be seen from certain directions. Only two of tombs are at the highest point of the locality, with all-round visibility. All the others

Carn Ingli – St Brynach's hill of angels and Lawrence Main's recumbent giant.
See also photograph of the summit on page 52.

have been located so that the views from the tomb (and therefore visibility of the tomb) are restricted, usually by being situated part-way up a rising slope.

Despite the tombs typically only being a few miles of each other, only a few of the most northern ones are intervisible. Nevertheless there is a sense of 'grouping', focussed around what might reasonably be considered the oldest of the tombs (although accurate dating evidence is not available).

First hand phenomenology

Tilley's discussion of these Neolithic tombs intrigued me, so in September 1995 I packed my camping gear and set off on what proved to be a most enjoyable week's holiday exploring these sites for myself.

Carn Ingli, the summit of the Preseli mountains, is visible from the Neolithic tombs to the north. In several cases if they were situated just a few hundred yards away this would not be possible (Tilley 1994: 105). As already noted in Chapter 3, the peak of Carn Ingli has many areas of remarkable geomagnetic anomalies. The name means 'hill of angels', a memory of the time when St Brynach lived on the summit towards the end of the 5th century CE and saw visions of what he took to be angelic beings. In 1992 anomalous lights were seen nearby, although local folklore suggests this was far from the first time. Locally they are known as *gorff connwyl* or *canwyll corf*, which translates as 'corpse candles', more often referred to in folklore as 'will 'o the wisps', while modern researchers have termed them 'earth lights', one of a number of inexplicable phenomena that tend to lumped together as UFOs in the popular

Pentre Ifan is the best-known and impressive of the Pembrokeshire chamber tombs, set on rising round above the Nevern Valley. Carn Ingli, just over two miles to the west, is clearly visible (on the right in this photograph). However the Preseli mountains to the south are only visible from the surviving chamber but not from the tail end of the mostly-destroyed long cairn running from the chamber (Cummings and Whittle 2004: 21; 143). This compares with the alignment of Windmill Hill and Silbury Hill near Avebury, which is visible from the tail end of the mound at West Kennett long barrow, but not from the forecourt to the chamber; see pages 72 and 145–6.

imagination (see Chapter 5). The locals also believe Carn Ingli is haunted by fairies and ghosts (Howard 1994: 72), which may be another way of conceptualising 'earth lights' (Bord 1997).

Lawrence Main, a modern day counterpart to St Brynach, has spent many years living in a tent at the top of Carn Ingli, recording the dreams he has while sleeping there, and immersing himself in local lore. This includes tales of a 'goddess' and a giant. Intriguingly he has recognised the profile of two such figures, formed from the natural outcrops (Main 1994). While the eye of faith is needed to see the rocks as recumbent humans, such simulacra can be found throughout the world.

Carn Menyn (or Meini) on the Preseli mountains is the geological source of the bluestones incorporated into Stonehenge. At least twenty-seven megalithic monuments broadly contemporary with Stonehenge incorporate these bluestones into their construction although nearly all are within sight of Carn Menyn (Souden 1997: 82). High-status polished axes (see Chapter 7) were also made from the same rock.

Over half the Pembrokeshire chamber tombs are located under half a mile from the sea but are in positions which seem deliberately selected so that the skyline completely blocks the view of the coast, or provides only a narrow sea view (Tilley 1994: 93; Cummings and Whittle 2004: 33). Carreg Coetan near Newport (also known as Arthur's Stone) is close to where the Afon Nyfer meets the sea, yet it was constructed in a place where the sea was barely visible (even allowing for the blocking of the view by nearby houses).

This photograph confirms that Carn Ingli is clearly visible just over a mile to the south; other chamber tombs (Cerrig y Gof) are a similar distance to the west. (Cummings and Whittle 2004: 141)

One musically inclined writer has noted that the rocks of the Preseli area have an unusual propensity to ring when struck (Fagg 1957). As already mentioned in Chapter 3, a village near the Preseli mountains is called Maenclochog, 'Ringing Rocks' (Devereux 2001a: 120). The ringing rocks at Maenclochog are thought to have been destroyed by quarrying in the late eighteenth century. However it raises the possibility that the Stonehenge 'blue stones' were originally significant as 'ringing rocks', before being silenced by being stood up in the ground.

Places of special virtue

Tilley's preliminary interpretation of these monuments has subsequently been followed up by other archaeologists, firstly Andrew Fleming (Fleming 1999) and more recently as part of the exemplary survey of Welsh megalithic sites by Vicki Cummings and Alasdair Whittle (Cummings and Whittle 2004). As already noted in Chapter 4, their book, *Places of Special Virtue: Megaliths in the Neolithic landscapes of Wales*, is a clear example of the way academic archaeologists are recognising

Carreg Sampson is situated at the head of a natural creek above Abercastle, one of the best natural harbours along this coast and presumably important for prehistoric travel.

The monument is positioned close to two natural outcrops (characteristic of many Pembrokeshire prehistoric monuments); another prominent outcrop is visible under half a mile to the east, and the Preseli mountains can be seen in the distance to the east. Two other chamber tombs and the outcrop associated with a third tomb are also visible. However, despite its coastal setting, the view of the sea is comparatively limited. (Cummings and Whittle 2004: 33; 156)

Two types of stone were used. One is the local stone, outcropping nearby. The other is not local although its geological source has not so far been identified. Such selection of non-local stones seems intentional and may 'echo' the trade in polished axes made from 'exotic'? (non-local) stone (see Chapter 7) (Cummings and Whittle 2004: 7). George Children and George Nash have gone further by suggesting that the prehistoric monuments of south-west Wales symbolically incorporate topographic features into the plans of the monuments (Children and Nash 1997: 28).

some of the ideas raised in the opening chapters, leading to more sophisticated interpretations of sites. However this excellent book was published only after I had drafted this book so, apart from the remarks at the end of Chapter 4, this section, and the captions to the Pembrokeshire 'places of special virtue' in this chapter, I have not adapted my remarks to include their ideas. Rather I would strongly recommend reading their book in its entirety, as their interpretations of these varied monuments (and how they relate to nearby outcrops and views of the sea, rivers, mountains and other features) are often discursive and subtle.

Although most Pembrokeshire chamber tombs are intentionally sited so the sea is obscured, a small number of chamber tombs built against natural outcrops have dramatic sea views. One of these is King's Quoit chamber tomb, overlooking Manorbier Bay, which is another good natural harbour and probably an important landing place during the Neolithic. In the hillside immediately behind the tomb are natural blow holes.

The three uprights and the 'earth fast' massive capstone have been erected but the large slabs forming the flat back wall of the chamber are natural (Cummings and Whittle 2004: 165). The overall impression is of a natural cave, a liminal place of entry to the Otherworlds.

King's Quoit is one of several Pembrokeshire chamber tombs that look like natural outcrops. Intriguingly, even the more 'architectural' tombs are often situated in close proximity to a pair of natural outcrops (Thomas 2004: 221; Cummings and Whittle 2004: 29–30). At other monuments, such as Pentre Ifan, specific outcrops are clearly visible from the forecourts.

Landscape locations in south-west Scotland

Another coastal area of Britain with a cluster of Neolithic monuments is south-west Scotland (Dumfries and Galloway with southern Ayrshire). There are 29 known chambered tombs and long cairns (most of them multi-phase), eight stone circles, several so-called 'four poster' megalithic structures, five cursuses, a henge and a recently-discovered series of palisaded enclosures, plus numerous standing stones (Cummings 2002: 125).

Llech y Dribedd chamber tomb is among the most magnificent prehistoric monuments in south-west Wales. The main view is over the Nevern valley, with Carn Ingli dominating the skyline to the south-south-west, as shown in this photograph. Turning around to face north-north-west you can just get a glimpse of the sea, and part of Fishguard Bay and Dinas Head is visible to the west. Such restricted views of the sea are clearly intentional because the location is less than a mile from the coast. However the view of Carn Ingli was probably important (Tilley 1994; Children and Nash 1997; Cummings and Whittle 2004: 139).

This site gives the impression that its builders intentionally 'turned their backs' to the nearby sea in favour of open views of the Nevern valley and Carn Ingli. The open views mean it would be difficult to locate a monument that did not have clear views of Carn Ingli; however as the photographs of other monuments in this chapter indicate, more typically the visibility of Carn Ingli is more subtle and therefore presumably intentional (contra Fleming 1999: 121).

Some of the tombs and cairns are located about a mile away from a river and less than 500 yards from a stream – often halfway between two streams. Almost all these monuments are also sited to have good views of Merrick mountain. Few monuments are situated near lochs and these have been carefully situated so the loch cannot be seen.

The monuments which are not located about a mile from a river are located near the coast, like their near-contemporaries in Pembrokeshire. All but two of these have clear views of the sea (whereas the sea can be seen from only half the Pembrokeshire ones). Some of these coastal monuments are intervisible, whereas none of the river valley ones are. Three mountains (but not Merrick) seem to have been important to

Cairnholy was perhaps 'the "interface" between wooden monuments to the east and indigenous stone-built monuments to the west' (Cummings 2002: 140–1).

The construction of the tombs seems relate to glimpses of the Isle of Man towards the south. However later phases of construction may have intentionally blocked visibility of the Isle of Man (Cummings 2002: 142–3).

at least some of these coastal monuments. However the main focus of interest of the coastal tombs and cairns seems to have been the Isle of Man, just discernible on the horizon in clear weather. For example, if the Cairnholy monuments were situated just a little lower down the hill then the Isle of Man would not be visible. (Cummings 2002: 132–5) The Isle of Man was the focus of Neolithic culture in Western Britain because it 'lies in a central position in the Irish Sea and many of the tidal streams of that region converge on the island.' (Noble 2003: 22) Certainly hand axes and other artefacts seem to have been traded throughout the coastal regions surrounding the Isle of Man (Cooney 2000).

Another of the Cairnholy chamber tombs.

Vicki Cummings also discusses the similarities and differences of the monuments of south-west Scotland and north-east Ireland, concluding that links between these two areas were formed after many of these monuments had been constructed, although before the final re-constructions.

Most interestingly, the view from all but two of these Neolithic tombs and cairns in south-west Scotland is quite 'closed' in one direction, meaning that 'all but the immediate landscape is hidden from view'. (Cummings 2002:134) The two exceptions have wide-ranging views in all directions, a characteristic of the stone circles in the area.

The siting of the monuments in Pembrokeshire and south-west Scotland reveals that the landscape had complex meanings for the early Neolithic people who created them. A variety of academic archaeologists are now adopting suitably open-minded approaches to develop subtly 'nuanced' interpretations of the significance of such sites for their creators. Inevitably their deliberations often raise more questions than the archaeological evidence can currently answer. I for one await future developments with keen interest.

12: Placing together

There is no way of telling what may yet become part of history. Perhaps the past is still essentially undiscovered! So many retroactive forces are still needed!
Friedrich Nietzsche *The Joyful Wisdom*

For several hundred years western culture has deluded itself that the past is something 'objective', something which – given enough surviving evidence and effort interpreting that evidence – would reveal the 'truth' of how people used to live and think. However, as any attempt to analyse recent political events quickly reveals, it is frustratingly difficult to establish the 'truth' about events well within living memory and fully documented by various journalists. The possibilities for differing interpretations grow exponentially as the 'facts' are increasingly diffused by the mists of time; we look back with the hindsight of the 'successful' outcome. The past is something we recreate according to present day concerns and, as such, is continually being recreated.

Each version of the past is concurrently created by and consumed by different groups of people – such as academics, pagans or 'mere tourists'. The identity of each of these groups is, in large part, defined by the version of the past they create and consume. Some of these recreations of the past are fairly resistant to change (such as the myth of the rural idyll which pervades the heritage industry), while others seem to almost wilfully adapt and mutate at a high rate (such as the latest thinking from the younger generation of academic archaeologists).

The neglected Greek philosopher Heraclitus (c.544–483 BCE) famously noted that 'We cannot step twice into the same river.' While we readily recognise that a river flows on and is not exactly the same from moment to moment, we may need to be prompted before realising that that the person who steps into the river has also 'flowed on'. Various recreations of the past are also akin to a river in that they are ever changing – although some are more like sluggish backwaters rather than fast-flowing torrents.

Different reconstructions and narratives about the past are rarely entirely distinct; instead they borrow from each other and overlap. This prevents clear distinctions and allows only tentative and liminal boundaries between the different approaches.

The past is akin to a constant conversation. If we stopped thinking about, talking about and recreating the past then – to all intents and purposes – the past does not exist. The past exists as some underlying story which helps to shape the present – although the present shapes the past to a far greater extent than the past shapes the present.

The physical presence of prehistoric monuments and sacred places is much less important than what these places signify within this constructed conversation. The exact archaeological and historical 'facts' are less important than a soft focus blur of oldness and specialness. Such places are meaningful principally because a person (or, more typically, a group of people) feels empowered in some way by relating to that oldness and specialness.

What makes a prehistoric monument into a sacred place is not some simplistic sacred:profane dualism. Rather the sense of sacredness is constructed by narratives created within a wide range of different meta-narratives or myths, most of them ever-evolving. Some of these meta-narratives have their origins in academic, some in 'fringe' research, and others reflect different aspects of modern paganisms. The term 'sacred places' is shorthand for a multiplicity of steadily changing distinctions.

What we *know* about the past is contained within the much bigger sense of what we *believe* about the past. Intriguingly, beliefs need not be exclusive and (as already noted in Chapter 6) our beliefs about the past might usefully be considered to be akin to a tool box. Just as different tools help us achieve different tasks, so a tool box of different beliefs allows us to access different pasts.

Many pasts, many landscapes

This means that the past is not something 'out there', some *thing* which can be objectively attained, but rather the past is an ever-changing process of constructing meaning and significance, and creating narratives which fit into the overall metanarrative of the group. Goddess-worshipping pagans simultaneously select and reinforce a different set of meanings about places such as the Avebury monuments than, say, more shamanic pagans, or most academic archaeologists.

However, there is self-referential circularity to the last sentence, as each of these labels ('goddess-worshipping pagans', 'more shamanic pagans', 'academic archaeologists' – and the list could be extended and sub-divided exhaustively) is defined by the version of the past each group creates and consumes. What is 'fact' to one group is 'fiction' (or 'outdated') to another – and, quite usually, vice versa!

Archaeologists and historians cannot recreate *the* past, they can only recreate 'their' past. Whether or not 'their' past is also 'our' past depends on the extent we share the same *present day* perspectives. This means there are as many pasts as there are present day perspectives. None are 'true', still less 'really what it was like'. And, just as there is not a single past, so there is 'never *a* landscape, always many landscapes' (Bender 1998: 7, 25). By extension this means that any one prehistoric monument is not *a* sacred place but always *many* sacred places.

Rather than a single past, there are many pasts, each depending on the viewpoint and prior assumptions of the person engaging with the past. This book has attempted to explore how we have created, and are continuing to recreate, significance and meaning for those aspects of the past we regard as prehistoric places and landscapes. Most of these include monuments deliberately erected to endure, to make a tangible statement about their creators' relationships with the place, evoking a sense of belonging that we can still relate to, and perhaps feel we still share.

Objects and places from the past are as much about what they are *not* as what they *are*. They are not part of a living culture, they are emblems of something we can only tentatively understand. They are not utilitarian, so an old pot or the remains of a stone circle have a different significance to a microwave oven or a supermarket. Ultimately, we see them as somehow different from the artefacts and locations that we regard as contemporary. Despite them continuing to exist in the present day they are somehow not of the modern world. Furthermore, the prehistoric places we regard as sacred are usually in open country, not part of everyday urban and suburban life.

Popular interest focuses on prehistoric monuments that are still visible (even if badly deteriorated). In many cases their survival has been 'against the odds'. Their setting now is one aspect of 'the landscape', 'the countryside', 'our heritage', and any number of other complex and far from neutral modern ideas.

Many players, no referee

The past has been compared to a book that has no author but only readers, each of whom trying to make their own sense out of the disparate pages. But this analogy is deeply flawed as it makes us think of the past as something that exists in the way a book exists. A better comparison is to think of our relationship with the past as being like a game. So, rather than readers, there are players – but no referee, and the rules depend on who is playing.

Games, by nature, are different every time they are played. They are one step removed from everyday experience, opening up new (if only temporary) ways of relating to other players – and that is as true for a game of rugby (tackling a passing stranger is not something you can get away with in the High Street) as it is for more conspicuous role playing in, say, *Dungeons and Dragons*. (Shanks 1992: 33; 80) Michael Shanks played with this approach to the past and noted:

> There can be good and bad matches, good and bad archaeological
> approaches and projects. These are judged not just according to how
> closely the rules are followed, but also according to how much the players
> (archaeologists) get out of the game, and how it looks to an audience.
> (Shanks 1992: 80)

We are accustomed to reading about the past, just as you have read this book. We are well aware of different genres of writing about the past, such as excavation reports, academic overviews, popular summaries and speculations, fantasy fiction, concise tourist guides, interpretation panels at sites, and the like. But perhaps we should swap the metaphor and start looking less at the literary genre adopted and more at the rules used by the writers to play with their ideas. Do they engage with the evidence and other peoples' ideas in the manner of shoot 'em up computer games? Or do they engage in team play and subtle strategies, akin to war games? Perhaps they approach the past as if it is like a cryptic adventure games (maybe with a bit of 'first person shooter' thrown in for fun, in the same way the *Tomb Raider* games combine genres). There are also writers who mix and match their ideas, akin to a fantasy sports team. Sophisticated computer simulations of past civilisations are being developed by academics seemingly inspired by *The Sims*. However, as the

Nietzsche quotation at the head of this chapter infers, we may have not yet found the most interesting rules for playing with the past. As our ideas develop in the future, so our ideas about the past will increase in complexity.

Meaning and significance matter

No matter how we think we engage with the past, the past has meaning and significance simply because we give it certain meanings and special significance. In Britain until about fifteen years ago there were deeply differentiated ideas about the past, with most academics having little in common with the various popular and alternative ideas. While extreme viewpoints still exist, the middle ground has become densely populated and provides an increasingly interesting perspective on how we give meaning and significance to all aspects of the past, not least its 'landscapes' and monuments.

Sadly there are few opportunities for these recent and exciting ideas to reach the attention of people with an interest in the past. This applies as much to those people who are fired up about archaeology after seeing *Time Team* as to, say, modern day pagans who seek a spiritual significance to megalithic sites, holy wells, and the like. This book has been intended as a start but is far too short to do more than skim the surface of the underlying ideas, and provides more detailed discussions of only a handful of specific places (although I have tried to leave sufficient bibliographical references to enable readers to follow up my sources).

The middle ground is far from uniform and contains a rich diversity of approaches. To some extent the only belief that unites them is that there cannot be One True Way of understanding the past, and the 'truth' cannot be discovered by finding enough evidence and applying enough scientific know how. Instead – to mix metaphors madly – the past is like a pick and mix sweet shop, where specific techniques are like ladders to be climbed to reach new ways of understanding, but then abandoned. Not only techniques but entire belief systems should be regarded as tools to achieve specific ways of understanding, then also abandoned. In this way our understanding of sacred places will keep up with the ever-changing cultures and societies within which they have meaning and significance.

Behaviour matters

This book can be regarded as principally a history of ideas – one person's account of how we have constructed meaning and significance about specific types of places that we think of as 'sacred', and how that meaning and significance has evolved.

Rather than being a guide book to such sacred places, I have attempted to offer a travelogue of the mental worlds in which we have created the idea of prehistoric sacred places.

However there is more to exploring sacred places than mindscapes and reading books. Direct experience of such places widens our awareness of how we give meaning and significance to the landscape and the past. This means getting out and about, preferably not just on pleasant summer afternoons – some of my most poignant experiences of prehistoric monuments have been in rain, mist, hoarfrost or snow. When you visit sacred places please comply with the ASLaN charter (see page 105). Above all, 'Don't change the site, let the site change you'.

Bibliography

ACKROYD, Peter, 2002, *Albion: The origins of the English imagination*, Chatto and Windus.

ADAMS, David, 1978, 'A modern myth', *Journal of Geomancy,* 2:iv, 105–8.

ADAMS, Douglas, 1979, *The Hitchhiker's Guide to the Galaxy*, Pan.

AITCHESON, Nicholas B., 1994, *Armagh and the Royal Centres in Early Medieval Ireland: Monuments, cosmology and the past*, Cruithne Press/Boydell and Brewer.

ALCOCK, Susan and Robin OSBORNE (eds), 1994, *Placing the Gods: Sanctuaries and sacred space in ancient Greece*, Clarendon.

ARNOLD, J., K. DAVIES and S. DITCHFIELD, 1998, *History and Heritage: Consuming the past in contemporary culture*, Donhead.

ASTON, Michael, 1985, *Interpreting the Landscape: Landscape archaeology and local history*, Batsford.

ASTON, Michael and Trevor ROWLEY, 1974, *Landscape Archaeology: An introduction to fieldwork techniques on post-Roman landscapes*, David and Charles.

AVENI, A.F., 1980, *Skywatchers of Ancient Mexico*, University of Texas Press.

BAKER, A.R.H., 1992, 'Introduction on ideology and landscape', in A.R.H. Baker and G. Biger (eds), *Ideology and Landscape: Essays on the meaning of some places in the past*, Cambridge UP.

BAKER, R.R., 1980, 'A sense of magnetism', *New Scientist*, 18 Sept.

BARRETT, John C., 1999, 'The mythical landscapes of the British Iron Age' in W. Ashmore and A.B. Knapp (eds), *Archaeologies of Landscape: Contemporary perspectives*, Berg.

BARRETT, J.C., R. BRADLEY and M. GREEN, 1991, *Landscape, Monuments and Society: The prehistory of Cranboune Chase*, Cambridge UP.

BATES, Brian, 1983, *The Way of Wyrd: Tales of an Anglo-Saxon sorcerer*, Century.

BAUDRILLARD, Jean, 1981, *For a Critique of the Political Economy of the Sign*, Telos.

BAUDRILLARD, Jean, 1983, *Simulations*, Semiotext(e).

BAUDRILLARD, Jean, 1990, *Revenge of the Crystal*, Pluto.

BEAUMONT, B. (trans), 1985, *Flaubert and Turgenev: The complete correspondence*, Athlone Press.

BELL, Catherine, 1992, *Ritual Theory, Ritual Practice*, Oxford UP.

BENDER, Barbara (ed), 1993a, *Landscape: Politics and perspectives*, Berg.

BENDER, Barbara, 1993b, 'Stonehenge – contested landscapes (medieval to present day)', in Bender 1993a; reprinted as chapters 4 and 6 of Bender 1998.

BENDER, Barbara, 1993c, 'Introduction: Landscape – meaning and action', in Bender 1993a.

BENDER, Barbara, 1998, *Stonehenge: Making space*, Berg.

BENDER, B., S. HAMILTON and C. TILLEY, 1997, 'Lesternick: stone worlds; alternative narrative; nested landscapes', *Proceedings of the Prehistoric Society*, 63, 147–78.

BENNETT, Gillian, 1993, 'Folklore studies and the English rural myth', *Rural History*, 4.

BETH, Rae, 1990, *Hedgewitch*, Hale.

BEY, Hakim, 1985, *T.A.Z.: The temporary autonomous zone, ontological anarchy, poetic terrorism*, Autonomedia; revised 1991.

BEY, Hakim, no date (mid-1990s), *Overcoming Tourism;*1st publ. France; various English translations on Internet.

BIRDWELL-PHEASANT, D. and D. LAWENCE-ZÚÑIGA, 1999, *House Life: Space, place and family in Europe*, Berg.

BILLINGSLEY, John, 2003a, 'Taking the Long view', *Northern Earth*, 94, 19–23.

BILLINGSLEY, John, 2003b, Editorial footnote to Edna Whelan 'In defence of the mystical consensus', *Northern Earth*, 96, 23.

BILLINGSLEY, John, 2004a, 'Earth mysteries is dead: Long live earth mysteries!', *Northern Earth*, 98, 22–5.

BILLINGSLEY, John, 2004b, 'A new line on the ley?', *Northern Earth*, 99, 8–9.

BLAIN, Jenny and Robert J. WALLIS, 2002a, 'A living landscape? Pagans, archaeology and spirits in the land', *3rd Stone*, 43, 20–7.

BLAIN, Jenny and Robert J. WALLIS, 2002b, 'Contemporary paganism and archaeology: irreconcilable?'. Paper at Archaeology in the Public Domain conference, Sheffield, 9 March 2002. Online at www.sacredsites.org.uk/papers/aypublic.html

BOLVIN, Nicole, 2004, 'Rock art and rock music: petroglyphs of the south Indian Neolithic', *Antiquity*, 78 (299).

BORD, Janet, 1997, *Fairies: Real encounters with little people*, Michael O'Mara.

BORD, Janet and Colin BORD, 1972, *Mysterious Britain*, Garnstone.

BORD, Janet and Colin BORD, 1976, *The Secret Country: More mysterious Britain*, Paul Elek.

BORD, Janet and Colin BORD, 1985, *Sacred Waters: Holy wells and water lore in Britain and Ireland*, Granada.

BORD, Janet and Colin BORD, 1995, *The Enchanted Land: Myths and legends of Britain's landscape*, Thorsons.

BOWDEN, Mark (ed), 1999, *Unravelling the Landscape: An inquisitive approach to archaeology*, Tempus.

BRACE, Catherine, 2002, *Landscape, Place and Identity*, Sage.

BRADLEY, Richard, 1993, *Altering the Earth: The origins of monuments in Britain and continental Europe*, Society of Antiquaries of Scotland.

BRADLEY, Richard, 1997, *Rock art and the prehistory of Atlantic Europe - signing the land*, Routledge.

BRADLEY, Richard, 1998, *The Significance of Monuments: On the shaping of human experience in Neolithic and Bronze Age Europe*, Routledge.

BRADLEY, Richard, 2000, *An Archaeology of Natural Places*, Routledge.

BRADLEY, Richard, 2002, *The Past in Prehistoric Societies*, Routledge.

BRADLEY, Richard, 2003, 'A life less ordinary: the ritualization of the domestic sphere in later prehistoric Europe', *Cambridge Archaeological Journal*, 13, 3–23.

BRENNAN, Michael, 1998, 'Juan for the money', *Fortean Times*, 117, 42–4.

BRENNEMAN, Walter J., 1991, 'Holy wells of Ireland', in Swan 1991.

BREWER, Teri, 1995, *The Marketing of Tradition: Perspectives on tourism and the heritage industry*, Hisarlik.

BROWN, Ian, 2002, 'More Seahenge', *3rd Stone*, 44, 65.

BRÜCK, Joanna, 1999, 'Ritual and rationality: some problems of interpretation in European archaeology', *European Journal of Archaeology* Vol. 2(3), 313–44.

BURCHARDT, Jeremy, 2002, *Paradise Lost: Rural idyll and social change since 1800*, Taurus.

BURKET, Walter, 1993, 'Concordia discors: the literary and the archaeological evidence on the sanctuary of Samothrace', in N. Marintos and R. Hägg (eds), *Greek Sanctuaries: New approaches*, Routledge.

BURL, Aubrey, 1979, *Prehistoric Avebury*, Yale UP; 2nd edn 2002.

BURTON, J., 1984, 'Quarrying in a tribal society', *World Archaeology*, 16, 234–47.

BURTON, Philip, 1993, 'Stone magnetism', *Gloucestershire Earth Mysteries*, 15, 5.

BURTON, Philip, 1995, 'Magalithic enquiries', *The Ley Hunter*, 124, 22–4.

BURTON, Philip, 2002, 'Magnetic megaliths', *3rd Stone*, 42, 48–53.

CAREY, John, 1987, 'The location of the Otherworld in Irish tradition', *Proceedings of the Harvard Celtic Colloquium*, 7, 1–27.

CARMICHAEL, D.L., J. HUBERT, B. REEVES and A. SCHANCHE (eds), 1994, *Sacred Sites, Sacred Places*, Routledge.

CARSTEN, J. and S. HUGH-JONES, 1995, *About the House: Lévi-Strauss and beyond*, Cambridge UP.

CASTANEDA, Carlos, 1968, *The Teachings of Don Juan: A Yaqui way of knowledge*, University of California Press.

CAVALLARO, Dani, 2001, *Critical and Cultural Theory*, Athlone.

CHADBOURNE, Kathryn, 1998,'The Celtic Otherworld', *Cosmos* 14, 157–77 [dated 1998 but appeared in 2002].

CHATWIN, Bruce, 1987, *The Songlines,* Jonathan Cape.

CHILDE, V.G., 1958, *The Prehistory of European Society*, Penguin.

CHILDREN, G. and G. Nash, 1997, *The Anthropology of Landscape: A guide to the Neolithic sites in Cardiganshire, Carmarthenshire and Pembrokeshire*, Logaston.

CHIPPINDALE, Christopher, 1983, *Stonehenge Complete*, Thames and Hudson.

CHIPPINDALE, C., P, DEVEREUX, P. FOWLER, P. JONES, R. AND T. SEBASTIAN, 1990, *Who Owns Stonehenge?*, Batsford.

CHOUDHURY, Anuradha Roma, 1994, 'Hinduism', in Jean Holm and John Bowker (eds), 1994, *Sacred Place*, Pinter.

CLASSEN, C., 1993, *Worlds of Sense: Exploring the senses in history and across cultures*, Routledge.

CLEAL, R., K. WALKER and R. MONTAGUE, 1995, *Stonehenge in its Landscape: Twentieth century excavations*. English Heritage.

COLLINGWOOD, Robin, 1960, *The Idea of Nature*, Oxford UP.

COONEY. Gabriel, 2000, *Landscapes of Neolithic Ireland*, Routledge.

COONEY. Gabriel, 2002, 'So many shades of rock: colour symbolism and Irish stone axeheads', in A. Jones and G. MacGregor (eds), *Colouring the Past*, Berg.

COPE, Julian, 1998, *The Modern Antiquarian: A pre-millennial odyssey through megalithic Britain,* Thorsons.

COPE, Julian, 2004, *Megalithic European: The 21st Century traveller in prehistoric Europe,* Element.

CORLETT, Chris, 1997, 'Prehistoric pilgrimage to Croagh Patrick', *Archaeology Ireland*, 11:2 (No.40),8–11.

COSGROVE, Denis, 1984, *Social Formation and Symbolic Landscape*, Croom Helm.

COSGROVE, Denis, 1993, 'Landscapes and myths, gods and humans', in B. Bender (ed), *Landscape: Politics and perspectives*, Berg.

COWAN, James, 1989, *Mysteries of the Dream-Time: The spiritual life of the Australian Aborigines*, Prism.

COWAN, James, 1992, *The Elements of the Aborigine Tradition*, Element.

COWAN, James, 1994, *Myths of the Dreaming*, Prism.

CUMMINGS, Vicki, 2002, 'Between mountains and sea: a reconsideration of the Neolithic monuments of south-west Scotland', *Proceedings of the Prehistoric Society*, 68, 125–46.

CUMMINGS, Vicki, and Alasdair WHITTLE, 2004, *Places of Special Virtue: Megaliths in the Neolithic landscape of Wales,* Oxbow.

DAMES, Michael, 1976, *The Silbury Treasure*, Thames and Hudson.

DAMES, Michael, 1977, *The Avebury Cycle*, Thames and Hudson.

DANIEL, Glyn, 1958, *The Megalith Builders of Western Europe*, Hutchinson.

DANSER, Simon, 2005, *The Myths of Reality*, Alternative Albion.

DARRAH, John, 1994, *Paganism in Arthurian Romance*, Boydell.

DARVILL, Tim, 1999, review of Julian Cope's *The Modern Antiquarian, Antiquity*, 73 (279), 236–8.

DE CUNZO, Lu Ann, 2003, 'Multilocal places: material systems, metaphors and lived experience', in Deborah L. Rotman and Ellen-Rose Savulis (eds), *Shared Spaces and Divided Places: Material dimensions of gender relations and the American historical landscape*, University of Tennessee Press.

DENNING, Kathryn, 1999a, *On Archaeology and Alterity*, unpublished PhD thesis, University of Sheffield.

DENNING, Kathryn, 1999b, 'Apocalypse past/future: Archaeology and folklore, writ large', in C. Holtorf and A. Gazin-Schwartz (eds), *Archaeology and Folklore*, Routledge.

DEVEREUX, Paul, 1982, *Earth Lights: Towards an explanation of the UFO enigma*, Turnstone.

DEVEREUX, Paul, 1989, *Earth Lights Revelation: UFOs and mystery lightform phenomena – the Earth's secret energy force*, Blandford.

DEVEREUX, Paul, 1990, *Places of Power: Secret energies at ancient sites – a guide to observed or measured phenomena*, Batsford.

DEVEREUX, Paul, 1991, 'Three-dimensional aspects of apparent relationships

between selected natural and artificial features within the topography of the
Avebury complex', *Antiquity*, 65, 894–8.

DEVEREUX, Paul, 1992a, *Shamanism and the Mystery Lines: Ley lines, spirit paths,
shape-shifting and out-of-body travel*, Quantum.

DEVEREUX, Paul, 1992b, *Symbolic Landscapes: The dreamtime Earth and
Avebury's open secrets*, Gothic Image.

DEVEREUX, Paul, 2001a, *Stone Age Soundtracks: The acoustic archaeology of
ancient sites*, Vega.

DEVEREUX, Paul, 2001b, *Haunted Land: Investigations into ancient mysteries and
modern day phenomena*, Piatkus.

DEVEREUX, Paul, 2002a, *Living Ancient Wisdom: Understanding and using its
principles today*, Rider.

DEVEREUX, Paul, 2002b, 'Soundings', *3rd Stone*, 44, 28–32.

DEVEREUX, Paul, 2004a, 'Dragon dreams', *Fortean Times*, 178, 30–5.

DEVEREUX, Paul, 2004b, 'Spirits in the stones', *Fortean Times*, 188, 46–50.

DEVEREUX, Paul and R.G. JAHN, 1996, 'Preliminary investigations and cognitive
considerations of the acoustical resonances of selected archaeological sites',
Antiquity, 70 (269), 665–6.

DICKINSON, Bob, 1990a, 'Sacred resonance', *Markstone*, 4, 12–16.

DICKINSON, Bob, 1990b, 'Sounding the landscape', *Markstone*, 4, 17–21.

DICKINSON, Bob, 1998a, 'Sounding the landscape', *At the Edge*, 9, 33–7.

DICKINSON, Bob, 1998b, Text Music Website; www.indigogroup.co.uk/txtmusic/

DICKINSON, Bob, 2001, *Music and the Earth Spirit*, Capall Bann.

DILLON, Matthew, 1997, *Pilgrims and Pilgrimage in Ancient Greece*, Routledge.

DRAYTON, Penny, 1995, 'Oxhide myths', *Mercian Mysteries*, 22, 9–13. Online at
www.indigogroup.co.uk/oxhide1.htm

DRYDEN, Alice, (ed), 1911, *Memorials of Old Leicestershire*, George Allen.

EADE, John and Michael J. SALLNOW (eds), 1991, *Contesting the Sacred: The
anthropology of Christian pilgrimage*, Routledge.

EARLE, F., A. DEARLING, H. WHITTLE, R. GLASSE AND GUBBY, 1994, *A Time to
Travel? An introduction to Britain's newer travellers*, Enabler.

EDMONDS, Mark, 1999, *Ancestral Geographies of the Neolithic: Landscape,
monuments and memory*, Routledge.

ELIADE, Mircea, 1964, *Shamanism: Archaic techniques of ecstasy*, RKP.

EVANS, John G., 1999, *Land and Archaeology: Histories of human environment in
the British Isles*, Tempus.

FAGG, Bernard, 1957, 'Rock gongs and slides', *Man*, 57, 30–2.

FELD, Steven, 1982, *Sound and Sentiment: Birds, weeping, poetics and song in
Kaluli expression*, University of Pennsylvania Press.

FIDLER, J. Havelock, 1983, *Ley Lines: Their properties and properties – a dowser's
investigation*, Turnstone.

FIELD, David, 2003, 'Great sites: Silbury Hill', *British Archaeology*, 70, 14–17.

FLEMING, Andrew, 1988, *The Dartmoor Reaves*, Batsford.

FLEMING, Andrew, 1999, 'Phenomenology and the megaliths of Wales: a
dreaming too far?', *Oxford Journal of Archaeology*, 18:2, 119.

FORD, Susan, 1991, 'Landscape revisited: a feminist reappraisal', in C. Philo (ed), *New Word, New Worlds: Reconceptualising social and cultural geography*, St David's University College.

FOSTER, Robert Fitzroy, 1988, *Modern Ireland: 1600–1972*, Allen Lane.

FOUCAULT, Michel, 1980, 'Questions on geography', in C. Gordon (ed.) *M. Foucault: Power/knowledge*, Pantheon.

FOWLER, Peter, 1995, 'Writing on the countryside', in I. Hodder *et al* (eds), *Interpreting Archaeology: Finding meaning in the past*, Routledge.

GADON, Elinor W., 1991, 'Sacred places of India: The body of the goddess', in Swan 1991.

GELL, Alfred, 1995, 'The language of the forest: landscape and phonological iconism in Umeda', in E. Hirsch and M. O'Hanlon (eds), *The Anthropology of Landscape: Perspectives on place and space*, Oxford UP.

GELLING, Margaret, 1984, *Place-names in the Landscape*, Dent.

GELLING, Margaret, 1988, *Sign posts to the Past: Place-names and the history of England*, Philimore.

GELLING, M. and A. COLE, 2000, *The Landscape of Place-names*, Shaun Tyas.

GIBSON, Alex, 1998, 'Introduction', in A. Gibson and D. Simpson, *Prehistoric Ritual and Religion*, Sutton Publishing.

GIBSON, A. and D. SIMPSON, 1998, *Prehistoric Ritual and Religion*, Sutton Publishing.

GIMBUTAS, Marija, 1974, *The Goddesses and Gods of Old Europe*, Thames and Hudson.

GOODY, Jack, 1977, 'Against "ritual": loosely structured thoughts on a loosely defined topic', in S.F. Moore and B.G. Myerhoff (eds), *Secular Ritual*, Van Gorcum.

GOMBRICH, Ernst Hans, 1966, 'The Renaissance theory of art and the rise of landscape' (first published in 1950), in E. Gombrich (ed) *Norm and Form: Studies in the art of the Renaissance*, Phaidon.

GOW, Peter, 1995, 'Land, people and paper in western Amazonia', in E. Hirsch and M. O'Hanlon (eds), *The Anthropology of Landscape: Perspectives on place and space*, Oxford UP.

GRAVES, Tom, 1978, *Needles of Stone*, Garnstone.

GRAVES, Tom, 1991, 'Energy Dowsing: Muddling with the meta-pattern', *The Ley Hunter*, 113, 1–6.

GREEN, Marian, 1991, *A Witch Alone: Thirteen moons to master natural magic*, Aquarian [page reference to Thorsons 1995 edition].

GRIGSON, Geoffrey, 1958, *Looking and Finding: and collecting and reading and investigating and much else*, Phoenix House.

GRIGSON, Geoffrey, 1966, *The Shell Country Alphabet*, Michael Joseph.

GRINSELL, Leslie V., 1936, *The Ancient Burial-Mounds of England*, Methuen.

GRINSELL, Leslie V., 1976, *Folklore of Prehistoric Sites in Britain*, David and Charles.

GYRUS (Steve Taylor), 2003, 'New developments in British rock art'. Online at http://norlonto.net/index.cfm/action/reviews.view/itemID/95/type/rvwsEvents

HALIFAX, Joan, 1979, *Shamanic Voices: A survey of visionary narratives*, Dutton.

HALSALL, Guy, 1997, 'Archaeology and historiography', in M. Bentley (ed), *Companion to Historiography*, Routledge.

HAMMOND, Norman and Matthew R. BOBO, 1994, 'Pilgrimage's last mile: Late Maya monumental veneration at La Milpa, Belize', in James Graham-Campbell, *Archaeology of Pilgrimage* (*World Archaeology* 26:1, 1–18), Routledge.

HARDING, Jan, 2003, *Henge Monuments of the British Isles*, Tempus.

HARNER, Michael, 1980, *The Way of the Shaman: A guide to power and healing*, Harper and Row.

HARTE, Jeremy, 1998, *Alternative Approaches to Folklore 1969–1996*, Heart of Albion. Available for free download from www.hoap.co.uk

HARTE, Jeremy, 1999, *Research in Geomancy 1990–1994: Readings in sacred space* (2nd edn), Heart of Albion. Available for free download from www.hoap.co.uk

HARVEY, Graham, 1997, *Listening People, Speaking Earth: Contemporary paganism*, Hust.

HAWKES, Jacquetta, 1951, *A Land*, Cresset.

HAWKES, Jacquetta, 1967, 'God in the machine', *Antiquity*, 41, 174–80.

HAWKINS, Gerald S., 1965, *Stonehenge Decoded*, Souvenir.

HAWKINS, Gerald S. and Vance TIEDE, 2004, 'Stonehenge computer', *British Archaeology*, 74, 20–21.

HAYMAN, Richard, 1997, *Riddles in Stone: Myths, archaeology and the ancient Britons*, Hambledon.

HEAD, Sarah J., 2002, 'Visiting sacred wells', *The Cauldron*, 105, 29–31.

HEAWORD, Rose, 2004, 'Watkins: the richest legacy', *Northern Earth*, 100, 11–14.

HESELTON, Philip, 1991, *The Elements of Earth Mysteries*, Element.

HESIOD, 1983, *Theogony* (translation by A.N. Athanassakis), Johns Hopkins University Press.

HEATH-STUBBS, John, 1984, 'The heros as a saint: St George', in H.R.E. Davidson (ed), *The Hero in Tradition and Folklore*, Folklore Society.

HEWISON, Robert, 1987, *The Heritage Industry*, Methuen.

HIRSCH, Eric, 1995, 'Introduction: Landscape – between place and space', in E. Hirsch and M. O'Hanlon (eds), *The Anthropology of Landscape: Perspectives on place and space*, Oxford UP.

HIRSCH, E. and M. O'HANLON (eds), *The Anthropology of Landscape: Perspectives on place and space*, Oxford UP.

HITCHING, Francis, 1976, *Earth Magic*, Cassell.

HODDER, Ian, 1986, *Reading the Past: Current approaches to interpretation in archaeology*, Cambridge UP (2nd edn 1991).

HODDER, Ian, 1990, *The Domestication of Europe*, Blackwell.

HOLM, Jean and John BOWKER (eds), 1994, *Sacred Place*, Pinter.

HOLTORF, Cornelius, 2000, 'Paul Feyerabend. Towards a Democratic Relativism in Archaeology' in *Philosophy and Archaeological Practice*, C. Holtorf and H. Karlsson (eds), Bricoleur Press.

HOLTORF, Cornelius, 2002, 'Richard Bradley's approach to monuments' in *Monumental Past: A hypermedia exploration of megaliths*, online at https://tspace.library.utoronto.ca/citd/holtorf/6.1.html

HOLTORF, Cornelius, 2003, 'Vandalism and the meaning of monuments', *3rd Stone*, 45, 64–5.

HOLTORF, Cornelius, 2004, 'Arkeologi som samprojekt' (with illustrations by Quentin Drew), in P. Andersson and S. Welinder (eds), *Mellan Thomsen och Däniken Oenig diskussion kring alternativ arkeologi*, Bricoleur. Original paper presented in English, 'Archaeology as a shared project', Från Thomsen till Däniken Workshop om alternativ arkeologi, Härnosand, Sweden (October 2003), unpublished.

HOSKIN, Michael, 2001, *Tombs, Temples and their Orientations: A new perspective on Mediterranean prehistory*, Ocarina.

HOSKINS, W.G.,1955, *The Making of the English Landscape*, Hodder and Stoughton.

HOSKINS, W.G. and C. TAYLOR, 1988, *The Making of the English Landscape* (revised edition), Hodder and Stoughton.

HOWARD, Michael, 1994, *Angels and Goddesses: Celtic Christianity and paganism in ancient Britain*, Capall Bann.

HOWKINS, Alun, 1986, 'The discovery of rural England' in Robert Colls and Philip Dodd, *Englishness: Politics and culture 1880–1920*, Croom Helm.

HOWKINS, Alun and C. Ian Dyck, 1987, '"The time's alteration": popular ballads, rural radicalism and William Cobbett', *History Workshop Journal,* 23, 20–38.

HUMPHREY, Caroline, 1995, 'Chiefly and shamanist landscapes in Mongolia', in E. Hirsch and M. O'Hanlon (eds), *The Anthropology of Landscape: Perspectives on place and space*, Oxford UP.

HUNTER, Michael 1996, *Preserving the Past: The rise of heritage in modern Britain*, Alan Sutton.

HUTTON, Ronald, 1991, *The Pagan Religions of the Ancient British Isles: Their nature and legacy*, Basil Blackwell.

HUTTON, Ronald, 1993, *The Shamans of Siberia*, Isle of Avalon.

HUTTON, Ronald, 1996, *The Stations of the Sun: A history of the ritual year in Britain*, Oxford UP.

HUTTON, Ronald, 1998, 'The Discovery of the Modern Goddess', in J. Pearson, R.H. Roberts and G. Samuel (eds), *Nature Religion Today: Paganism in the Modern World*, Edinburgh UP.

HUTTON, Ronald, 1999, *The Triumph of the Moon: A history of modern pagan witchcraft*, Oxford UP.

JAHN, Robert George, 1995, 'The old stones speak', *The Ley Hunter*, 123, 1–8.

JAHN, R.G., P. DEVEREAUX, M. IBSON, 1996, 'Acoustical resonances of assorted ancient structures', *Journal of the Acoustical Society of America*, 99:2.

JAYNES, Julian, 1976, *The Origin of Consciousness in the Breakdown of the Bicameral Mind*, Houghton Mifflin.

JOHNSTON, Robert, 1998, 'Approaches to the perception of landscape: philosophy, theory, methodology', *Archaeological Dialogues*, 5, 54–68.

JOLLY, Karen Louise, 1996, *Popular Religion in Late Saxon England*, University of North Carolina Press.

JONES, Leslie Ellen, 2001, 'Everybody must get stoned… : Megaliths and movies', *3rd Stone* 40, 6-14. (Completists should also see *3rd Stone* 41 p5 and p59 for obscure movies-with-megaliths missed from Jones' survey.)

KAISER, David, 2003, 'Sacred Preseli', *3rd Stone*, 43, 34–7.

KEDAR, B.Z. and R.J.Z. WERBLOWSKY (eds), 1998, *Sacred Space: Shrine, city, land*, New York UP.

KEITH, William J., 1975, *The Rural Tradition: William Cobbett, Gilbert White and other non-fiction prose writers of the English countryside*, Harvester/University of Toronto Press.

KELLEY, Klara Bonsack and Harris FRANCIS, 1994, *Navajo Sacred Places*, Indiana UP.

KEESING, Roger, 1982, *Kwaio Religion: The living and the dead in a Solomon Island society*, Columbia UP.

KIMMIS, Jim, 2004, 'Places, people and perception: a model?', *Northern Earth*, 100, 23–5.

KITCHIN, Rob and Mark BLADES, 2002, *The Cognition of Geographic Space*, Tauris.

KLIMO, Jon, 1987, *Channeling*, Tarcher. (Published in UK as *Psychics, Prophets and Mystics: Receiving information from paranormal sources*, Aquarian, 1991.)

KNAPP, A. Bernard and Wendy ASHMORE, 1999, 'Archaeological landscapes: constructed, conceptualized and ideational' in W. Ashmore and A.B. Knapp (eds), *Archaeologies of Landscape: Contemporary perspectives*, Berg.

KRIPPNER, Stanley, Paul DEVEREUX and Adam FISH, 2003, 'The use of the Strauch scale to study dream reports from sacred sites in England and Wales', *Dreaming*, 13:2.

LACHMAN, Gary Valentine, 2001, *Turn Off Your Mind: The mystic Sixties and the dark side of the Age of Aquarius*, Sidgwick and Jackson.

LACHMAN, Gary Valentine, 2003, *A Secret History of Consciousness*, Lindisfarne.

LAQUEUR, T, 1994, 'Memory and naming in the Great War', in J. Gillis (ed.), *Commemorations: The politics of national identity*, Princeton UP.

LARKMAN, Brian and Philip HESELTON, 1985, *Earth Mysteries: An exploratory introduction*, Northern Earth Mysteries Group.

LAWLOR, Anthony, 1994, *The Temple in the House: Finding the sacred in everyday architecture*, Tarcher Putnam.

LAWSON, Graeme, 2003, paper at Acoustics, Space and Intentionality conference, MacDonald Institute, Cambridge, 27–29 June.

LEFEBVRE, Henri, 1991, *The Production of Space*, Blackwell (1st publ. in French 1974).

LETCHER, Andy, 2000, '"Virtual paganism" or direct action? The implications of road protesting for modern paganism', *Diskus*, 6. Online at www.uni-marburg.de/religionswissenschaft/journal/diskus

LETCHER, Andy, 2001, 'The scouring of the Shire: fairies, trolls and pixies in eco-protest culture', *Folklore*, 112, 147–161.

LETHBRIDGE, Tom, 1957, *Gogmagog: The buried gods*, RKP.

LETHBRIDGE, Tom, 1961, *Ghost and Ghoul*, RKP.

LETHBRIDGE, Tom, 1976, *The Power of the Pendulum*, RKP

LEWIS-WILLIAMS, J.D., 2002, *The Mind in the Cave,* Thames and Hudson.

LEWIS-WILLIAMS, J.D. and T.A. DOWSON, 1988, 'The signs of the times: entoptic phenomena in Upper Palaeolithic art', *Current Anthropology,* 29 (2), 201–45.

LODGE, Sir Oliver, 1925, *Ether and Reality: A series of discourses on the many functions of the ether of space*, Hodder and Stoughton.

LONEGREN, Sig, 2004, 'The role of dowsing in the future of earth mysteries', *Northern Earth*, 100, 15–19.

LOVELOCK, James, 1979, *Gaia: A new look at life on Earth*, Oxford UP.

LOW, Mary, 1996, *Celtic Christianity and Nature: Early Irish and Hebridean traditions*, Edinburgh UP.

LOWE, Philip, 1986, *Countryside Conflicts*, Gower.

LOWENTHAL, David, 1985, *The Past is a Foreign Country,* Cambridge UP.

LOWENTHAL, David, 1996, *The Heritage Crusade,* Free Press.

LUNDQUIST, John M., 1993, *The Temple: Meeting place of heaven and Earth*, Thames and Hudson.

LYLE, Emily (ed), *Sacred Architecture in the Traditions of India, China, Judaism and Islam, (Cosmos* 8), Edinburgh UP.

MABEY, Richard, 1980, *The Common Ground*, Hutchinson.

MACDERMOTT, Mercia, 2003, *Explore Green Men*, Heart of Albion.

MCKAY, George, 1996, *Senseless Acts of Beauty: Cultures of resistance since the Sixties*, Verso.

MACLELLAN, Gordon, 1996, 'Dancing on the edge: shamanism in modern Britain' in G. Harvey and C. Hardman (eds), *Paganism Today: Wiccans, Druids, the Goddess and ancient earth traditions for the twenty-first century*, Thorsons.

MCMANAMON, Francis, 2000, 'Archaeological messages and messengers', *Public Archaeology,* 1, 5–20.

MAIN, Lawrence, 1994, 'A sleeping angel, goddess and giant', *The Ley Hunter,* 122, 34–5.

MALONE, Caroline, 1989, *Avebury*, Batsford/English Heritage.

MANDLER, Peter, 1997a, *The Fall and Rise of the Stately Home*, Yale UP.

MANDLER, Peter, 1997b, 'Against "Englishness": English culture and the limits to rural nostalgia 1850–1940', *Transactions of the Royal Historical Society* 6th series, 7.

MARSH, Jan, 1982, *Back to the Land: The pastoral impulse in England, from 1880 to 1914*, Quartet Books.

MATTHEWS, John, 1991, *The Celtic Shaman: A handbook*, Element.

MAVOR, James W. and Byron E. DIX, 1989, *Manitou: The sacred landscape of New England's native civilization*, Inner Traditions International.

MEINIG, D.W., 1979, 'The beholding eye: ten versions of the same scene', in D.W. Meinig (ed), *The Interpretation of Ordinary landscapes: Geographical essays*, Oxford UP.

MESKELL, Lynn, 1995, 'Goddesses, Gimbutas and New Age archaeology', *Antiquity,* 69, 74–86.

MESKELL, Lynn, 1999, 'Feminism, paganism, pluralism', in C. Holtorf and A. Gazin-Schwartz (eds), *Archaeology and Folklore*, Routledge.

MICHELL, John, 1969, *The View Over Atlantis*, Sago.

MICHELL, John, 1970, 'Alfred Watkins: a note', in A. Watkins *The Old Straight Track*, Sago.

MICHELL, John, 1977, *A Little History of Astro-Archaeology*, Thames and Hudson.

MOLYNEAUX, Brian Leigh and Piers VITEBSKY, 2001, *Sacred Earth, Sacred Stones*, Duncan Baird.

MOORE, Michael J.,1995, 'A bronze age settlement and ritual centre in the Monavullagh Mountains, County Waterford, Ireland', *Proceedings of the Prehistoric Society*, 61, 191–244.

MORPHY, Howard, 1991, *Ancestral Connections: Art and the Aboriginal system of knowledge*, University of Chicago Press.

MORPHY, Howard, 1993, 'Colonialism, history and the construction of place: the politics of landscape in northern Australia', in B. Bender (ed), *Landscape: Politics and perspectives*, Berg.

MORPHY, Howard, 1994, 'Landscape and the reproduction of the ancestral past', in E. Hirsch and M. O'Hanlon (eds), *The Anthropology of Landscape: Perspectives on place and space*, Oxford UP.

MORRIS, Michael, 1992, 'The rise and fall of Bronze Age studies in England 1840–1960', *Antiquity*, 66 (251), 419–26.

MORTIMER, Neil, 2003, 'Acoustics, space and intentionality: McDonald Institute, Cambridge, 27–29 June 2003', *3rd Stone*, 47, 7.

NEWBY, Howard, 1988, *The Countryside in Question*, Hutchinson.

NOBLE, Gordon, 2003, 'Islands and the Neolithic revolution', *British Archaeology*, 71, 21–2.

NORTH, John, 1996, *Stonehenge: Neolithic man and the cosmos*, HarperCollins.

OBLEKEVICH, James, 1976, *Religion and Rural Society: South Lindsey 1825–1875*, Clarendon.

OLIVIER, E., 1951, *Wiltshire*, Hale.

OLWIG, Kenneth, 1984, *Nature's Ideological Landscape: A literary and geographic perspective on its development and preservation on Denmark's Jutland heath*, George Allen and Unwin.

OLWIG, Kenneth, 1993, 'Sexual cosmology: nation and landscape at the conceptual interstices of nature and culture; or, what does landscape really mean', in B. Bender (ed), *Landscape: Politics and perspectives*, Berg.

ONG, Walter J., 1982, *Orality and literacy*, Methuen.

PARKER PEARSON, Mike and Colin RICHARDS, 1994, *Architecture and Order: Approaches to social space*, Routledge.

PATTON, Mark, 1993, *Statements in Stone: Monuments and society in Neolithic Brittany*, Routledge.

PENNICK, Nigel, 1969, 'Geomancy', in *The Other Britain: A record of pre-Doomsday resistance*, published as a supplement to *Cambridge Voice*, series 2 No. 4.

PENNICK, Nigel, 1979, *The Ancient Science of Geomancy*, Thames and Hudson.

PENNICK, Nigel, 1995, *The Oracle of Geomancy: The divinatory arts of Raml, Geomantia, Síkídy and I Ching*, Capall Bann.

PENNICK, Nigel, 1997, 'Leys as ideology', *At the Edge*, 7, 1–3.

PENNICK, Nigel and Paul DEVEREUX, 1989, *Lines on the Landscape: Leys and other linear enigmas*, Hale.

PENNY. A. and J. WOOD, 1973, 'The Dorset Cursus complex: a Neolithic astronomical observatory?', *Archaeological Journal*, 130, 44–76.

PITTS, Mike, 2001, *Hengeworld* (2nd edn), Arrow.

PITTS, M. and J. RICHARDS, 2003, 'A future for Stonehenge', *Current Archaeology*, 185, 197–201.

PLUSKOWSKI, Aleks, 2002, 'Mapping neo-medieval forests in the popular Western imagination', *3d Stone*, 44, 22–7.

POLLARD, J and A. Reynolds, 2002, *Avebury: The biography of a landscape*, Tempus.

PRENDERGAST, Kate, 2003, 'Neolithic solar ritual at Stonehenge: mad midsummer or bleak midwinter?', *3rd Stone*, 45, 38–43.

PRIOR, Francis, 1996, 'Archaeology and the public'; British Archaeological Awards lecture. Online at http://briac3.britac.ac.uk/cba/prjects/baalect.html

PYE-SMITH, Charlie and Chris ROSE, 1980, *Crisis and Conservation*, Penguin.

QUINN, Phil, 1999, *Holy Wells of Bath and Bristol Region*, Logaston.

RACKHAM, Oliver, 1986 *The History of the Countryside*, Dent.

RAFTERY, Barry, 1994, Pagan Celtic Ireland: The enigma of the Irish Iron Age, Thames and Hudson.

RAMSEY, David A., 2002, *Time Line... Old John* (2nd edn), Bradgate Books.

RATTUE, James, 1995, *The Living Stream: Holy wells in historical context*, Boydell.

R.C.H.M.E., 1979, *Stonehenge and its Environs: Monuments and land use*, Edinburgh UP.

RENFREW, Colin, 1994, 'Towards a cognitive archaeology', in C. Renfrew (ed.) *The Ancient Mind*, Cambridge UP.

RICHARDS, Julian, 1984, 'The development of the Neolithic landscape in the environs of Stonehenge', in R. Bradley and J. Gardiner (eds), *Neolithic Studies*, BAR.

RICHARDS, Julian, 1990, *The Stonehenge Environs Project*, English Heritage Archaeological Report 16.

RICHARDS, Julian, 1991, *Stonehenge*, Batsford/English Heritage.

RICHARDSON, R.C., 2004, 'William Camden and the re-discovery of England', *Transactions of the Leicestershire Archaeological and Historical Society*, 78, 108–123.

RIPPON, Stephen, 2004, *Historic Landscape Analysis: Deciphering the countryside by Stephen Rippon*, Council for British Archaeology.

ROBERTS, Andy, 'A saucer full of secrets', *Magonia*, 87, 3–8.

ROBINS, Don, 1985, *Circles of Silence*, Souvenir.

ROMANO, Jack, 2002, 'Beyond archaeology: Tom Lethbridge', *3rd Stone*, 44, 16–21.

RONEY-DOUGAL, Serena, 1991, *Where Science and Magic Meet*, Element.

RONEY-DOUGAL, S. and G. VOGL, 1993, 'Some speculations on the effects of geomagnetism on the pineal gland', *Journal of the Society for Psychical Research*, 59 (830).

ROTHWELL, Peter and Christopher MARTYN, 2000, 'Reproducibility of peer review in clinical neuroscience. Is agreement between reviewers any greater than would be expected by chance alone?', *Brain,* 123, 1964–9.

ROTMAN, Deborah L. and Ellen-Rose SAVULIS (eds), 2003, *Shared Spaces and Divided Places: Material dimensions of gender relations and the American historical landscape,* University of Tennessee Press.

SAMUEL, Raphael, 1994, *Theatres of Memory: Past and present in contemporary culture,* Verso.

SANDELL, Roger, 1988, 'Notes towards a social history of ley-hunting', *Magonia,* 29, 3–7.

SCHAMA, Simon, 1995, *Landscape and Memory*, Harper Collins.

SCHULZE, Gerhard, 1993, *Die Erlebnis-Gesellschaft. Kultursoziologie der Gegenwart,* 3rd edition, Campus.

SCREETON, Paul, 1974, *Quicksilver Heritage: The mystic leys – their legacy of ancient wisdom*, Thorsons.

SCREETON, Paul, 1984–5, 'Seekers of the Linear Vision', serialised in *Stonehenge Viewpoint* no's 44 to 51.

SCREETON, Paul, 1993, *Seekers of the Linear Vision including The Science of Ley Hunting* by Donald L. Cyr, Stonehenge Viewpoint.

SCHREIBER, Laurel and John NICHOLSON, 1987, *An English Figure*, Bozo.

SCULLY, Vincent, 1979, *The Earth, the Temple and the Gods: Greek sacred architecture*, Yale UP (3rd edn; 1st edn 1962).

SEMPLE, Sarah, 1998, 'A fear of the past: the place of the prehistoric burial mound in the ideology of middle and later Anglo-Saxon England', *World Archaeology,* 30:1 (*The Past in the Past*), 109–26.

SHANKS, Michael, 1992, *Experiencing the Past: On the character of archaeology,* Routledge.

SHANKS, Michael, 1997, 'Introduction', in I. Hodder *et al* (eds), *Interpreting Archaeology: Finding meaning in the past*, Routledge.

SHANKS, M and C. TILLEY, 1987, *Re-constructing Archaeology*, Cambridge UP.

SHELDRAKE, Rupert, 1989, 'Life in a living world', *Beshara,* 10.

SHELDRAKE, Philip, 2001, *Spaces for the Sacred*, SCM Press.

SHOARD, Marion, 1980, *The Theft of the Countryside*, Temple Smith.

SHOARD, Marion, 1998, *This Land is Our Land*, Paladin.

SILVERMAN, Helaine, 1994 'The archaeological identification of an ancient Peruvian pilgrimage center', in James Graham-Campbell, *Archaeology of Pilgrimage (World Archaeology* 26:1, 1–18), Routledge.

SKEATES, Robin, 2000, *Debating the Archaeological Heritage*, Duckworth.

SOLOMON, Anne, 1997, 'The myth of ritual origins? Ethnography, mythology and interpretation of San rock art', *South African Archaeological Bulletin,*165, 1–11.

SOUDEN, David, 1997, *Stonehenge Revealed*, Facts on File.

STOLLER, Paul, 1989, *The Taste of Ethnographic Things: The sense in anthropology,* University of Pennsylvania Press.

STONE, Christopher James, 1996, *Fierce Dancing,* Faber and Faber.

STONE, Alby, 1998, *Straight Track, Crooked Road: Leys, spirit paths and shamanism,* Heart of Albion.

STONE, Alby, 2003, *Explore Shamanism,* Heart of Albion.

STOUT, Adam, 2001, 'Making the past: the politics of prehistory', *3rd Stone,* 40, 34–42.

STOUT, Adam, 2003, 'The world turned upside down: Stonehenge's summer solstice before the hippies', *3rd Stone,* 46, 38–42.

STRONG, Roy, 1996, *Country Life: 1897–1997: The English arcadia,* Boxtree.

SWAN, James A., 1990, *Sacred Places: How the living Earth seeks our friendship,* Bear and Co.

SWAN, James A., (ed), 1991, *The Power of Place: Sacred ground in natural and human Environments,* Quest; reprinted Gateway 1993.

TAÇON, P.S.C., 1994, 'Socialising landscapes: the long-term implications of signs, symbols and marks on the land', in L. Head, C. Gosden and J.P. White (eds), *Social Landscapes,* Archaeology in Oceania, 29 (3), 117–29.

TAYLOR, David, 1993, 'Earthing the paranormal', *Mercian Mysteries,* 17, 12–13.

THOMAS, Keith, 1983, *Man and the Natural World: Changing attitudes in England 1500–1800,* Allen Lane.

THOMAS, Julian, 1991, *Rethinking the Neolithic,* Cambridge UP.

THOMAS, Julian, 1993, 'The politics of vision and the archaeologies of landscape', in B. Bender (ed), *Landscape: Politics and perspectives,* Berg.

THOMAS, Julian, 2004, *Archaeology and Modernity,* Routledge.

TILLEY, Christopher, 1993, 'Art, architecture, landscape [Neolithic Sweden]', in B. Bender (ed), *Landscape: Politics and perspectives,* Berg.

TILLEY, Christopher, 1994, *A Phenomenology of Landscape: Places, paths and monuments,* Berg.

THOM, Alexander, 1967, *Megalithic Sites in Britain,* Clarendon.

THORN, Richard, 1997, 'Hearing is believing', *Resonance,* 5:2, 11–14 (reprinted *At the Edge,* 9 (1998), 27–32.

TOTH, N, D. CLARK and G. LIGABUE, 1992, 'The last stone axe makers', *Scientific American,* 261, 66–71.

TRUBSHAW, Bob, 1991a, *Standing Stones and Mark Stones of Leicestershire and Rutland,* Heart of Albion.

TRUBSHAW, Bob, 1991b, 'Does magnetism distort your dreams?', *Mercian Mysteries,* 6, 30–1.

TRUBSHAW, Bob, 1991c, 1991, 'Losing my innocence in Wiltshire', *Touchwood* 4:13; reprinted in *Mercian Mysteries* 18 (1994), 25–26, and *Towards 2012,* 4 & 5 (1998), 7–8. Online at norlonto.net/index.cfm?action=articles.view&itemID=81

TRUBSHAW, Bob, 1992, 'Magnetism does distort your dreams', *Mercian Mysteries,* 10, 21–4.

TRUBSHAW, Bob, 1993, 'Dowsing – the good, the bad and the muddled', *Mercian Mysteries,* 15, 26–29. Online at www.indigogroup.co.uk/edge/dowsing.htm

TRUBSHAW, Bob, 1994a, 'Landscapes and mindscapes', *Mercian Mysteries,* 19, 1–5. Online at www.indigogroup.co.uk/edge/mindscap.htm

TRUBSHAW, Bob, 1994b, 'Monuments as ideas', *Mercian Mysteries,* 21, 1–3. Online at www,indigogroup.co.uk/edge/monument.htm

TRUBSHAW, Bob, 1994c, 'Them and us', *The Ley Hunter,*120, 17–19.

TRUBSHAW, Bob, 1995, 'The metaphors and rituals of place and time: an introduction to liminality', *Mercian Mysteries,* 22, 1–8. Online at www.indigogroup.co.uk/edge/liminal.htm

TRUBSHAW, Bob, 1996a, 'Who's fringe now?', *Assemblage,*1. Online at www.shef.ac.uk/assem.trub2.html

TRUBSHAW, Bob, 1996b, 'The fifth direction: sacred centres in Ireland', *At the Edge,* 2, 14–19. Online at www.indigogroup.co.uk/edge/5dirns.htm

TRUBSHAW, Bob, 1997a, 'Cosmic homes', *At the Edge,* 5, 13–16.

TRUBSHAW, Bob, 1997b, 'Beyond Indiana Jones *versus* the Mother Goddess', *At the Edge,* 6, 1–5. Online at www.indigogroup.co.uk/edge/beyondig.htm

TRUBSHAW, Bob, 1997c, 'Making time', *At the Edge,* 7, 26–30. Online at www.indigogroup.co.uk/edge/makingt.htm

TRUBSHAW, Bob, 2002, *Explore Folklore,* Heart of Albion.

TRUBSHAW, Bob, 2003a, *Explore Mythology,* Heart of Albion.

TRUBSHAW, Bob, 2003b, 'Dream incubation', *3rd Stone,* 46, 24–7.

TRUBSHAW, Bob, 2003c, 'Geomagnetism: from dream incubation to dowsing', *3rd Stone,* 47, 32–7

TUAN, Yi-Fu, 1974, *Topophilia: A study of environmental perception, attitudes and values,* Prentice-Hall.

TUAN, Yi-Fu, 1977, *Space and Place: The perspective of experience,* Edward Arnold.

TUAN, Yi-Fu, 1986, 'Strangers and strangeness', *Geographical Review,* 76, 10–19.

TUNBRIDGE, Dorothy, 1988, *Flinders Range Dreaming,* Aboriginal Studies Press.

TURNER, V., 1974, 'Pilgrimages as social processes', in V. Turner (ed), *Dramas, Fields and Metaphors,* Cornell UP.

TURNER, V., 1979, *Process, Performance and Pilgrimage: A study in comparative symbology,* Concept.

TURNER, V. and E. TURNER, 1978, *Image and Pilgrimage in Christian Culture: Anthropological perspectives,* Columbia UP.

UCKO, P., M. Hunter, A.J. Clark and A. David, 1991, *Avebury Reconsidered: From the 1660s to the 1990s,* Unwin Hyman.

UNDERWOOD, Guy, 1969, *The Pattern of the Past,* Museum Press.

VAYNE, Julian, 2003, 'Holding back the years', *The Cauldron,* 107, 12–16.

VENKATESH, M.R., 2004, 'In Shiva's temple, pillars make music', *Telegraph India,* July 26.

VOSS, Jerome A., 1987, 'Antiquity imagined: cultural values in archaeological folklore', *Folklore,* 98(1), 80–90.

WAGSTAFF, J. Malcolm, (ed), 1987, *Landscape and Culture,* Blackwell.

WALLER, Steven, 1993a, 'Sound and rock art', *Nature*, 363, 501.

WALLER, Steven, 1993b, 'Sound reflection as an explanation for the content and context of rock art', *Rock Art Research*, 10:2, 91–101.

WALLIS, Robert J., 2000, 'Queer shamans: autoarchaeology and neo-shamanism', *World Archaeology*, 32(2) (*Queer Archaeologies*), 252–62.

WALLIS, Robert J., 2001, 'Waking ancestor spirits: neo-shamanic engagements with archaeology', in N. Price (ed), *The Archaeology of Shamanism*, Routledge.

WALLIS, Robert J., 2003, *Shamans/Neo-Shamans: Ecstasies, alternative archaeologies and contemporary pagans*, Routledge.

WALLIS, R.J. and J. BLAIN, 2003, 'Site, sacredness, and stories: interactions of archaeology and contemporary paganism', *Folklore*, 114, 307–21.

WALLIS, R.J. and K. LYMER, 2001, 'Introduction', in R.J. Wallis and K. Lymer (eds), *A Permeability of Boundaries? New approaches to the archaeology of art, religion and folklore*, BAR International Series 936.

WATKINS, Alfred, 1922, *Early British0Trackways, Moats, Mounds, Camps and Sites*, Simpkin, Marshall, Hamilton, Kent and Co.

WATKINS, Alfred, 1925, *The Old Straight Track: Its mounds, beacons, moats, sites and mark stones*, Methuen.

WATSON, W. and D. KEATING, 1999, 'Architecture and sound: an acoustic analysis of megalithic monuments in prehistoric Britain', *Antiquity*, 73 (280), 325–36.

WATSON, W. and D. KEATING, 2000, 'The architecture of sound in Neolithic Orkney', in A. Ritchie (ed) *Neolithic Orkney in its European Context*, McDonald Institute Monographs.

WESTWOOD, Jennifer, 1987, *Albion: A guide to legendary Britain*, Paladin.

WHEATLEY, Paul, 1971, *The Pivot of the Four Quarters: A preliminary enquiry into the origins and character of the ancient Chinese city*, Aldine.

WHITWORTH, Michael H., 2003, 'Physics: "a strange footprint"', in David Bradshaw (ed), *A Concise Companion to Modernism*, Blackwell.

WILK, Richard, 1985, 'The ancient Maya and the political present', *Journal of Anthropological Research*, 41, 307–26.

WILLIAMS, Howard, 1998, 'Monuments and the past in early Anglo-Saxon England', *World Archaeology*, 30:1 (*The Past in the Past*), 90–108.

WILLIAMS, Raymond, 1972, 'Ideas of Nature' in J. Benthall (ed), *Ecology, the Shaping Enquiry*, Longman; reprinted in Williams 1980.

WILLIAMS, Raymond, 1973, *The Country and the City*, Chatto and Windus; reprinted Hogarth Press 1985.

WILLIAMS, Raymond, 1980, *Problems in Materialism and Culture*, Verso.

WILLIAMS, Rosalind, 1990, *Notes on the Underground: An essay on technology, society and the imagination*, MIT Press.

WILLIAMSON, Tom and Liz BELLAMY, 1983, *Ley Lines in Question*. World's Work.

WILSON, C.B., 1992, 'Dwelling at the centre of the world', in E. Lyle (ed), *Sacred Architecture in the Traditions of India, China, Judaism and Islam*, (*Cosmos* 8), Edinburgh UP.

WILSON , Peter Lamborn, 1998, *Escape from the Nineteenth Century and other essays*, Autonomendia.

WILTON, Andrew and Anne LYLES, 1993, *The Great Age of British Watercolours 1750–1880*, Prestel.

WOOD, Chris, 2002, 'The meaning of Seahenge', *3rd Stone*, 43, 49–54.

WOOD, Christopher S., 1993, *Albrecht Altdorfer and the Origins of Landscape*, Reaktion.

WOOLF, Virginia, 1929, *Mrs Dalloway*, Tauchnitz.

WOOLF, Virginia, 1931, *The Waves*.

WOOLLEY, Mark, 1999, 'Beyond simulation: production and the nostalgia industry', *SSPP.net*, 2(1), www.sspp.net/archive/papers/2(1)woolley.htm

WORTHINGTON, Andy, 2002a, 'A brief history of the summer solstice at Stonehenge', *3rd Stone*, 42, 41–7.

WORTHINGTON, Andy, 2002b, 'No to menhirland! Conservation and conflict at Carnac', *3rd Stone*, 43, 40–4.

WORTHINGTON, Andy, 2002c, 'A Mediterranean madness: threats to Malta's Neolithic heritage', *3rd Stone*, 44, 52–6.

WORTHINGTON, Andy, 2004, *Stonehenge: Celebration and subversion*, Alternative Albion.

WRIGHT, Patrick, 1985, *On Living in an Old Country*, Verso.

WUNDERLICH, H.G., 1975, *The Secret of Crete*, Souvenir.

ZINTZEN, Christiane, 1998, *Von Pompeji nach Troja: Archäologie, literatur und ööffentlichkeit im 19. jahrhundert*, WUV Universitätsverlag.

Index

Places are listed under **country**.

3rd Stone xi, 81, 91, 103, 114

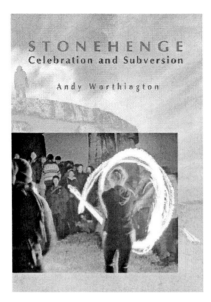

Stonehenge:
Celebration and Subversion

Andy Worthington

This innovative social history looks in detail at how the summer solstice celebrations at Stonehenge have brought together different aspects of British counter-culture to make the monument a 'living temple' and an icon of alternative Britain. The history of the celebrants and counter-cultural leaders is interwoven with the viewpoints of the land-owners, custodians and archaeologists who have generally attempted to impose order on the shifting patterns of these modern-day mythologies.

The story of the Stonehenge summer solstice celebrations begins with the Druid revival of the 18th century and the earliest public gatherings of the 19th and early 20th centuries. In the social upheavals of the 1960s and early 70s, these trailblazers were superseded by the Stonehenge Free Festival. This evolved from a small gathering to an anarchic free state the size of a small city, before its brutal suppression at the Battle of the Beanfield in 1985.

In the aftermath of the Beanfield, the author examines how the political and spiritual aspirations of the free festivals evolved into both the rave scene and the road protest movement, and how the prevailing trends in the counter-culture provided a fertile breeding ground for the development of new Druid groups, the growth of paganism in general, and the adoption of other sacred sites, in particular Stonehenge's gargantuan neighbour at Avebury.

The account is brought up to date with the reopening of Stonehenge on the summer solstice in 2000, the unprecedented crowds drawn by the new access arrangements, and the latest source of conflict, centred on a bitterly-contested road improvement scheme.

ISBN 1 872883 76 1
Perfect bound, 245 x 175 mm, 281 + xviii pages, 147 b&w photos, **£14.95**

Also from Heart of Albion Press

Myths of Reality

Simon Danser

'This liberal author's knowledge of contemporary society is amazingly broad. He exposits the mythic depths (and appearances) of everything from 'the myth of science' to superhero attitudes of contemporary American nationalism.

'Along the way he challenges many superficial trivialities about myths functioning in culture. He regards the mythic as a primary, highly effective agent of social ideology, and is never hesitant about demanding that the garments of our truly mythological capitalism are ill-fitting and socially harmful.

'This is the best book I know in terms of disclosing the pragmatic functioning of myth in society.'

William Doty, Professor Emeritus, The University of Alabama and author of *Mythography: The study of myths and rituals*

Simon Danser asks us to think of myths as like the lenses in spectacles – we see the world through them, but rarely see them in their own right. He then systematically focuses on the myths at the core of the belief systems which create every aspect of what we take to be reality: religion, politics, commerce, science, knowledge, consciousness, self-identity, and much else that we take as 'given'.

This book reveals how reality is culturally constructed in an ever-continuing process from mythic fragments transmitted by the mass media and adapted through face-to-face and Internet conversations.

Published by Alternative Albion, an imprint of Heart of Albion Press.
ISBN 1 872883 80 X. 215 x 175 mm, 205 + xiv pages, paperback. **£12.95**

Explore Mythology

Bob Trubshaw

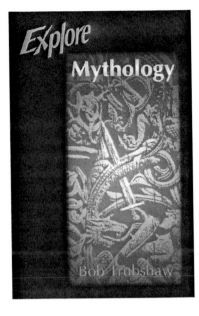

Myths are usually thought of as something to do with 'traditional cultures'. The study of such 'traditional' myths emphasises their importance in religion, national identity, hero-figures, understanding the origin of the universe, and predictions of an apocalyptic demise. The academic study of myths has done much to fit these ideas into the preconceived ideas of the relevant academics.

Only in recent years have such long-standing assumptions about myths begun to be questioned, opening up whole new ways of thinking about the way such myths define and structure how a society thinks about itself and the 'real world'.

These new approaches to the study of myth reveal that, to an astonishing extent, modern day thinking is every bit as 'mythological' as the world-views of, say, the Classical Greeks or obscure Polynesian tribes. Politics, religions, science, advertising and the mass media are all deeply implicated in the creation and use of myths.

Explore Mythology provides a lively introduction to the way myths have been studied, together with discussion of some of the most important 'mythic motifs' – such as heroes, national identity, and 'central places' – followed by a discussion of how these ideas permeate modern society. These sometimes contentious and profound ideas are presented in an easily readable style of writing.

ISBN 1 872883 62 1

Perfect bound. Demi 8vo (215 x 138 mm), 220 + xx pages, 17 line drawings. **£9.95**

Explore Shamanism

Alby Stone

Shamanism is a complex and confusing subject. There are many different ideas about what shamanism is, who is a shaman, and what a shaman does. *Explore Shamanism* provides a much-needed up-to-date guide to the study of shamanism.

Focusing mainly on the shamans of Siberia and Central Asia, *Explore Shamanism* includes a historical survey of academic approaches to shamanism, an overview of the various theories about shamanism, and a discussion of the origins of shamanism based on the latest ideas. There are also more detailed explorations of the initiation of shamans; the costumes, drums and other tools of the shaman's trade; journeys to the spirit world; and the place of trance, spirit possession and ecstasy in shamanic performance.

Explore Shamanism also surveys revived and reconstructed shamanisms in the world today.

Alby Stone has been studying and writing about shamanism for twenty years.

ISBN 1 872883 68 0.
Perfect bound, Demi 8vo (215 x 138 mm), 184 + x pages, 2 photographs; 17 line drawings, **£9.95**

Explore Folklore

Bob Trubshaw

'Highly Recommended'
by the Folklore Society's
Katharine Briggs Folklore Award 2003

**'A howling success, which plugs a big
and obvious gap'**
Professor Ronald Hutton

There have been fascinating developments in the study of folklore in the last twenty-or-so years, but few books about British folklore and folk customs reflect these exciting new approaches. As a result there is a huge gap between scholarly approaches to folklore studies and 'popular beliefs' about the character and history of British folklore. *Explore Folklore* is the first book to bridge that gap, and to show how much 'folklore' there is in modern day Britain.

Explore Folklore shows there is much more to folklore than morris dancing and fifty-something folksingers! The rituals of 'what we do on our holidays', funerals, stag nights and 'lingerie parties' are all full of 'unselfconscious' folk customs. Indeed, folklore is something that is integral to all our lives – it is so intrinsic we do not think of it as being 'folklore'.

The implicit ideas underlying folk lore and customs are also explored. There might appear to be little in common between people who touch wood for luck (a 'tradition' invented in the last 200 years) and legends about people who believe they have been abducted and subjected to intimate body examinations by aliens. Yet, in their varying ways, these and other 'folk beliefs' reflect the wide spectrum of belief and disbelief in what is easily dismissed as 'superstition'.

Explore Folklore provides a lively introduction to the study of most genres of British folklore, presenting the more contentious and profound ideas in a readily accessible manner.

ISBN 1 872883 60 5
Perfect bound, demi 8vo (215x138 mm), 200 pages, **£9.95**

Footprints in Stone

The significance of foot- and hand-prints and other imprints left by early men, giants, heroes, devils, saints, animals, ghosts, witches, fairies and monsters

Janet Bord

'A delightful exploration of a truly mysterious subject. 9 out of 10'
Bob Rickard *Fortean Times*

'Fascinating stuff and highly recommended.' Mike Howard *The Cauldron*

'... a good and wide-ranging first step into investigating the significance of the foot imprint.' John Billingsley *Northern Earth*

From the earliest humans to the present day, there has always been a compulsion to 'leave one's mark': early cave art includes thousands of hand outlines, while many churches in Britain have foot outlines inscribed in lead and stone. These two extremes span almost 30,000 years during which time all kinds of persons, real and legendary, have left visible traces of themselves. But 30,000 years ago seems almost recent, when compared with the finding of some (admittedly controversial) fossilized human footprints in rocks apparently contemporary with dinosaur footprints that are tens of millions of years old.

Most of the footprints – and hand-prints, knee-prints, and impressions of other body parts – are clearly not real, having allegedly been impressed into rocks around the world by such high-profile figures as the Buddha, Vishnu, Jesus Christ, and the Virgin Mary, as well as a vast panoply of saints, whose footprint traces and associated stories occupy two chapters. Their horses also left hoof-prints, and other animals are represented too. Not surprisingly, the ubiquitous Devil has a whole chapter to himself – but giants, villains and heroes, such as King Arthur, also feature strongly. Witches, fairies, ghosts and assorted spirits have made their mark: there are many modern instances of phantom hand- and foot-prints, the latter often bloodstained and indelible.

Hundreds of imprints are described in this book, which concludes with location details for more than 100 imprint sites all around the world.

ISBN 1 872883 73 7. 245 x 175 mm, 263 + x pages, 112 b&w photos, 26 line drawings, paperback. **£14.95**

Further details of all Heart of Albion titles online at
www.hoap.co.uk

All titles available direct from Heart of Albion Press.

Please add 80p p&p (UK only; email
albion@indigogroup.co.uk for overseas postage).

To order books or request our current catalogue
please contact

Heart of Albion Press

2 Cross Hill Close, Wymeswold
Loughborough, LE12 6UJ

Phone: 01509 880725

Fax: 01509 881715

email: albion@indigogroup.co.uk

Web site: www.hoap.co.uk